SECRETS, LIES, AND CONSEQUENCES

SECRETS, LIES, AND CONSEQUENCES

A GREAT SCHOLAR'S HIDDEN
PAST AND HIS PROTÉGÉ'S
UNSOLVED MURDER

BRUCE LINCOLN

OXFORD
UNIVERSITY PRESS

OXFORD
UNIVERSITY PRESS

Oxford University Press is a department of the University of Oxford. It furthers
the University's objective of excellence in research, scholarship, and education
by publishing worldwide. Oxford is a registered trademark of Oxford University
Press in the UK and certain other countries.

Published in the United States of America by Oxford University Press
198 Madison Avenue, New York, NY 10016, United States of America.

CIP data is on file at the Library of Congress
ISBN 978–0–19–768910–3

DOI: 10.1093/oso/9780197689103.001.0001

Printed by Sheridan Books, Inc., United States of America

For Louise,

Martha, and Rebecca

That which is hidden, from the simple fact that it is dissembling, becomes a peril for the individual and the collective. A "sin" is surely serious, but if it is not confessed, it becomes terrible, as the magic forces provoked by the secret end by menacing the entire community.

—MIRCEA ELIADE, "Secrets" (1935)

CONTENTS

———◦◦◦◦———

ACKNOWLEDGMENTS

———◦◦◦———

AT VARIOUS POINTS IN THE course of my research, I was fortunate to have been able to speak or exchange emails with a number of people who knew Mircea Eliade and Ioan Culianu personally or have done serious research on them. I would like to express my gratitude to Sorin Alexandrescu, Sorin Antohi (whose generosity was enormous and whose help invaluable), Ted Anton, Alexander Arguelles, Stefan Arvidsson, Cristina Bejan, Liviu Bordaş, T. David Brent, Raul Cârstocea, Alin Constantin, Wendy Doniger, Jaš Elsner, Chris Gamwell, Clark Gilpin, Carlo Ginzburg, Cristiano Grottanelli, Eric Heath, Moshe Idel, Mark Krupnick, Marcello de Martino, Russell McCutcheon, Daniel McNally, Jason Merchant, Bernard McGinn, Frank Reynolds, Mac Linscott Ricketts, Martin Riesebrodt, Gianpaolo Romanato, Roberto Scagno, Greg Spinner, Ivan Strenski, Dorin Tudoran, Florin Ţurcanu, Steve Wasserstrom, Anthony Yu, and Kenneth Zysk. Unless cited directly by name, they hold no responsibility for the opinions expressed in the pages that follow.

I

A Sheaf of Papers

(1991–2017)

IN MAY 1991 IOAN CULIANU, associate professor of history of religions at the University of Chicago Divinity School, approached a colleague with a request to safeguard some papers. Less than a week later, Culianu was shot to death in the Divinity School men's room. The papers he sought to protect would eventually come into my hands. This is their story.

THE ACT OF WRITING THIS book has been not just technically difficult, but emotionally fraught. The text that follows is the result of more than a quarter century of what might euphemistically be called incubation, but is more accurately characterized as evasion, repression, and some haunted mix of half-knowledge, anxiety, and sorrow.

The dreams I had while writing it suggest how disturbing I found—and still find—this material. In one, I saw myself with a band of ragged *milicianos* in the Spanish Civil War, under fire and terrified, but determined to halt fascism at any cost. In another, while gardening in my backyard I unearthed a corpse that stirred slowly and revealed itself to be barely alive. "What should I do?" I cried, in a state of panic. "How can I help?" To which the aged, filthy figure replied: "Just leave me alone. Cover me up and let me rest."

From 1971 to 1976, it was my privilege to study under Mircea Eliade and serve as his research assistant. Eliade was the world's foremost historian of

FIGURE 1.1 Mircea Eliade, circa 1976

Photo from the Mircea Eliade archive of Regenstein Library, Box 165, Folder 4.

religions at the time and remains one of the giants of the field (Figure 1.1). I cannot say enough good things about the way he treated me. Despite his accomplishments and stature, I found him remarkably approachable, modest, and unassuming. In our dealings, he was unfailingly generous, kind, supportive, and encouraging. What I said of Professor Eliade in my first book (which grew out of the dissertation he directed) remains heartfelt and true: "His insight and genius are available to all in his many books, but his warmth, enthusiasm, and friendship are a particularly treasured memory for me."[1]

There was, however, another side to the lovely man I knew. During the years I studied with him, it came to light that in his younger days he had been involved with Romanian fascism. Those revelations sparked controversy that runs hot to this day.[2] For years, I sought to avoid the ugly debates that followed, telling myself (and others, when necessary): "Mr. Eliade was my second father, whom I loved and to whom I am indebted in countless ways. Like all fathers, he was not perfect. Having become aware of his failings, I cannot continue to sing his praises without reservations, but it is hardly my job to denounce him in public. Honesty requires that I acknowledge—and regret—those charges that are true, while rejecting those that are unfounded or exaggerated. Conversely, loyalty does not mean defending the indefensible. Rather than getting embroiled in polemics, my preference is simply to remember all that I found most admirable in him."

There is also a specific incident that inclined me toward that position. When Professor Eliade agreed to supervise my dissertation, he expressed some sentiments that he recorded in his journal on other occasions. "When I take on new students," he began, in what was clearly a well-rehearsed speech, "I prepare myself for the day they will betray me. I have come to expect that, since it is a necessary step if they are to become creative in their own right."[3] I found this statement confusing at the time. Decades later, I still do. On the surface it is high-minded and generous, granting preemptive absolution for a yet-to-be-committed offense, one that he saw as the inevitable climax of a successful initiatory process. At the same time, it was an incredibly manipulative gambit, to which I responded as was no doubt expected: "Oh no, sir! You have no need to worry. I could never be so ungrateful." And in some sense it worked. Although my own work has changed much since my student days, advancing values and views markedly different from those of my teacher, I have always taken pains not to write anything that might be construed as betrayal.

Several things prompted me to reconsider my position. First was an article I wrote with my daughter, Martha Lincoln, a medical anthropologist whose fieldwork in Vietnam alerted her to a veritable epidemic of ghosts and haunting.[4] In our paper, we sought to understand this and other "hauntological" phenomena as a set of beliefs, practices, and experiences that manifest the enduring power of the past in the present, forcefully reminding survivors of their unfulfilled obligations to, ongoing relations with, and ultimate accountability to the dead.

Second, an observation Eliade made in one of his early works caught my attention. It suggested that—his later reticence notwithstanding—Eliade understood full well that even the most shameful and painful secrets must be disclosed. In 1935 he wrote: "That which is hidden, simply by being hidden, becomes dangerous to the individual and the collective. A 'sin' is surely serious, but a 'sin' that is unconfessed and is kept hidden becomes terrible, as the magic forces unleashed by the act of concealment in time menace the whole community."[5] Magic or not, the secrets he struggled to preserve had terrible consequences for those who became aware of them, some of whom sacrificed their careers, their scholarly integrity, perhaps even their lives.

The most immediate stimulus, however, was a serious mistake I made, one involving those papers that Ioan Culianu (Figure 1.2) had entrusted to a colleague all those years ago: papers that have bearing not only on Eliade's past, but on Culianu's murder.

II

Ioan Petru Culianu was just forty-one years old when he was killed, on the afternoon of May 21, 1991. He had gained his position at the University of Chicago's Divinity School just three years earlier and was widely seen as Eliade's successor. The crime was shocking and remains unsolved, although

FIGURE 1.2 Ioan Culianu, circa 1988

By permission of the Hanna Holborn Gray Special Collections Research Center, University of Chicago Library.

multiple theories have been offered, including those that focus on disgruntled students, jealous spouses, drug cartels, Chicago gangs, and occult covens. Most widely accepted is the theory popularized by Ted Anton: that agents of the Romanian secret service (*Securitate*) killed Culianu in response to critical articles he wrote for the émigré press, which threatened their postcommunist hold on power.[6]

Those articles drew complaints and threats, and in the week before Culianu's murder, the threats became sufficiently serious that he entrusted the papers to our colleague Mark Krupnick, whom he asked to safeguard them. Shortly before his own death in 2003, Krupnick gave me the manuscripts and explained how he came to have them. He was not sure what to make of the papers themselves, nor did he understand why Ioan entrusted them to his care, since the two men were not particularly close. Perhaps it was a chance result of their offices' proximity. Mark speculated that his own identity as a Jewish scholar whose research centered on Jewish fiction, testimonial, and autobiography, might also have had some relevance.

The papers, it turned out, were English translations of articles Eliade had written in the 1930s, including a good number in which he voiced his support for a movement known under two names that signaled its religious and militant nature: the Legion of the Archangel Michael and the Iron Guard. Although these articles were key pieces of evidence in the debate about Eliade's past, few people had actually read them. In Communist Romania, surviving copies of the right-wing dailies in which they originally appeared were consigned to the special collections of select libraries, access to which was tightly controlled. Requests to view such material triggered state suspicion, and few were foolhardy enough to take that risk.

The articles contained passages that shed light on the bitterly contested question whether—and to what extent—Eliade shared the Iron Guard's virulent anti-Semitism.

When I received these manuscripts, I was not prepared to deal with them or the serious issues they raised. I gave them a cursory reading and persuaded myself that on the crucial question they were neither damning, nor exculpatory, but sufficiently nuanced, ambiguous, and elusive to admit rival interpretations. Determined to continue my own work and avoid entanglement in the endless, acrimonious debates about Eliade, I put the papers in a manila folder and buried them in my files. There they remained until June 2017, when I retired from teaching. While cleaning out my office—a task I found inconvenient and annoying, and thus undertook hastily—I carelessly let that folder go to the dumpster, along with many others of no great importance. Freudians will say this was hardly an accident, and I am in no position to disagree.

A few days later, realizing the enormity of what I had done, I resolved to do whatever I could to rectify it. Since the papers could not be recovered, I decided that the only responsible course of action was to learn Romanian, locate the original articles, translate and study them myself, and make the results available. As I made this vow, I could hear the voice of my *Doktorvater*, for Professor Eliade was always urging me to learn new languages. "You could pick up X easily," he would say, "since it's just like Y, which you already know, with some added vocabulary from Z."

Finding the original Romanian articles proved easier than I expected, as they had been collected and republished in 2001, but there was much in their content that I did not initially comprehend.[7] And so I continued to gather material, translating numerous related texts that helped me understand the context of these old publications: Romania's situation between the two world wars; Eliade's position in the intellectual, cultural, and political life of his country; the role played by Nae Ionescu, his mentor and patron, and the turbulent group that had Nae and Eliade at its center. Beyond this, I was led to other texts that show how Culianu got drawn into the Eliade controversies, how he became aware of the legionary articles, what he made of them, and what he was planning to do with them at the time of his murder. Most of this was written in Romanian and Italian, with occasional pieces in German and French. As a result, monoglot anglophones have had to rely on the way these materials have been characterized by the few scholars writing in English who had competence in these languages—Culianu, Mac Linscott Ricketts, and Adriana Berger—each of whom interpreted the evidence in ways strongly inflected by a desire to defend or prosecute Eliade.

Wading through this material, I came to believe that my chief responsibility is to make the relevant documents more fully and readily available. It was thus my intention to include translations of the texts Culianu entrusted to Mark Krupnick as an appendix to this book and to make them easily available online. Culianu's own efforts to publish this material had run into determined opposition from Christinel Eliade, who inherited the copyrights from her husband. My efforts were similarly checked by Sorin Alexandrescu, Eliade's nephew and one of two literary executors to the Eliade estate, who similarly refused permission, despite the strong support of his coexecutor, David Brent, for the translations' publication. Fortunately, copyright to all these articles will expire in 2028, at which time I plan to make my translations available in one form or another.

In the following chapters, I thus can do no more than quote from those documents and offer the inferences I have drawn from them, along with the interpretations and hypotheses I consider most likely. My own views are less important, however, than the evidence itself. Experience suggests that what I have to say will not resolve the debate about Eliade, nor identify Culianu's killer. The material is revealing, however, and holds more than a few surprises.

2

A Hidden Past

Part I (1927–1937)

I

The Treaties of Trianon and Paris were signed on June 4, 1920, and October 28, 1920, respectively. Among the last steps concluding the First World War, they ceded Transylvania, Banat, Bukovina, and Bessarabia (previously Hapsburg, Romanov, and Bulgarian territories) to Romania, virtually doubling its territory (Figure 2.1). The territory was a reward for Romanians, who had contributed much and sacrificed greatly during the Great War. But it was also the result of shrewd maneuvering by Queen Marie, who persuaded the victorious powers that a strong Romania would provide a secure barrier against Bolshevism. This expansion realized long-standing ambitions for a "Greater Romania" (*România Mare*). But it also brought new ethnic groups into the nation—Hungarian, German, Slavic, Turkic, Roma, and Jewish—that aroused xenophobic resentment and seriously destabilized national politics. Further, as a condition of these territorial grants, the victorious allies obliged Romania to confer full rights of citizenship on its Jews. Article VII of the country's postwar constitution (adopted March 1923) fulfilled that commitment but was resented and resisted by a great many ethnic Romanians. Those involved in several potent right-wing parties accused the country's political class of having surrendered to foreign pressure or, worse yet, having been corrupted by Jewish money.[1]

FIGURE 2.1 Territorial expansion of Romania after World War I

Ever since the revolutions of 1848, Romanians had been divided on whether to modernize and westernize or, alternatively, to defend and emphatically reassert key features of their distinctive national identity.[2] In the postwar period, this long-standing conflict acquired new urgency, and passions became more heated.

Political debate on virtually all issues, including urbanization, industrialization, rationalism, cosmopolitanism, banking, the press, education, culture, and parliamentary democracy, consistently broke down along this same line. Over the course of the 1920s, however, the ultranationalist Right increasingly saw Jewish interests, conspiracies, and corrupting power as the source of all the nation's problems.[3]

It was during this period that Mircea Eliade, the son of an army officer, was schooled at the elite Spiru Haret Lycée along with a group of talented youths who would remain his friends and colleagues for many years.[4] While still in lycée, he began publishing short articles, drafting novels, and keeping a journal, some entries from which register his political opinions—strong at times, but also in adolescent flux. On January 31, 1923, he wrote: "Like all the boys, I'm anti-Semitic out of intellectual conviction and I tremble that the anti-Semitic demonstrations aren't succeeding."[5] Within a year, however, he was reading Marx, Engels, and Kautsky, while toying with leftist ideas under the influence of a close Jewish friend, Mircea Mărculescu.[6] After lycée, he advanced to study at the University of Bucharest, where his copious writings included fiction, literary criticism, topical commentary, semischolarly articles, and polemic pieces. During these years, he mostly affected a stance above "politics," construing the latter as the dirty business of parties, elections, and government offices. In complementary fashion, he understood "culture"— the realm of philosophy, religion, literature, the arts, journalism, and all spheres of the imagination—as the most potent means to reshape society.

Many of the values he championed in his early publications, particularly those voicing his sense of Romania's unique national character and destiny, were consonant with those of the indigenist Right, an affinity that grew stronger over time. Like these rightists, he considered "modernity" a disaster imported from the West by political elites and misguided cosmopolitan intellectuals. Being foreign—both literally and figuratively—"modern" fashions and institutions threatened to undermine the unique spiritual values that were core to Romania's greatness. As he saw it, modernity's characteristic disregard for the sacred had distanced humanity from the wellsprings of its creativity, an error that could be reversed in some measure through such premodern (and antimodern) technologies of the sacred as mysticism, asceticism, and magic.[7]

Consistent with this critique, Eliade celebrated the "primacy of the spirit" (a phrase taken from Catholic philosopher Jacques Maritain) and felt that the task of restoring his nation's endangered spiritual values fell to himself and others in the "Young Generation." Most broadly, this included those who experienced the Great War at a critical remove—having been too young for combat—and could thus perceive how modernity's trust in science, progress, and secular reason helped produce the war's dehumanizing horrors. In contrast to the older generation, who fought the war and realized historic ambitions for a Greater Romania, he understood his own generation's mission to be cultural, not military, economic, or political.

Although he used the term "Young Generation" as a slogan and branding mechanism, Eliade acknowledged he was speaking more narrowly about (and on behalf of) a relatively small group of intellectuals who styled themselves an elite (Figures 2.2 and 2.3).[8] Central to this group were a few dozen students of Nae Ionescu, the charismatic, influential, and well-connected professor of philosophy and logic at the University of Bucharest.

Reacting against the positivistic strains of philosophy previously dominant in the Romanian academy, Ionescu (Figure 2.4) introduced discussions of faith, salvation, authenticity, and experience into his classes. Here, as in his public lectures and journalistic salvos, he maintained that the Orthodox faith—particularly its mystical aspects—was central to Romanian identity. As such, it provided the best antidote to the shallow rationalism and selfish

FIGURE 2.2 Some members of the "Young Generation" circa 1933. Eliade is the figure in glasses seated at the head of the table. On the left are Floria Capsali, Mihail Sebastian, Mihail Polihroniade, and Mary Polihroniade. On the right, Marietta Sadova and Haig Acterian.

Photo courtesy of the Archives of the National Museum of Romanian Literature.

materialism he identified with western Europe, other forms of Christianity (which he considered defective), and parliamentary democracy, a form of governance that produced partisanship, corruption, and fragmentation, undermining any nation's unity and spirit.[9]

Ionescu made a point of recruiting his best and most loyal students to write for *Cuvântul* ("The Word"), the popular right-wing newspaper he edited from 1926 until its suppression in March 1934. Among the first and most important of those to do so was Eliade, who published a manifesto of sorts under the title "Spiritual Itinerary," which appeared across twelve issues of *Cuvântul* during the autumn of 1927.[10] Here and in numerous subsequent articles, Eliade argued that the political goal of creating a Greater Romania having been accomplished by their predecessors, the mission falling to his generation was to establish Romania's cultural greatness by producing literary and artistic works of extraordinary spiritual depth in which they would synthesize tradition and innovation in ways informed by their daring experimentation with myriad forms of religious experience: mystical, ecstatic, meditative, magical, alchemical, ascetic, erotic, and so on.[11] Writing with an extraordinary mix of zeal, passion, erudition, impatience, and swagger, he rapidly gained an enthusiastic following and

FIGURE 2.3 Some members of the "Young Generation" circa 1934. Eliade is the seated figure in glasses. Seated next to him is Haig Acterian. Standing, from left to right, are Mihail Sebastian, an unidentified woman, Mary Polihroniade, Floria Capsali, Mihail Polihroniade, Marietta Sadova, and Prince Alexandru Cantacuzino.

Photo courtesy of the Archives of the National Museum of Romanian Literature.

was widely acclaimed as the leader (Romanian *șef,* literally "chief") of the Young Generation.

For nearly a decade, Eliade continued to regard politics and the political class with disdain while urging his contemporaries toward the spiritual endeavors and cultural accomplishments he considered vitally important. Implicit in many of his publications from this period is the ambition he shared with others in his group who wished to elevate Romania to the status

FIGURE 2.4 Nae Ionescu, circa 1934
Photo courtesy of the National Library of Romania—Special Collections.

of a "major" culture. Thus, in an article titled "Romania in Eternity," he argued that the true goal of nationalism is to raise a country from the transient plane of history to that of the eternal. This is something that can be done only when a country's creative geniuses express their people's distinctive values in such novel, compelling ways that the whole world is brought to recognize, celebrate, and remember them forever. Aeschylus and Plato accomplished that for Greece in antiquity, as did Leonardo, Michelangelo, and Dante for Italy during the Renaissance, but Eliade believed a single genius could accomplish the same miracle, as Kierkegaard had more recently done for the Danes. The implication, of course, was that he—and perhaps others of his generation—would do the same for Romania.[12]

Despite the grandiosity manifest in this text, a certain insecurity creeps into its closing passages, where Eliade acknowledged the anxieties underlying his ambitions. It is not just that he aspired to immortalize Romanian culture: more poignantly, he hoped to rescue his country from a situation in which it was ignored—or worse yet, ridiculed.

I think with horror that another kind of "eternity" awaits us Romanians: the proverb. We enter into the proverbs of other nations, just as the Scots, Irish, Jews, and in the Balkans, the Gypsies have done. We are stereotyped, and until we are known beyond our borders through our masterpieces and our Romanianism, we are known through our politics and inner shamelessness. I don't know if any of you has recognized how seriously we are compromised. Only a few steps and we will enter an irremediable state, from which no one will ever extract us. The proverb will become our lord; and just as it is said, rightly or wrongly, that Bulgarians are stupid, Poles are vain, and Spaniards exceptional lovers, just so it will be said that Romanians are *thieves*. It has begun to be said, not only in newspapers and European political circles, but also through proverbs. Listen to one of them, collected by Knickerbocker: "When someone steals, it's kleptomania. When many people steal, it's mania. When a whole people steal, it's Romania!" Doesn't that make you blush with shame? This is the eternity that is being prepared for us. This is all that politics, the administration, and our official national culture have done for us since the end of the war.[13]

What emerges from this unintentionally revealing article is a portrait of its author as a young, ambitious intellectual who feels burdened by the fact of his birth in a relative backwater, who dreams of international fame but fears becoming the butt of jokes. By way of defensive reflex, he lashes out at those he blames for putting him and his country at such risk: Romania's politics and political class. By the mid-1930s, he had identified democracy as a significant part of the problem.

We must choose between a slow, larval, humiliating evolution—meanwhile being ridiculed by our neighbors—and a violent, heroic, risk-filled revolution, a revolution that will make people speak about Romania as they have never done before. The former—the larval and humiliating evolution—is the ideal of Romanian democracy. The other—revolution, chauvinism, inexhaustible faith in the destiny of Romania—is the ideal of the rest of the Romanian populace. Little do I care whether what will come will be dictatorship or not, whether it will be tyranny, anti-democracy, or who knows what. Only one thing matters to me: whether the problem of Romania will be the dominant problem—whether, in the name of this Romania, which began several thousand years ago and will end only in the Apocalypse, social reform will be achieved with sufficient severity, whether the corners of the provinces overrun with foreigners will be recolonized, whether all traitors will be punished, whether the myth of our state will be spread everywhere within our borders and the news of our country will be carried across our borders... . To me, then, it is entirely immaterial what will happen in Romania after the liquidation of democracy. If, by leaving democracy behind, Romania becomes a strong national state, armed, conscious of its power and destiny—history will take account of this deed. It would be ridiculous for us to place any hope in formulas, to say to ourselves: "We know that democracy hasn't done anything much for us, we know we're deluged with lackeys and traitors, we know that politicianism has paralyzed us—but we can't give up a modern and civilized formula to go back to tyranny." In fact, it is not a return to tyranny, but rather a great national revolution. Obviously, such national revolutions don't suit anyone but the nations that make them. Neither our neighbors nor the great powers will like it if we become a *powerful* state. And that is why they encourage us, gently or with force, to maintain the most blessed sociopolitical system, democracy, which classes us, fatally, with Afghanistan, Albania, and Lithuania.[14]

II

In the same year that Eliade published his "Spiritual Itinerary," Corneliu Zelea Codreanu, who also yearned for Romanian greatness of a spiritual sort, led a small splinter group out of A. C. Cuza's National Christian Defense League, then the most important party of the ultranationalist Right.[15] While Codreanu (Figure 2.5)—who styled himself "the Captain"

(a)

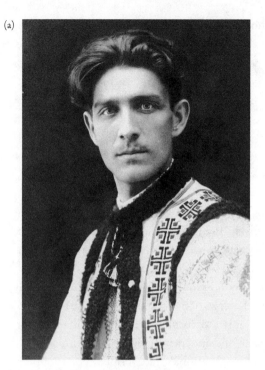

(b)

FIGURE 2.5A AND B (a) Corneliu Zelea Codreanu in traditional costume and (b) leading a demonstration, 1925

(*Căpitanul*)—shared Cuza's ideology and fierce anti-Semitism, he found the older man's tactics too restrained.[16]

Codreanu chose to name his new group the Legion of the Archangel Michael, drawing on the Orthodox tradition's understanding of this dragon-slaying archangel as commander of the heavenly forces, defender of the faith, and protector of Christian nations. By defining themselves in this fashion, its members consciously constructed themselves not as a political party, but a martial religious order sworn to protect the faithful, an orientation that helps explain the appeal it came to have for Eliade.

Recent studies of fascism have devoted considerable attention to the legionary movement as historians and political scientists have come to recognize that fascist regimes did not rely on force, intimidation, and indoctrination alone, but also cultivated—and enjoyed—broad popular support for much of their duration. As scholars began exploring the ways fascist culture, aesthetics, myth, and ritual helped produce such support, Romania provided a telling example.[17]

Two related themes emerge from what has been termed the "new consensus" in fascist studies: the sacralization of politics and a mythology embodying the conviction that a nation must return to its original, authentic nature in order to achieve its destined greatness.[18] Fascist movements that fit this mold regard their nation (including its ethnic identity, bodily substance, unique culture, landscape, and spirit) as having fallen into decadence, corruption, and humiliation at the hands of sinister forces (foreign enemies, internal traitors), in response to which they promise to produce a national rebirth through their struggles and sacrifices.

Codreanu's Legion offers a telling example. On the one hand, it took the Romanian nation (*neam*) and homeland (*ţară*) to be a sacred entity, whose spiritual identity was grounded in and defined by its Orthodox faith.[19] On the other, it demonized those it defined as the nation's enemies: Ottomans, Hapsburgs, Muslims, Phanariots, Catholics, and Protestants in the past; Russians, Hungarians, communists, liberals, corrupt politicians, lying journalists, and Jews (above all) in the present.[20] Against such forces, legionaries construed themselves as a mystic order of soldiers and would-be martyrs, bound to one another and their leaders by sacred oaths and solemn rituals designed to transform dispirited, confused youths into bold, virile "new men" who would accomplish not just a reform of the Romanian nation, but its resurrection.[21]

The Legion's distinctive blend of religion and nationalism included a mystic bond to the land itself, eagerness to sacrifice oneself for the nation, a sense of ongoing communion with heroic ancestors, and militance in the salvific mission of rescuing an afflicted people from religio-ethnic others. As a convenient example, consider Codreanu's account of the proceedings through which the first legionaries constituted—and consecrated—themselves as a group.

> The ceremony began with the mixture of earth taken from the tomb of Michael the Brave in Turda, the earth of Moldavia from the battlefield where Stefan the Great fought his most serious battles, and from all those places where the blood of our ancestors was mixed with the soil in the course of cruel battles. . . . When this earth had been mixed, many small sacks were filled and given to everyone who had taken the vow, to be worn on their chest. This vow consisted of five questions and responses, to wit:
>
> 1. Do you commit yourself, for the Justice of the endangered Fatherland, to overcome all your personal interests and desires? Response: Yes!
> 2. Recognizing that domination by Yids (*jidani*) leads us to spiritual and national destruction, do you commit yourself as a brother with us to struggle for the defense, cleansing, and emancipation of the ancestral land? Response: Yes!
> 3. In this struggle, will you support the Legion of the Archangel Michael? Response: Yes!
> 4. Will you carry this earth on your breast with devotion? Response: Yes!
> 5. And will you leave us? Response: I will not leave.[22]

III

If the Legion's induction ceremonies reflected—and reproduced—its self-understanding, so, too, did the story of its origins, as recounted by Codreanu. His small band of militants originally called themselves *Văcăreșteni*, with reference to their October 1923 incarceration in the Văcărești Prison, where they took solace in religious devotions.

> Every morning at seven, we would go to the church in the prison's courtyard in order to pray. We gathered, all on our knees before the altar and recited "Our Father," and Tudose Popescu sang "Holy Mother of God." Here we found consolation for our sad life in prison and hope for tomorrow. . . . On November 8, the day of the archangels Michael and Gabriel, we discussed what name we should give to the organization of the youth we were planning to form. I said, "The Archangel Michael."

My father said, "There is an icon of St. Michael in the church, by the door to the left of the altar." I went, along with the others. We looked and were truly amazed. The icon exhibited to us an incomparable beauty. I had never been attracted by the beauty of any icon. Here, however, I felt connected to this one with all my soul, and it gave me the impression that the Sainted Archangel is alive. From here, I began to love that icon. Whenever we found the church open, we entered and prayed at that icon. Our souls were filled with peace and joy.[23]

The aura of sanctity and tranquility is hard to reconcile, however, with Codreanu's earlier account of how the Văcăreșteni (Figure 2.6) came to be imprisoned. Apparently, one of their group informed authorities of his comrades' plan to transform earlier student protests into a campaign of assassinations.[24] Here again is Codreanu's description.

The first problem that presented itself to us is this: to whom must one respond first? Who are more responsible for the disastrous state in which

FIGURE 2.6 The *Văcăreșteni*, 1924. Back row, left to right: Corneliu Georgescu, Tudose Popescu, Ion Moța. Front row: Radu Mironovici, Corneliu Codreanu, Ilie Gârneață.

Photo courtesy of the National Library of Romania—Special Collections.

the country is floundering: Romanians or Yids? Unanimously, we fell into agreement that the guiltiest are those Romanian scoundrels who betrayed the country for Jewish silver. The Yids are our enemies, and in this capacity they hate us, they poison us, they exterminate us. Romanian leaders who align themselves with them, however, are worse than enemies: they are traitors. The harshest punishment is deserved by traitors in the first place, enemies in the second. If I have only one bullet and an enemy and a traitor are in front of me, I would send the bullet into the traitor.[25]

Ultimately, the group decided to execute six cabinet ministers in the liberal government, starting with Gheorghe Mârzescu, the minister of justice, who was responsible for the laws that secured citizenship rights for Jews and outlawed "extremist" political parties. Had they succeeded in killing Mârzescu and his fellow "traitors," the group planned to dispatch those Jews they identified as the nation's foremost "enemies": rabbis first, then bankers, publishers, and journalists.[26]

Chilling though the passage is, it fits neatly into Codreanu's writings, which seethe with rants against Jews and the political class, along with calls to violence and a commitment to "propaganda of the deed." In October 1924, Codreanu himself shot and killed a police chief, then defended himself as having taken proper vengeance on an enemy of the people, winning acquittal on all charges.[27] Later assassinations were carried out by legionary "punishment squads," who were trained to await the police after dispatching a victim, thereby offering themselves as a sacrifice on behalf of the nation. Their victims included three prime ministers, two heads of the secret service, two leaders of opposition parties, and apostates from the legionary movement, along with scores of others.[28]

Singular in its brutality was the murder of Mihail Stelescu, a former legionary commander and member of parliament who had broken with Codreanu to lead his own movement. A punishment squad of ten members (accordingly mythologized as the "Decemviri") entered the hospital room where Stelescu was recovering from surgery, shot him more than a hundred times, dismembered his body with an ax, then sang and danced around his mangled corpse while waiting for the police.[29] This and other less grisly acts figured prominently in legionary propaganda and in legal defenses that, in several well-publicized cases, led to acquittal. Treatment of "enemies" (i.e., Jews) was equally self-confident in its violence, and the Legion's brief period of state power (September 1940–January 1941) featured pogroms of obscene brutality, in which seven synagogues were sacked, several hundred victims killed, and many more robbed, beaten, and tortured. Most grisly of all was the fate of thirteen Jews killed in the Bucharest slaughterhouse, who were suspended on meathooks and fitted with a placard identifying them as "Kosher meat."[30]

IV

In the years when the Legion first took shape, Eliade was absorbed in other pursuits (Figure 2.7). From 1925 to 1928 he studied at the University of Bucharest in the Faculty of Philosophy and Letters, taking his degree under Nae Ionescu with a thesis on the Neoplatonists of Renaissance Italy, who—as both teacher and student saw it—offered a mystic alternative to rationality at the dawn of the modern era.[31] During the same years, he served on *Cuvântul*'s editorial board, where he published a great number of cultural, literary, and philosophical articles, building on the success of his "Spiritual Itinerary." Then, having become interested in Indian philosophy for some of the same reasons that inspired his thesis, he traveled to India in 1928, where he spent the next three years studying, traveling, learning

FIGURE 2.7 Mircea Eliade, circa 1934

languages, engaging in ill-fated love affairs, and gathering material for subsequent publications.

Returning to Bucharest in 1931, Eliade resumed whirlwind activities at the University and at *Cuvântul*. His involvement with the latter continued when Nae shifted the paper's political orientation sharply rightward. Previously supportive of King Carol II and aligned with the National Peasant Party, in 1933 *Cuvântul* became one of the most vigorous and influential champions of the Legion, sufficiently so that the government closed the paper the following year, when it rallied support for the Legion and its three members who carried out the assassination of Prime Minister Ion Duca. Eliade rejoined the editorial board of *Cuvântul* during the brief period in 1938 when it was permitted to resume publication, having contributed a steady stream of articles to other right-wing venues in the meantime.[32] In this period, he continued to work closely with Nae Ionescu, who supervised his groundbreaking dissertation on yoga (1933).[33] Thereafter, he served as assistant professor for Ionescu's courses, for which he was paid out of his mentor's own pocket, since the University of Bucharest considered him too controversial a figure to be granted an official position.[34] At the same time, he produced a steady stream of journalistic articles, along with three volumes of essays, eight novels, three scholarly monographs, a translation of T. E. Lawrence's *Seven Pillars of Wisdom*, and long introductions to the collected works of the two Romanian scholars he most admired, B. P. Hasdeu and Nae Ionescu.[35]

Conditions in Romania were changing quickly, however, in ways that affected Eliade and his circle. Most broadly, the economic effects of the Great Depression made it increasingly difficult for young intellectuals to earn a decent living or anticipate a productive career, which drove many to more radical politics. At the same time, the Legion expanded beyond its base in the provinces and began courting intellectuals in Bucharest. Among the first to lend support was Nichifor Crainic, one of Romania's best-known, most militant theologians, who embraced the Legion in 1932.[36] Two schoolmates and close friends of Eliade's quickly followed: Mihail Polihroniade and Ion Victor Vojen, who founded the journal *Axa* ("Axis") in October 1932 and made it the leading vehicle through which the Legion cultivated intellectuals.[37] Late in the following year Nae Ionescu, who had been a close adviser to King Carol II, became frustrated by his inability to persuade the monarch that parliamentary democracy should be replaced by an authoritarian regime. Whether acting out of wounded pride, on principle, or some mixture of the two, Ionescu shifted his support and that of *Cuvântul* to the legionary movement, bringing many of his students and admirers with him.

Like those he influenced, Ionescu was impressed by the emphatically spiritual nature of the Legion and the fact that its anti-Semitism was based—properly, in his view—on religious grounds (i.e., Jews' refusal to accept Christ as Messiah) and not racial considerations of the Nazi sort. Once committed to the Legion, Ionescu, Crainic, Polihroniade, and other intellectuals from the Young Generation reshaped legionary discourse in ways that fueled the movement's explosive growth in the second half of the 1930s.

Initially, Eliade was not among these recruits, although others expected him to follow his mentor's lead. A week after he published two articles with relatively anodyne nationalist sentiments, Polihroniade reprinted them in *Axa*, along with an article welcoming Eliade—"who has played with ideas and attitudes toward life . . . been brilliant always and everywhere, but who has refused any definitive anchorage in Romanian realities"—as a convert to right-wing "Romanianism."[38] In response, Eliade rejected any talk of "conversion," asserting that he remained what he always had been: a proud Romanian. Further, he insisted that the things he consistently championed were not irrelevant, as Polihroniade suggested, but indispensable to the national cause, since "only experiences, authenticity, and culture can clarify someone's ethnic substance, can lead him to a full understanding of himself, to full mastery of all ethnic force." Deflecting his friend's attempt to flatter and recruit him, Eliade remained convinced that "purely spiritual activity is more necessary and more fruitful than the political." And in the closing paragraph of his rejoinder, he distinguished "Romanianism," which he embraced, from anti-Semitism (or at least its excesses), from which he kept his distance.[39]

V

Eliade's articles of the mid-1930s show his position in flux. As others around him rallied to the Legion with the raucous enthusiasm and herd mentality Eugène Ionesco described as "rhinocerization," Eliade sought to maintain his position of generational leadership without firmly committing to a faction. Beneath his surface bombast, one can perceive indecision, as he tries out new ideas and phrases, while struggling to maintain a semblance of consistency in a rapidly shifting situation.

Thus, in December 1933, he denounced government actions against the Legion as "barbaric and inhuman," but said nothing about the movement itself.[40] In February 1934, he ventured more of an opinion, rejecting ideologies of the Left and the Right as equally foreign, equally odious.

> And for all that, intelligent people persist in introducing this gentle land to the Code of the Good Hitlerist Hangman or the Code of the Red Marxist Beast. No, gentlemen, do not let yourselves be deceived by words. Just as much innocent blood will flow in the streets should "power" be conquered by the "Left" or the "Right." We will see old men with cracked skulls, people put up against the wall, and women raped in both cases. And we will awake more sinful, more burdened with this sad life on the morning of the red flag, just as on the morning of the green shirts [the uniform of Codreanu's Legion]. There are the same barbarities on both sides. There is the same dictatorship of brutes, imbeciles, and incompetents in Russia and in Germany.[41]

Six months later, Eliade embraced revolution, while rejecting what others called by that name. The kind of revolution he had in mind, he explained, was not simple regime change, but a messianic transformation made possible by spiritual vision and great sacrifice. Not the revolution of a Lenin, Hitler, Marx, or Mussolini, but that of Jesus and Gandhi.[42] It was, moreover, a distinctly antipolitical revolution (in his narrow sense of politics) and antimodern (in its promise to restore Romania to its authentic, primordial past while achieving its destined grandeur).[43] Having made those points, Eliade went on to identify his preferred model of revolution with the "new man" that was a centerpiece of fascist discourse in Romania, as elsewhere.[44]

> Revolution? Why not? Everyone who wants to endow his life with meaning is born through revolution. But let us remember that a true revolution (not a politicianized pseudorevolution, a change of nobles and rulers) begins with a very full soul, with a sacred, biological fury against lies and hypocrisy, with a pagan thirst for a new life, a new man, a new world. The man who prepares himself for revolution is a man of mystery. He goes shouting the new spirit in the streets only after he has accomplished the revolution himself, after he has seen and tasted it. A new man! But, by God, this new man is our salvation, he is the sense of our

existence! The new man is made, not awaited. Above all, the new man means a complete break with the hypocrisy and cowardice of the society in which we live. A young man unattached to anything, without fear and without stain, with eyes on the future, not the practices of the past.[45]

However appealing Eliade found the virile energy of the "new man," he did not yet identify this figure with any specific group, nor did his general enthusiasm lead him to view the Legion with particular favor. On the contrary, in November 1934, he expressed contempt for those who rallied to the movement for reasons he judged unworthy.

Christian intellectuals were afraid of the successes of the "Iron Guard" and they began to endorse it, not because the program of "the Guard" was congenial to them, but because they feared being suspected and persecuted after its eventual victory. I have nothing to say against "intellectuals" who feel obliged by a certain social or national consciousness to take the part of or mount the barricades on one side or the other. But I find repugnant the cowardice of apolitical intellectuals, who suddenly reveal themselves adherents of a social movement when it is on the threshold of success (or only seems to be so).[46]

A few months later, Eliade emphatically reasserted his commitment to "Romanianism," while observing that those who reject strong nationalism—is he speaking of Jews? leftists? the timid and lukewarm? nonlegionaries?—effectively condemn themselves to exclusion, expulsion, and death. His language is charged but allusive and sufficiently ambiguous that it could be taken as a metaphor, prophecy, or call to action.

To renounce "Romanianism" means for us Romanians to renounce life and take refuge in death. There are people who have done this. God forgive them! But since when are the majority of us who live in this country obliged to debate the case of hundreds or thousands of unfortunates who have, through stupidity or lack of masculinity, chosen their own death? Romanianness, that is, this living organism in which we all participate, eliminates them from itself. All the inertia of their dead corpuscles is in vain; sooner or later, they will naturally be undone and they will fall.[47]

Does this mean Romanian patriots should rid their country of those insufficiently committed to the national cause or, alternatively, that there is no need to do so, since the "living organism" of the nation will automatically expel them? When the foolish, effeminate nonpatriots are said to have "chosen their own death," does one expect their death to come from natural causes or at the hands of the more fervent Romanians they have offended? The passage is sufficiently unclear to permit either conclusion.

Equally indecisive is a rambling article of May 1935, in which Eliade wrestled with the "Jewish question." Here he endorsed Zionist aspirations for a Jewish state, celebrated Romania's (putative) tolerance and skill at assimilation, voiced sympathy and respect for the Jews, observed similarity between Jewish and Romanian insecurities, and told Romanians they have nothing to fear, only to conclude with the assurance that, should Jews or other minorities become too numerous or powerful, "we will extract them by means of competition, by our own forces, and by administrative laws as necessary."[48]

In these publications of the mid-1930s, Eliade shifted his position gradually rightward, while insisting he had no interest in and scant regard for conventional politics. In 1935, however, Eliade began speaking of "politicianism," a term he used to decry politics as a corrupt business with "criminal influence . . . over all forms of civil, cultural, and spiritual life over all Romania."[49] The term figures more prominently in his legionary publications of the late 1930s and writings by others on the extreme Right, where it was infused with strong anti-Semitic content.[50] Witness, for example, Codreanu's summary of Romania's ills, which follows his usual insistence that the nation must dispose of its politician traitors before it can take care of its Jewish enemies.

1. *The Jewish problem* is not imaginary, but a serious question of life and death for the Romanian people; the country's leaders, grouped in political parties, increasingly become a plaything in the hands of Judaic power.
2. *This politicianism*, through its conception of life, through its morality, through the democratic system from which it derives its being, constitutes a true curse fallen on the head of the country.
3. The Romanian people will not be able to resolve the Jewish problem until its *problem of politicianism* is resolved.[51]

At times, Eliade seemed to voice similar views without making explicit reference to the Jews, as in a December 1936 article, where he described

Romania as "a country full of impudent minorities, swindlers and spies, and with a state mixed up in shady dealings involving a dozen Romanian, Parisian, and minority newspapers, a thousand deputies, and who knows how many bank directors."[52] Whether Eliade was implicitly accepting, rejecting, or dodging discussion of the anti-Semitism that was central to Codreanu's use of the term, he consistently treated "politicianism" as a ubiquitous horror, in opposition to which he championed an incorruptible ideal, which he termed "messianism." This, he explained, would be a movement possessing a "powerful spiritual effervescence," capable of restoring a nation's historic mission, "an apocalyptic exertion of the collective, in which the individual is lost and his immediate interests (economic, social, political) are annulled."[53] Pondering the question of whether messianism of this sort could take shape in his country's moment of crisis, he called attention to one man and one movement.

> A political leader of the youth says that the goal of his movement is "to reconcile Romania with God." Here is a messianic formula. Here is a formula that does not appeal to class struggle, political interests, economic instincts, or the bestial instincts in man. I ask myself, however, how many have understood the sense of this formula among all those who have heard it? Because a "reconciliation of Romania with God" means, in the first place, an overthrow of values, a clear primacy of the spiritual, an invitation to creation and spiritual life.[54]

Although this singular man went unnamed, readers would immediately have recognized Codreanu, about whom Eliade continued to hedge his bets. Having characterized the Captain's message as messianic, Eliade went on to worry that only elites like himself had properly understood it. In subsequent passages, he voiced further reservations, worrying whether the Legion—like other "revolutionary" movements on the right and left— was so concerned with discipline, dogma, ritual interdictions, and critique as to be "Puritan" and "Talmudic," rather than truly "messianic."[55] Here, as in all his publications of the period, Eliade struck ambiguous, even contradictory, postures that kept his options open.

VI

Exactly when Eliade gave full and active support to the Legion remains uncertain. Some scholars believe there were signs of his formal affiliation as early as 1934, while the Romanian security services dated it to 1935, without citing concrete evidence.[56] His first article of full-throated praise for the Legion appeared in January 1937.[57]

This article followed on a chain of events that began the previous month, when eight legionaries joined Franco's forces in Spain as a show of fascist solidarity against what they took to be the anti-Christian barbarism of the Spanish republic and the Left in general (Figure 2.8).[58]

Within a month, Ion Moța—translator of *The Protocols of the Elders of Zion* into Romanian, cofounder of the Legion, Codreanu's brother-in-law and second-in-command—and Vasile Marin, one of its leading intellectuals, were killed in battle on the Madrid front.[59] Exploiting the symbolic significance of their "sacrificial" deaths to the fullest, the Legion organized their funeral as a religio-political ritual of unprecedented scale and spectacle. For several days, a train bearing the martyrs' bodies circled

FIGURE 2.8 Legionary volunteers headed to Spain, December 1936. From left to right: General Gheorghe Cantacuzino (about whom Eliade contributed an elegiac obituary in a legionary daily, "Mitul Generalului" ("The Myth of the General"), *Buna Vestire* 1, no. 189 [October 16, 1937]: 2), Ion Moța, Gheorghe Clime, Father Ion Borșa-Dumitrescu, Nicolae Totu, Banica Dobre, Vasile Marin, and Prince Alexandru Cantacuzino. Moța and Marin were killed in battle on the Madrid front, January 13, 1937.

through Romania, stopping in numerous cities and villages. Everywhere, large demonstrative crowds gathered, as legionary officials and hundreds of Orthodox priests presided over ceremonies building to mass recitation of "the Moța-Marin oath."

> Moța and Marin, I swear before God and before your holy sacrifice for Christ and the Legion, I will forsake my earthly pleasures and tear myself away from human affections, and I stand ready to die at any time for the resurrection of my nation![60]

When the train finally reached Bucharest on February 11, tens of thousands welcomed it, including many in legionary uniform. Italy, Germany, and Nationalist Spain sent diplomatic representatives, while hundreds of Romanian priests, politicians, professors, and other luminaries stood in rapt attendance. In the funerary celebration itself, massive outpourings of grief and militant displays of force built to the emotional climax of a roll call in which the crowd thundered "Prezent!" when the names of Moța and Marin were called, signaling the unbreakable solidarity of the living and dead (Figure 2.9).[61]

Eliade knew Moța and Marin personally and had considerable respect for both men. Within days of their death, he published an article celebrating their sacrifice and openly voicing support for the Legion, to

FIGURE 2.9 Funeral cortège for Moța and Marin in Bucharest, February 11, 1937

which he now attributed the same virtues and mission he earlier associated with his Young Generation.

> Ion Moţa and Vasile Marin gave countless proofs of their spirit of sacrifice: imprisonments, sufferings, moral oppressions—a youth lived heroically, responsibly, ascetically. . . . The voluntary deaths of Ion Moţa and Vasile Marin have a mystical sense: sacrifice for Christianity. A sacrifice that validates the heroism and faith of a whole generation. A sacrifice destined to be fruitful, strengthening Christianity and energizing the young. . . . Like his leader and friend, Corneliu Codreanu, Ion Moţa believed that the mission of the Young Generation is to reconcile Romania with God. To transform the dead letter into Christian life. To struggle by every means against the powers of darkness.[62]

Eliade wrote fifteen articles of enthusiastic support for the Legion between January 1937 and February 1938, when King Carol established a royal dictatorship and suppressed all legionary activity. Among the first of these articles was a commentary on the Moţa-Marin oath, in which Eliade demonstrated his ability to focus on those aspects of the Legion that were most consonant with his ideals, while overlooking its less savory aspects.

> Seldom has a youth movement, born of a will to make history, but not politics, expressed itself so fully as in this oath. . . . The struggle, action, effort, and all the gestures that imply "politics" have now acquired a new, Christian, and mystical sense. . . . This oath, which expresses so clearly the thought of Codreanu, demonstrates how far the legionary movement is from some "nationalist revolution." There is no talk of seizing power at any price, but above all of a new man, a man for whom spiritual life exists. . . . A movement based on such an oath is, above all, a Christian revolution: a spiritual revolution, ascetic and masculine, such as European history has not yet known.[63]

In subsequent articles, Eliade championed the Legion, consistently embellishing its religious aspirations, while downplaying its anti-Semitism and erasing its violence, of which he—like all Romanians—was well aware. By way of example, consider two passages that show Eliade's knowledge of (and shifting reactions to) legionary brutality. The first comes directly from Eliade:

> The circumstances of Stelescu's assassination absolutely disgusted me. One does not do away with an adversary lying on a hospital bed, with no means to defend himself. God forgive us![64]

The other was recorded by Mihail Sebastian, whose posthumously published journal bears witness to the unraveling of their once-close friendship as Eliade embraced the Legion with increasing fervor.

> As regards Gogu Rădulescu (Mr. Gogu, as Mircea ironically calls him), the liberal student who was beaten with wet ropes at the Iron Guard headquarters, that was all well and good. It's what should be done to traitors. He, Mircea Eliade, would not have been content with that; he'd have pulled his eyes out as well. All who are not Iron Guardists, all who engage in any other kind of politics, are national traitors and deserve the same fate.[65]

Violence notwithstanding, in an article of February 28, 1937, Eliade continued to celebrate the legionary oath and the Legion's "new men" as instruments for the "total Christianization" of a Europe, in which Romania would emerge as the New Jerusalem and New Geneva.[66]

In many ways, Eliade saw the Legion as the continuation and fulfillment of his generation's efforts. Witness, for instance, an article of June 1937 that he published in *Buna Vestire*, the Legion's flagship publication.

> The year 1927 recorded the beginning of a struggle between "generations." Not a struggle between old and young, as has been said and believed many times, but a war between two worlds: on the one side, the old world that believes in the belly (above all economics and politics), on the other side, the new world that dares to believe in the soul (above all, the spiritual). The youth movement of 1927 was born with consciousness of this historic mission: to change the heart of Romania, subordinating all values to a single supreme value: the Spirit. . . . Only now does one begin to understand the sense of this Christian revolution, which attempts to create a new Romania by first creating a new man, a perfect Christian, and which replaces the old

"political life" with a "civic life," that is, the restoration of human relations and of Christianity in the breast of this community of blood.[67]

Eliade's legionary articles occasionally include semiveiled racist discourse, as when he called Romania a "community of blood" in the passage just quoted. For the most part, however, he tried to keep his language abstract and uplifting, without the blunt aggression that characterized legionary discourse. Thus, instead of reviling Jews as corrupters and enemies of the people or denouncing politicians as traitors and dupes, Eliade mostly wrote in a positive register, hailing the Legion as a messianic order of unprecedented spiritual depth and selfless nobility, whose goals and tactics he compared to those of Gandhi.[68]

There are some exceptions, however, as in an article of September 19, 1937, in which he denounced Romania's political class as "blind pilots" whose incompetence let the homeland be overrun with foreigners: Slavs in the south, Hungarians in the north, and Jews in the east.[69] In turn, he decried each incursion with roughly equal vehemence, focusing more blame on cowardly, corrupt, and irresponsible politicians than on the "ethnic elements" in question. Here, as in his other publications, Eliade consistently used the respectful term *evrei* (literally "Hebrews"), rather than the derogatory *jidani* ("Yids") that was common in legionary discourse. His superficially respectful gesture—"I understand their struggle and admire their vitality, tenacity, and genius"—also contrasts with legionary norms, but this sentence must be read in connection with the paragraph that precedes it.

> I know very well that Jews will scream that I am an anti-Semite; and the democrats, that I am a hooligan or fascist. . . . And it does not irritate me when I hear loud Jews screaming "anti-Semitism," "fascism," "Hitlerism"! These people, who are lively and farsighted, defend their economic and political primacy, which they gained with so much hard work and on which they have squandered so much intelligence and great sums of money. It would be absurd to expect the Jews to resign themselves to being a minority, with certain rights and very strong obligations, after they have tasted the sweetness of power and have conquered so many positions of command.[70]

Even while tilting far to the right—"Blind Pilots" is among the most aggressive of his legionary articles—Eliade sought to temper his language and hedge his bets. Toward that end, in the same moment he evinced admiration for the "vitality, tenacity, and genius" of Jews in the struggles they waged, he deployed standard anti-Semitic stereotypes without resorting to the coarse language of his legionary brethren. As Marta Petreu trenchantly observed, "In anti-Semitism, [Eliade] had neither the range nor the intensity of Cioran, but only some legionary slogans he imitated and recycled mechanically in a state of moral anaesthesia."[71]

However awkward and artificial it may have been, Eliade's swipe at the (purportedly) rich, loud, shrewd, and power-hungry Jews resonated with the broader attack he and the Legion aimed at Romania's democratic system and political class.

> If a good idea has ever had a terrible result for a nation, in the Romanian case that good idea was democracy. Through democracy, the modern Romanian state was begun: through a democracy that was at that time fiercely nationalistic. . . . Since the war, democracy here has managed to thwart any attempt at national reawakening. Through the blind pilots at the helm of the fatherland, democracy today has brought us to the place where we are today.[72]

A few months later, he returned to the same issues, no longer treating Romania's political classes as simply "blind" in their inability to recognize the threat minorities posed to the nation. Now, consistent with other legionaries, he denounced the country's "pilots" as "unconscionable traitors" and called for their execution.

> From all the regions, the same groans come to us, the same rumor of death. Never was our Romanian nation so close to perishing. Never were unconscionable traitors and imbecilic pilots so much the masters of the country's controls. What court-martial will be able to pass judgment on so many thousands of traitors—and how many forests will we have to transform into gallows for all the scoundrels and imbeciles of these twenty years of "Romanian politics"?[73]

The ambiguity of his earlier writings is no longer in evidence.

VII

Eliade's legionary articles make for tedious reading. Repetitive, bombastic, and shrill, they recycle slogans and buzzwords, rarely developing

any sustained argument. Over time, however, one can see him gradually modifying the schema he developed in earlier writings, where he
maintained that (a) the modern world is a disaster, since (b) it has lost sense
of the spirit's primacy, whereupon (c) its salvation falls to an elite group of
the young who will resist materialism and a narrow scientistic rationality,
while restoring spiritual values to their rightful prominence. Most of this
schema remained unchanged, although he no longer envisioned the Young
Generation as the agents of salvation. He now accorded this role to the
"new man," whom he defined in such a way as to bring legionary ideology
and rhetoric into alignment with his own (and vice versa).

> The new man is never born from a political movement—but always from
> a spiritual revolution, from a vast internal transformation. A new man of
> this sort was born from Christianity, from the Renaissance, etc.—from a
> perfected primacy of the spiritual against the temporal, from a triumph
> of the soul against the flesh. The new man is born from a genuine experi-
> ence and the generative power of freedom. I believe in the victory of the
> legionary movement because I believe in freedom, in the power of the
> spirit against biological and economic determinism.[74]

After the war, Eliade shifted slightly once more, now placing his hope in
the academic discipline he helped popularize, which he expected to intro-
duce a "new humanism" rather than a "new man."[75] Otherwise the schema
remained more or less intact.

3

A Hidden Past

Part II (1938–1979)

I

Eliade's legionary involvement ended abruptly—but in another sense, it never ended.

In the period leading up to the December 1937 elections, Eliade actively campaigned on behalf of the Legion, which had been barred from participating in the previous national elections of December 1933 and had grown dramatically in the meantime.[1] The electoral results were complex, and understanding them requires some background (Table 3.1). First, in the month preceding the elections, the Legion negotiated an "electoral nonaggression pact" with two other parties, which enhanced its influence and share of the vote. Second, laws of the time stipulated that any party receiving 40% of the popular vote would have its parliamentary representation significantly increased to ensure a majority. It would therefore automatically be called to form the next government. The National Liberal Party reached that mark in 1933 and had governed since, but its support fell below 40% in 1937, and it could not find coalition partners to produce an absolute majority.

Rather than see the Legion gain a share of state power, King Carol maneuvered frantically. After appointing a minority government that quickly proved unstable, he dissolved parliament and scheduled new elections. Before these could be held, however, he assumed dictatorial power, abrogated the

Table 3.1 Results in the national elections of December 1937

Party	Popular vote	Change from 1933	Seats in Chamber of Deputies	Change from 1933	Seats in Senate	Change from 1933
National Liberal	36.5%	−15.5%	152	−148	97	−8
National Peasant	20.7%	+1.3%	86	+57	10	+10
Legion of the Archangel Michael	15.8%	+13.4% (from 1932)	66	+61 (from 1932)	4	+4 (from 1932)
Liberal	9.3%	+0.5%	39	+21	0	0
Magyar	4.5%	+0.4%	19	+11	2	−1
Liberal	3.9%	−1.2%	16	+6	0	0
Radical Peasants	2.3%	+0.2%	9	+3	0	0
Minor Parties	7.0%	−2.7%	0	0	0	0

Note: Parties aligned in an "electoral nonaggression pact" appear in small capital letters.

constitution, gained ratification of a new one, and abolished the political arm of the Legion. On March 6, 1938, his minister of the interior (and later prime minister) Armand Călinescu issued an order for legionaries to be kept under state surveillance. On March 21, all political parties save the National Renaissance Front hastily organized by the king were formally abolished, and on April 19, Călinescu had Codreanu, Nae Ionescu, and forty-two other legionary leaders arrested, with more arrests and repression to follow. By late May, Eliade had gone into hiding, fearing imminent arrest as he explained to Cezar Petrescu, an influential author and journalist of the nonlegionary Right, from whom he sought sympathy and assistance.

> You know how Nae Ionescu was arrested: with a wagon full of gendarmes and four cars full of agents. You probably know how they ransacked his library.... Nae Ionescu was led to [the concentration camp at] Miercurea Ciuc, where he cannot even read and cannot be seen by anyone. All these

things you know. Undoubtedly, however, you do not know and do not even imagine what is happening to Nae Ionescu's assistant, your humble friend. To be Nae's assistant, it is understood, is to be of the subversive Right. To be an editor on *Cuvântul* is even worse. As a result of these two guilts, I and my family have been constantly watched by agents over the last six weeks. Five visits and searches, a search of our landlady, gendarmes in the street, a sergeant at the door. My wife and our child no longer sleep. For the past five days, from the time they came to arrest me—without a warrant, naturally—I have been fleeing like a hunted beast, from house to house, railway station to station, town to town.[2]

Archived reports from the Romanian Secret Services, including the following testimony obtained from Marietta Sadova, show that Mircea and his first wife, Nina, were supporters of the Legion from 1933 or 1934 and actively participated in meetings with Codreanu and other leading figures of the movement beginning in 1937.

In 1933–34, when I took part in the Criterion association in Bucharest, I entered into a circle of legionaries and legionary sympathizers, like Mihai Polihroniade, Mircea Vulcănescu, Petrişor Viforeanu, [Ion] Belgea, Mircea Eliade, Constantin Noica, Emil Cioran, Haig Acterian, and others. This circle exercised a nationalistic-chauvinistic influence on me. Rapidly accepting the legionary doctrine, I remained close to the legionary organization. Owing to this fact, in 1937, together with Haig Acterian, I participated in the first legionary meeting organized at the home of Mihai Polihroniade, in which the legionaries Mircea Eliade, Anton Hoitaş, C. Z. Codreanu, Nina Eliade, and Mary Polihroniade took part alongside us. At this meeting, a series of problems were discussed regarding legionary activities, including expropriation of the goods Jews possess and legionary electoral propaganda along with the National Peasant Party. Beginning from that date, I began to participate regularly at legionary sessions that were organized at the homes of the legionaries Mircea Eliade, Mihai Polihroniade, and at my home with Haig Acterian. In these legionary sessions, a set of legionary leaders took part, like Mircea Vulcănescu, Mihai Polihroniade, Alexandru Tell, Ion Belgea (legionary commander), and the legionaries Emil Bulbuc, Anton Hoitaş, Mircea Eliade, Horia Cosmovici and his brother, Constantin Ionescu, Petrişor Viforeanu, Nina Eliade, Mary Poihroniade, and myself. Within these legionary sessions, problems of legionary doctrine were discussed, and comments were offered on the actions of King Carol II, the situation of arrested legionaries, the identity of those executed. It was also established who would write in the future and what they would say, what actions needed to be taken to raise legionary aid, measures were established that needed to be undertaken against citizens of Jewish nationality, the activities of the Romanian Communist Party were slandered, and sometimes we sang legionary songs.[3]

Secret police reports filed in the immediate aftermath of Codreanu's arrest identify Eliade as a "legionary leader" (*fruntaș Legionar*) and describe him as having helped circulate information and instructions through a hastily assembled network of those movement intellectuals who had not yet been arrested.[4] Reports from the security forces in April 1938 treat these contacts as informal, but that of May 2 states, "The Legionary commander Nicoleta Nicolescu has succeeded in organizing a service of contacts for the entire capital for the Legionary movement" and places Eliade first on the list of those participating in the network.[5] Nicolescu was the highest-ranking woman in the legionary movement and served as an adviser to Codreanu. Arrested toward the end of 1938, she was tortured to death by the authorities, after which she achieved mythic status among the legionaries.[6]

Secret police accounts of Eliade's role in the Nicolescu group show him concerned, but relatively calm. Consistent with instructions given by Codreanu, he counseled legionaries to abstain from any serious action until after the trial, believing that Nazi Germany and fascist Italy would intervene and secure the Captain's release.[7] While actively working within these covert legionary circles, Eliade engaged in self-protective camouflage, portraying himself to Cezar Petrescu and others as the innocent victim of unfounded suspicions, a narrative he would cultivate and deploy many times in the future.[8]

In his letter to Petrescu, Eliade did not lie, but his account was selective and designed to mislead. He did not deny his legionary activities and commitments. But when he wrote, "To be Nae's assistant, it is understood, is to be of the subversive Right. To be an editor on *Cuvântul* is even worse," he used irony to portray himself as an innocent man suffering persecution at the hands of ignorant, biased authorities. That picture is complicated, however, by a subsequent passage, in which his anger, fear, and sense of solidarity with other victims interfered with his artful discourse.

I ask you to believe me, I'm not complaining. Think about it, if all this is happening to me—a university assistant, member of the Executive Committee of the Society of Romanian Writers, commentator on the radio—what must be happening to other legionary writers and scholars? I'll tell you what is happening to them. Constantin Virgil Gheorghiu, arrested and kept on his feet for two nights, brought before the "chief" from hour to hour in order to make a speech about what he didn't know. Arşavir Acterian arrested, Valeriu Cârdu arrested. I'm telling you only the names that you know. Monday night, there were five hundred of us arrested. All subversives. All my students in the Seminar in Metaphysics have been arrested or followed. Again, I am considered so dangerous that a colonel came to my house to "take me in." I'm sorry, but I'm still not able to surrender myself. My family isn't in the habit of begging.[9]

The word "other" leaps out from Eliade's rhetorical question—"What must be happening to *other* legionary writers and scholars?"—as does the first-person plural in his response, "there were five hundred *of us* arrested." Here his usage implicitly acknowledges what he simultaneously sought to conceal: the fact that he was—in that moment and for the foreseeable future—committed to and active in the legionary movement, consistent with the authorities' suspicions.

Eliade was ultimately arrested on July 14, 1938, having returned home after receiving assurances—which proved mistaken—from Armand Călinescu, transmitted through General Nicolae Condeescu, who was Nina Eliade's uncle.[10] In a letter written two weeks after her husband's arrest, Mrs. Eliade described these events and protested his detention, insisting on her husband's innocence and repeating what Mircea told his captors under interrogation: "He had not taken part in politics and would not do so, because it doesn't interest him." By way of elaboration, she provided an admirably succinct and precise summary of his views, which placed his legionary commitments outside—and above—the grubby sphere of the political: "He believes only in *the salvation of the nation through sacrifice and faith*."[11]

Upon his arrest, Eliade was asked to sign a declaration of "desolidarization," formally dissociating himself from the Legion. He refused, and in his auto-biography he offered two explanations for that refusal. In the first place, he said he could not sign any such document, "since I did not consider myself a 'political man.'"[12] In the second: "A declaration of dissociation from the legionary movement seemed not only unacceptable but downright absurd. I could not conceive of dissociating myself from my generation in the midst

of its oppression, when people were being prosecuted and persecuted un-
justly."[13] In his most important novel, *Forbidden Forest* (1955), he has the
protagonist, Ștefan Viziru, go further, standing on principle while asserting
his absolute innocence.

> Two days later he was again taken to be questioned, this time by a young
> commissar who regarded him absently. "You have influential protectors,"
> was his greeting. "Who has intervened for you? I have orders to let you
> go. Sign this declaration and you are free."
>
> He held out a piece of paper which Ștefan accepted with a smile.
> The inevitable administrative complications, he said to himself. But as
> he began to read it his face suddenly grew red. "I can't sign this!" he
> said firmly. "It's a declaration of my separation from the Legion of the
> Archangel Michael. I can't be separated from it if I never belonged to it."
>
> "It's just a formality," the inspector said wearily.
>
> "It's more than that. Why should I lie, saying I am no longer some-
> thing I never was? Something, besides, that I could not be, because it
> opposes my fundamental ideas, both ethical and political."
>
> "So much the better. This is precisely what we ask you to declare."
>
> "Then let me write my own declaration. I'm ready to sign a criticism
> any time because these are my views. But I can't confess that I regret
> having been a member of the Legion and that from now on will have
> nothing to do with it."[14]

Given his refusal, Eliade was consigned to the concentration camp at
Miercurea Ciuc, where other legionaries were being held and where Nae
Ionescu held seminars on the movement's doctrine and goals. Meanwhile,
fearing for her husband's life, Nina Eliade continued to seek help from her
uncle and others.[15] Finally, after months of sustained effort, she succeeded
in securing Mircea's release, ostensibly on medical grounds.[16] Formal
desolidarization remained a condition, however. His initial protests notwithstanding, Eliade signed the required document on October 28, 1938—
an act he never acknowledged in any of his later writings. Preserved in the
files of successive Romanian security services, it came to light only in the
postcommunist era when the Securitate Archives were made public, years
after Eliade's death.

> I, the undersigned Mircea Eliade, declare on my honor and conscience,
> of my own free will and for the future, I understand that I will abstain

from any political activity, whatever it might be, and will not undertake any action or agitation forbidden by law.[17]

One day after Eliade was released from the camp, Lt. Col. Ştefan Gherovici, chief of Gendarmerie, filed a related document, stating as follows: "As the named subject has given a declaration on his honor and conscience that he will abstain from any political activity, whatever it might be, and that he will undertake no more action or agitation forbidden by law, let us respectfully request that he be held under strict surveillance."[18] Presumably, Eliade would have known or suspected that such would be the case. One way or another, he honored the declaration. A police report of May 5, 1939—the result of such surveillance—describes a conversation he had "with a close circle of friends," explaining why he had refused employment with *România*, a paper sympathetic to the Legion, in favor of a position on the more centrist *Timpul* ("The Times"). The questions others raised went straight to the point, eliciting an answer simultaneously truthful and evasive.

Asked if he had definitively renounced the legionary movement, MIRCEA ELIADE responded: "The times, and especially external events, oblige all conscientious Romanians to close ranks and be united, in order to be able to confront the dangers outside, which still persist in great measure."[19]

Here, as would be true many times thereafter, Eliade spoke guardedly and obliquely, making it difficult to tell what his beliefs and commitments were, either at core or in that moment. In doing so, he sought to shield himself against two antithetical dangers that would haunt him for the rest of his life: (a) the possibility that the authorities or those hostile to the Legion would recognize the extent of his earlier involvement and believe—rightly or wrongly—that he remained loyal to the movement; (b) the possibility that his former legionary comrades would consider him a traitor. Maintaining that two-sided defense was no easy matter. We saw him rework the details of his arrest and internment in the fictive account of *Forbidden Forest* in ways designed to guard against the first of these dangers. Some years later, worrying that he might have gone too far in that direction, he revised things again to protect him from the second.

I utilized many of my memories from the Security headquarters and Miercurea Ciuc in *Forbidden Forest* and I regret now that I did; it could leave the impression that Ştefan Viziru is an alter-ego of mine, which isn't true.[20]

One is left not knowing what to believe, and that is probably just the point.

II

As it turned out, Eliade emerged from Miercurea Ciuc just in the nick of time. A few weeks earlier, Horia Sima, a rising, particularly militant legionary commander and one of the few not in prison, decided that aggressive action was the best way to advance the movement's interests (and not coincidentally, his own). Thus, on October 13, 1938, the Legion committed terrorist attacks in Bukovina and Transylvania. These were followed, in rapid succession, by student demonstrations in Cernăuţi (October 24), anti-Semitic violence in Cluj (November 1–5), and an assassination attempt on Florian Ştefănescu-Goangă, dean of the University of Cluj and former minister of education (November 28). In the midst of this violent upsurge, King Carol met with Hitler in Obersalzberg and came away convinced the Führer would not object if he took harsh steps against the Legion.

Five days after that meeting, on the night of November 29/30, acting on orders from Călinescu and the king, prison guards killed Codreanu and the thirteen legionaries responsible for the murders of Prime Minister Duca and the legionary apostate Mihail Stelescu, under pretext of thwarting an attempted escape. An accelerating cycle of reprisals and counterreprisals followed, culminating in the assassination of Prime Minister Călinescu, in vengeance for Codreanu's murder. Then, in the week following Călinescu's murder, 242 legionaries were summarily executed by the state's "forces of order," who left corpses on public display in all of Romania's major cities.[21]

Some of the victims were among Eliade's closest friends. Fearing that he could meet the same fate, several influential colleagues hastened to get him out of danger.[22] Toward that end, they secured a position for him in the Romanian diplomatic service, which sent him to London in March 1940 and, after the British refused to recognize his credentials, to Lisbon in February 1941.[23] While Eliade was in England, Stalin and Hitler pressed King Carol to cede important territories to the Soviet Union, Hungary, and Bulgaria. When he did so, the subsequent outcries and political pressure forced him to abdicate on September 6, 1940. Thereafter, a "National Legionary State" was proclaimed, in which state power was shared between the Legion and the military, with General Ion Antonescu as *Conducător* ("leader," parallel to *Duce* and *Führer*) and Horia Sima—who had become the Legion's most potent leader—as deputy prime minister. Legionaries controlled several important ministries, including that of the interior, within which they created an independent Legionary Police who visited bloody reprisals on old enemies, terrorized Jews, and profited from various corrupt dealings.[24] Most scandalous, perhaps, were the events of November 27, 1940, when legionaries summarily executed sixty-four officials of the old regime who were being held at the Jilava Prison, awaiting trial for earlier actions against the Legion. Not content with these victims, legionary death squads also sought, captured, and murdered former prime minister Nicolae Iorga and Virgil Madgearu, a leading economist who served in many ministerial positions and consistently opposed the Legion. When such excesses prompted resistance from their coalition partners, Sima and his followers attempted the coup d'état he had long been planning. Three days of street battles shook the country from January 21 to January 23, 1941, in the course of which the army crushed the insurrection, while legionaries staged a series of vicious pogroms.[25] Thereafter, Sima and most of the movement leaders who managed to avoid arrest fled Romania for Germany, where Hitler sheltered but kept a tight leash on them.[26] By that time, however, Eliade was safely on assignment abroad, where he saw out the war.

Multiple entries in Eliade's *Portuguese Journal* of 1941–45 show him hoping for German victory, understanding that Allied success would mean Soviet domination of Romania.[27] At the same time, his 1942 book celebrating the Portuguese dictator António Salazar makes clear his preference for a style of fascism in which religion enjoys a privileged position.[28] Although he previously identified the Legion as the ideal of that type, his journal entries during the war years contain relatively few comments on the Legion itself. The most significant exception is an entry of July 1942, describing a conversation he had with a group of friends during his last trip home to Bucharest.

> A vehement discussion at Mircea Vulcănescu's between Dinu Noica and all the others, concerning the Legion. Dinu accuses them of making themselves a comfortable bed under the shelter of the formula, "We're content to be technicians and serve the state under whatever form it may have." Dinu demands: "What did you do when Codreanu was killed? When you voted for the Constitution? For the Plebiscite?" etc. I intrude episodically in the discussion, declaring that I, although a legionary, have

suspended any judgment concerning internal politics so long as the war with Russia lasts."[29]

Noica accused his comrades of having abandoned the movement in the aftermath of defeats and having settled for a comfortable, but cowardly and unprincipled accommodation with their enemies. Eliade's conduct was surely at issue, and, in responding, he deployed the two-sided defense he was in the process of perfecting. Thus, he let the authorities know (should any informers be present) that he was no longer politically active, consistent with his declaration of desolidarization, while simultaneously assuring legionaries—who were clearly present—that he remained loyal and was no traitor.[30]

Other evidence suggests his position may have been more complicated still. Circumstances had changed, he told Noica and the others, such that he felt he could no longer speak out publicly or take direct action. But the Legion itself had also changed, as had his attitude toward it. Thus, the Legion to which Eliade was—and remained—committed was that of Codreanu, whom he continued to idealize in later years, as indicated by the way he described "the Captain" in his autobiography.

> I don't know how Corneliu Codreanu will be judged by history. . . . For him, the legionary movement did not constitute a political phenomenon but was, in its essence, ethical and religious. He repeated time and again that he was not interested in the acquisition of power but in the creation of a "new man." He had known for a long time that the king was planning to kill him, and had he wished he could have saved himself by fleeing to Italy or Germany. But Codreanu believed in the necessity of sacrifice; he considered that every new persecution could only purify and strengthen the legionary movement, and he believed, furthermore, in his own destiny and in the protection of the Archangel Michael.[31]

By voicing his continued admiration for the Captain, Eliade let those so inclined believe that he remained loyal to the movement as a whole. Later in the autobiography, however, he made clear that his loyalty did not extend to the elements of the Legion that assumed leadership after Codreanu's death.

> With horror I learned of the assassination of Nicolae Iorga and V. Madgearu, plus a group of "detainees" awaiting questioning at the

Văcăreşti Prison. By these assassinations on the night of November 29, [1940], the legionary squads who committed them believed they were avenging Codreanu. In fact, they had nullified the religious meaning of "sacrifice" held by the legionaries executed under Carol, and irreparably discredited the Iron Guard, considered *from then on* as a terrorist and pro-Nazi movement. The murder of Iorga, the great historian and brilliant cultural prophet, would be a blot for years to come on the name of Romania.[32]

Here, Eliade deployed another version of his two-sided defense, using the phrase "from then on" to draw a sharp distinction between the "good" Legion of Codreanu and the "bad" one of Horia Sima.[33] Accordingly, he portrayed the original movement as nearly ideal, for which he felt something like "nostalgia for paradise," while rejecting its historic successor as morally and spiritually fallen. Committed legionaries could understand that he remained loyal to the movement's founder and true values, while critics were assured that he never supported anything unworthy, for the violence, rabid anti-Semitism, and fascist aspirations of Codreanu's Legion had no place in his account.

Although one might consider these passages from the second volume of Eliade's autobiography (published posthumously in 1988) as an attempt to disarm his latter-day critics, much the same views appear in his letter of October 15, 1948, to Brutus Coste, a diplomat who had been his colleague in Lisbon.

> I know that nothing pure can be kept pure. In 1938, I joined the Iron Guard out of consideration for Moţa's memory, only to see in 1940 a Guard led by outlaws, loafers, and half-educated types, who were also compromising the memory of Moţa's ideal. Such is "History"—and therefore, I opt for Metaphysics.[34]

Writing in confidence to a trusted friend, Eliade acknowledged something he never admitted in his published works, that is, that he actively joined (*am aderat*) the Legion, while fudging the date, which could have been no later than January 1937 and was possibly some years earlier. The immediate context of his letter to Coste was their collaboration in postwar attempts to create a unified anticommunist front among expatriate Romanians. Legionaries, however, were wary of cooperating with people who had been their mortal enemies a few years earlier, and the task of persuading them fell to Eliade, who thus ran "the risk of being considered a 'traitor'" (*riscul de a fi considerat "trădător"*).[35] Knowing the way legionaries dealt with traitors, this was no trivial matter.

Eliade may have developed reservations about the post-Codreanu Legion earlier still, as antagonism between "Codrenist" old-timers and the emergent "Simist" mainstream initially took shape.[36] In 1964, Cristofor Dancu, an Orthodox priest and militant legionary, was imprisoned at the Aiud Penitentiary in Communist Romania. Asked to provide information on Eliade, whom he had known in earlier years, Dancu gave the authorities a mixed picture. He did not hesitate to praise his former colleague as "a beehive full of talent," "one of the truly tumultuous representatives of his generation," and "the type of scholar without time for quotidian problems, who loved books and had a passion for their explication." Such praise was leavened by remarks designed to please the Communist authorities, suggesting that Eliade's work on religion had no great importance, as it ignored material realities. At other points, Dancu made scabrous accusations, as when he charged Eliade with having taken money from the German I.G. Farben cartel and of having been sexually involved with his own stepdaughter.[37] On the question of the Legion, however, Dancu's accusations were relatively muted. Thus, when the issue first arose, he distanced Eliade from the Legion's violence: "In the Iron Guard, he was not a militant on the march, but he was a mentor through his writings for those of us who were younger than himself, who idolized him."[38] In the final paragraph of his statement, Dancu also suggested there were temporal—and moral—limits to Eliade's legionary involvement.

> In 1943, when I saw him for the last time, on the occasion of his return to the country for the printing of his monograph on Salazar, he was disgusted with legionarism, which he rightly criticized as a minor phenomenon, being disgusted with what he heard had happened in the country under the legionary government, while he was out of the country.[39]

Dancu was mistaken on the date of Eliade's last visit home, which took place in July 1942 and on the motive for that visit, which we will treat later. But his account of Eliade's disgust at the offenses of the post-Codreanu Legion is consistent with what Eliade wrote to Coste in 1948 and in his autobiography. It also suggests that the proper question is not just whether Eliade was a legionary, but what kind of a legionary he was and for how long.

III

After the war, Eliade made his way to France rather than returning to a Romania liberated by the Red Army. In Paris he eked out a living, made connections, and published the books that won him international fame.[40] His attempts to secure a university position were checked, however, by opposition from the Romanian ambassador, several knowledgeable Romanians living in Paris, and leftist students outraged at reports of his legionary past who painted swastikas on the posters announcing his course.[41] His circumstances improved dramatically in 1956 when he was named to a prestigious chair at the University of Chicago, where he quickly established himself as a scholar of exceptional breadth, erudition, and imagination. Given that few Americans knew anything of Romania's history or his entanglements in it, he was received in much the same spirit as the other European intellectuals Chicago welcomed, including Enrico Fermi, Hannah Arendt, Leo Strauss, and Arnaldo Momigliano. Kindly, brilliant, rumpled, and occasionally befuddled—he was famed for never reading newspapers, having no interest in politics, and frequently appearing lost in his thoughts—Eliade was regarded by his colleagues and students with uncritical admiration and affection.[42]

Some people have long memories, however. In 1972, a "dossier" on Eliade's legionary involvement appeared in the inaugural issue of an obscure Israeli journal published in Hebrew and Romanian.[43] Its author was Theodor Lavi, a journalist, historian, educator, and Zionist activist in Romania, who left the country in 1957 after being imprisoned by the Communist régime. Once settled in Israel, he worked as a researcher at Yad Vashem, with responsibility for the anguished history of Jews in his native country (Figure 3.1).[44]

Lavi felt moved to publish this article—which is virtually a prosecutorial brief—upon learning that Gershom Scholem, one of Israel's most distinguished academics and the world's foremost expert on Jewish mysticism, had contributed to a Festschrift honoring Eliade.[45] "The presence of a professor of our Hebrew University in the chorus of those singing the praise of Mircea Eliade is painful, to put it mildly," Lavi stated at the beginning of his article, since

Mircea Eliade took part in the Iron Guard, an extremist anti-Semitic organization, whose murderous activity is inscribed in our history with the blood of thousands, even tens of thousands of victims in the breast of the Jews of Romania.[46]

FIGURE 3.1 Theodor Lavi at the trial of Adolf Eichmann, 1961
Photo courtesy of the Central Archives for the History of the Jewish People.

Lavi charged that Eliade gave philosophical cover to unspeakable crimes, using his prestige to advance the legionary cause. To support his case, he marshaled the testimony of a privileged eyewitness, quoting extensively from the not-yet-published journal of Mihail Sebastian, an exceptionally talented playwright and novelist, who was the sole Jew in the circle around Nae Ionescu, a coeditor of *Cuvântul*, and one of the young Eliade's closest friends (Figure 3.2).[47]

Sebastian was a well-positioned observer who wrote about life under fascism with rare acuity, texture, and precision. His journal provides an intimate day-by-day account of the humiliations, injustices, and assaults Jews suffered.[48] Numerous passages detail his pain as he watched friends and colleagues embrace the Legion. Most wrenching was the case of Eliade, whom Sebastian held in high esteem and from whom he expected better.

The passages Lavi cited begin with Sebastian's September 25, 1936, account of Eliade voicing support for Codreanu, Mussolini, and Franco, while raging against Nicolae Titulescu, the Romanian minister for foreign

FIGURE 3.2 Mihail Sebastian, circa 1938

Photo courtesy of the Archives of the National Museum of Romanian Literature in Bucharest.

affairs, whose policies favoring France and the Soviet Union Codreanu had recently denounced as "an act of betrayal ... before God, the moral order of this world, and those who serve that order in a war against the destructive powers of evil."[49] Eliade opined that Titulescu "should be executed. Put in front of a machine-gun firing squad. Riddled with bullets. Strung up by the tongue."[50] Subsequent entries report Eliade's enthusiastic support for the Legion, his advocacy of violence against its enemies, and his authorship of a play (*Iphigenia*, which premiered in February 1941) that Sebastian understood as a celebration of legionary sacrifice.[51]

Toward the end of his dossier, Lavi observed, "I don't think it's necessary to comment very much on Sebastian's notes. Mircea Eliade's anti-Semitic attitude is evident."[52] Sebastian had indeed provided rich testimony about the depth of Eliade's legionary commitment, and it is probably a legitimate inference that any strong supporter of the Legion had to share—or at an absolute minimum, condone—its anti-Semitism. Yet Sebastian reported no instances of anti-Semitic acts on Eliade's part and only three instances of explicitly anti-Semitic comments. Most immediately, on December 17, 1937, he quoted without comment several ugly passages from Eliade's article "Why I Believe in the Victory of the Legionary Movement," to which we will shortly return.[53] The other two incidents Sebastian had on hearsay from Petru Comarnescu, who founded the Criterion group and was close to both Sebastian and Eliade. His testimony on these episodes—in which Eliade voiced opinions he would surely have hidden from Sebastian—is probably reliable.[54]

According to Sebastian's journal entry of March 25, 1937, Comarnescu reported Eliade's reactions to a ballet performance they had attended: "He found it disgusting because of its 'Jewish spirit.' He thought the show was Semitic." Although neither Sebastian nor Comarnescu make this explicit, Eliade's judgment was as much political as choreographic, the performance in question having been given by the avant-garde, antiwar Neue Tanzbühne, which had been forced out of Germany in 1933 when its founder, Kurt Jooss, refused Nazi orders to dismiss Jewish members of the troupe.[55] More disturbing still are remarks Comarnescu relayed to Sebastian shortly after the German invasion of Poland in September 1939.

> Comarnescu tells me of a political conversation he had recently with Mircea, who is more pro-German than ever, more anti-French and anti-Semitic. "The Poles' resistance in Warsaw," says Mircea, "is a Jewish resistance. Only Yids are capable of the blackmail of putting women and children in the front line, to take advantage of the Germans' sense of scruple. The Germans have no interest in the destruction of Romania. Only a pro-German government can save us. . . . What is happening on the frontier with Bukovina is a scandal because new waves of Jews are flooding into the country. Rather than a Romania again invaded by Yids, it would be better to have a German protectorate." Comarnescu assures me that these are Mircea's exact words.[56]

For the most part, Lavi's text simply cites or summarizes Sebastian's account of these episodes, with an occasional caustic comment. On one point, however, he ventured well beyond Sebastian's testimony to draw some strong conclusions. The incident is one Sebastian recorded on July 23, 1942, when he learned Eliade had returned to Bucharest from Lisbon for a brief visit; it was, in fact, the last time he would set foot in his homeland.

> I heard a while ago—but omitted to mention it in this journal (is it becoming so unimportant to me?)—that Mircea Eliade is in Bucharest. He did not try to get hold of me, of course, or show any sign of life. Once that would have seemed odious to me—even impossible, absurd. Now it seems natural. Like that, things are simpler and clearer. I really no longer have anything at all to say to him or ask him.[57]

Sebastian took Eliade's silence as a sign that their personal relations had ended, for reasons he found obvious. The two had grown apart as their political commitments and religious identities, previously matters of lesser importance, came to determine who they were, what opportunities were open (or closed) to them, and whose company they would keep. Writing from a post-Holocaust perspective, Lavi perceived something more sinister.

> Mihail Sebastian had no way to know that in summer 1942 an agreement was signed between Mihail Antonescu [then Romania's deputy prime minister] and Gustav Richter, Eichmann's delegate to Bucharest, for the deportation of all Jews to the extermination camps in Poland. Afterward, the measure was annulled, following a complex set of circumstances. As a diplomat, Mircea Eliade surely understood the fate being prepared for the Jews. What was the use of seeing his former friend, fated for death?[58]

Based on Sebastian's testimony and the conclusions he drew from it, Lavi accused Eliade of an anti-Semitism that was not "a temporary, opportunistic, or strictly theoretical adherence," but "a very deep defect of inner character" tantamount to "moral infamy."[59]

IV

Upon publication of his article, Lavi sent a copy to Gershom Scholem (Figure 3.3). Scholem responded politely and promised to send a copy to Eliade for comment. At the same time, he expressed the view that Lavi's dossier gave no evidence of anti-Semitic *activity* on Eliade's part and characterized Lavi's suggestion that Eliade knew of the coming Holocaust

FIGURE 3.3 Gershom Scholem, 1962
Photo courtesy of the Leo Baeck Institute.

in 1942 as "pure speculation." Cultural attachés were unlikely to be well informed on such matters, he observed, although "these things will surely be ascertainable."[60]

Scholem wrote to Eliade on the same day, transmitting a photocopy of the article. Like Lavi and many who have since entered the debate, Scholem's perspective was informed by acute consciousness of the Holocaust, such that he focused almost entirely on the question of anti-Semitism while ignoring other important issues, including fascism, violence, antidemocratic sedition, and Eliade's efforts to hide his past. But in marked contrast to Lavi's prosecutorial tone, the eminent Israeli scholar spoke sympathetically and reassuringly, while requesting an explanation.

> You will understand that I am most concerned about these things, and I would like to react to these accusations, to state your attitude at those times and, if necessary, your reasons for changing your mind. In those long years I have known you I had no reason whatsoever to believe you to have been an anti-Semite, and even more so, an anti-Semitic leader. I consider you a sincere and upright man whom I regard with great

respect. Therefore, it is only natural to ask you to tell me, and through me those concerned, the mere truth. If there is anything to be said on this score, let it be said, and let the atmosphere of general or specific accusations be cleared up.[61]

A month later, Eliade sent Scholem a carefully crafted letter in which he made eight individually enumerated points.[62] Some of these correct errors of detail in Lavi's article, undermining confidence in its accuracy and overall argument. Others rework the line of defense Eliade first advanced in his 1938 letter to Cezar Petrescu, dismissing accusations of his legionary involvement as instances of guilt by association because of his relationship with Nae Ionescu.

To demonstrate his independence from his mentor and rebut the charge of anti-Semitism, Eliade recalled the 1934 controversy that followed publication of Mihail Sebastian's autobiographical novel *For Two Thousand Years*, whose protagonist struggles to achieve an identity simultaneously Jewish and Romanian in the face of rising anti-Semitism. Some years earlier, Nae Ionescu (who is lovingly portrayed in the novel as Prof. Ghiță Blidaru) had agreed to write a preface for this work, although he had long maintained that Orthodox Christianity was indispensable to proper Romanian identity.[63] What is more, by the time the novel was finished, Ionescu had become one of the most prominent public champions of the Legion. In the year before the book appeared, he had published articles calling for the removal of all Jews from positions of political leadership (*retragerea tuturor evreilor de la posturile de conducere politică*) and suggesting that criticism of Nazi Germany in the liberal press constituted philo-Semitic aggression that threatened Romania's national interests.[64] Consistent with such views—and with the Legion's principle of confronting enemies directly— he delivered an offensively provocative text, assuming it would never be published.

Ionescu wrote that although Sebastian wanted "to discuss the problem of Judaism," he had shown only "that Judah suffers and is tormented; and it cannot be otherwise." It thus became the professor's task to show *why* Jewish suffering is inevitable and irreversible. Having rejected Christ, he explained, in a tone simultaneously pedantic, condescending, and aggressive, Jews remain permanent outsiders in the lands they inhabit. Accordingly, they are doomed to suffer, unless and until they reverse their error by accepting the Messiah, solving their problem by ceasing to be Jewish.[65]

Having rehearsed these theological arguments, to which he added a few sociological and philosophical wrinkles, Ionescu closed, speaking directly to Sebastian and addressing him by his Jewish birth name, rather than the pseudonym he employed as an author. His language was blunt and deliberately callous, as he condemned his protégé—along with his people—to eternal damnation.

> Iosef Hechter, you are sick. You are substantially sick because you can only suffer and because your suffering is unfounded. Everyone suffers, Iosef Hechter. We Christians also suffer. But for us there is a way out because we can be saved. I know that you hope; you hope that one day the long-awaited Messiah will come on a white horse, and then you will rule the world. Hope, Iosef Hechter. It is the only thing that remains for you.
>
> I, however, can do nothing for you because I know this Messiah will not come. The Messiah has come, Iosef Hechter, and you didn't recognize him. In return for all the good things God gave you as yours, you were asked to be watchful. And you were not watchful—or you did not see—because pride put scales on your eyes.
>
> Iosef Hechter, don't you feel that the cold and the dark overwhelm you?[66]

Contrary to Ionescu's expectations, Sebastian included this preface in the published volume and a sharp controversy followed. On the one hand, the Jewish community attacked Sebastian for letting a hateful screed see light of day. Liberals attacked Ionescu with equal fervor, while legionaries and others on the right rallied to his defense.[67] Describing his own role in this debate forty years after the fact, Eliade wrote to Scholem as follows.

> I was among the few authors who, in two long articles published in the journal *Vremea*, not only defended Sebastian, but criticized the preface, showing that Nae Ionescu's arguments could not be justified theologically, as he had thought. In turn, I was savagely attacked by the press of the right.[68]

Once again, this is not an outright falsehood, but it omits some things and overstates others. Rather than a defense of Sebastian against Ionescu and of Jews against anti-Semites, Eliade's 1934 article is better understood as an attempt to straddle the issue by defending his friend and his teacher alike. To those who believed Sebastian a self-hating Jew and a traitor to his people, Eliade praised his friend's courage in permitting publication of the preface, then proceeded to defend Ionescu against the charge of anti-Semitism. It was a labored, specious argument, in which he distanced himself from his mentor on just one point, suggesting that although the Jews had failed to recognize Christ as Messiah, one could not conclude they were categorically excluded from salvation as a result, since that would deny God's freedom to extend grace even to them, should he mysteriously choose to do so.[69]

Eliade simply ignored the moral issues raised in Sebastian's book: how widespread and violent anti-Semitism had become in Romania; the effects it had on its victims; its prime causes and prime agents; the way decent people ought judge and respond to it.[70] Rather than considering any of these points, he devoted the great bulk of his discussion to Ionescu's defense.

> As an orthodox thinker, Nae Ionescu cannot be an anti-Semite in any form. And in fact, *he is not*. This seems a bit paradoxical and yet it is very simple. The preface is not anti-Semitic. It *appears* otherwise because it includes bitter pages concerning the Jewish destiny. In fact, however, these pages do not include *an anti-Semitic attitude*—but only an unjustified transition from the plane of philosophy of history to that of Christian theology. That which was mistakenly interpreted as "anti-Semitism" is only a serious lapse of the distinguished dialectician. . . . Being anti-Semitic does not mean believing that the Jews suffer because they denied the Messiah—this is only a theological problem, erroneously resolved—rather, being anti-Semitic means taking a decisive attitude against the Jews, reckoning them inferior, scoundrels, dangerous, etc. In Prof. Nae Ionescu's preface, we do not discern this intransigent attitude toward the Jews.[71]

In Eliade's view, Ionescu would have done better to keep his discussion "on the plane of philosophy of history." Elsewhere in the article, he expanded on this point, observing that Nae's preface "says unpleasant things about Jews . . . because . . . it has the ill misfortune to have been written from the viewpoint of philosophy of history. But what do you want? *This* is how philosophy of history is written, without sweet words, without everyday things, without wordplay."[72] What he meant becomes clear from other articles in which he listed the authors he regarded as the leading "philosophers of history," most of whom were notorious anti-Semites: Artur, Comte de Gobineau, whose *Essai sur l'inégalité des races humaines* (1853) introduced the concept of "scientific racism," within which Semites figured as the chief threat to Aryan supremacy; Houston Stewart Chamberlain, Richard Wagner's pugnacious son-in-law, whose *Grundlagen des neunzehnten Jahrhunderts* (1899) popularized Gobineau's racism in Germany; and Alfred Rosenberg, whose *Der Mythus des 20. Jahrhunderts* (1929) picked up where Chamberlain left off and was the most influential Nazi ideological work after *Mein Kampf*.

Beginning with his "Spiritual Itinerary," Eliade repeatedly cited these men as the foremost "philosophers of history," following what he had absorbed from his professors, Nae Ionescu and Constantin Rădulescu-Motru.[73] The position he took differed markedly from that of the latter, however, who in 1922 observed that the "progress of biology . . . has debunked all the arguments invoked in support of the existence of human races," rendering Gobineau and Chamberlain obsolete.[74] Six years later, Eliade made Chamberlain's *Grundlagen* the very first book he recommended to readers, describing it as follows.

A grand synthesis, based on a vast and immense body of historical, philosophical, and scientific material. It provides orientation for all problems of culture. It enjoys a false reputation of "anti-Semitic dogma." That is only a superficial impression; the book is based on the theory of races, verifying Gobineau in light of the most recent research. A book that must be read twice (it has 1,200 pages), the first time without notes; the second, with notes and meditation on its essential chapters. It revivifies political, religious, and cultural history, from the Greeks to the French Republic.[75]

This was the same judgment Eliade would offer in 1934 with regard to Nae Ionescu: not an anti-Semite, just mistakenly regarded as such.

V

In his letter to Scholem, Eliade responded in some detail to two other points raised by Lavi's dossier. The first of these was the article "Why I Believe in the Victory of the Legionary Movement," published under Eliade's name on December 17, 1937, in the legionary paper *Buna Vestire*. Upon reading this text, Mihail Sebastian copied several passages into his journal.

> Can the Romanian people end its life . . . wasted by squalor and syphilis, overrun by Jews and torn apart by foreigners . . . ?
>
> . . . the legionary revolution has the nation's salvation as its supreme goal . . . as the Captain has said.
>
> . . . I believe in freedom, in personality, and in love. That is why I believe in the victory of the legionary movement.[76]

Reading these extracts, Lavi took them as conclusive proof of Eliade's anti-Semitism and reproduced them in his dossier, where they are the only material quoted directly from Eliade's writings. Since legionary publications were strictly controlled in the libraries of Communist Romania, the selections by Sebastian provided rare and precious evidence from Eliade's own pen.

The context in which this article appeared is also significant. Published on the eve of the crucial 1937 elections, Eliade's ringing endorsement contributed to the Legion's success. Its importance is further established by the fact that in May 1938, at the trial where Codreanu would lose his freedom, the Captain read this article to the court in its entirety, citing it as an accurate summary of the Legion's high ideals and spiritual nature.[77] By contrast, Sebastian quoted the piece without comment, but with unmistakable dismay. Reading these snippets decades later with full knowledge of the Holocaust's horrors, Lavi was enraged and Scholem troubled. Confronted with this seemingly incontrovertible piece of evidence, Eliade manufactured an audacious defense when responding to Scholem.

> I do not recall having written a single page of legionary doctrine or propaganda. But Sebastian cites several lines from a text that appeared in the daily of the Iron Guard, *Buna Vestire* (14 December 1937) titled: "Why I Believe in the Victory of the Legionary Movement." I never collaborated on this newspaper. However, this text exists, since Sebastian cites it. Probably it was the oral response made to an inquiry, which was then "edited" by the editor. It is impossible for me to be more precise.[78]

Eliade's assertion that he never wrote "a single page of legionary doctrine or propaganda" is patently false—as we have seen, he wrote fifteen such articles in the late 1930s. The opening "I do not recall" was a hedge against the then-unlikely event these documents would come to light. His claim that he never "collaborated on" *Buna Vestire* was also carefully phrased. True, he never served on the paper's editorial board or had any official position on it, but beyond the disputed piece, he published three other articles in what was then the Legion's most popular publication.[79]

In crafting his explanation, Eliade apparently drew on the sentence that introduced the article when it was initially published: "Mircea Eliade, member of the Society of Romanian Writers, was pleased to give us the following in response to the question put by our paper: 'Why do I believe in the victory of the Legionary movement?'"[80] Presumably written by Mihail Polihroniade, who edited *Buna Vestire*, this framing sentence leaves unclear whether Eliade gave a written response to the question, or whether—as he suggested to Scholem—he made some remarks to his friend Polihroniade, who produced a written text on that basis, introducing some of his own attitudes and language in an article he attributed to Eliade.

Speaking with Mac Linscott Ricketts almost a decade after the exchange with Scholem, Eliade developed his story further. While his letter to Scholem addressed the question "How could you have written this awful screed?" his remarks to Ricketts moved to the obvious follow-up: "If the article wasn't yours, why didn't you say so at the time?" Table 3.2 reveals the way Eliade reworked his story to shore up points where he felt vulnerable. However, the newer version—which had him firmly reject *Buna Vestire*'s invitation, only to be betrayed by its editor, a friend whom he was too noble to denounce—is no more verifiable and even less plausible than its predecessor.

Eliade's defenders have felt obliged to accept his denials, occasionally justifying their position by claiming that the prose style of the disputed article differs from Eliade's. Their assertions, however, are backed by no serious analysis of vocabulary, syntax, average sentence and paragraph length, or other stylistic features. Accordingly, they resemble professions of faith more than scholarly arguments.

The fullest attempt at a linguistic analysis was made by Culianu, who identified one term ("nation," Romanian *neam*) and two expressions ("squalor and syphilis," "overrun by Jews and foreigners") as foreign to Eliade's vocabulary.[81] On the contrary, *neam* appears in scores of Eliade's

Table 3.2 Eliade's attempts to distance himself from the December 1937 article bearing his name, titled "Why I Believe in the Victory of the Legionary Movement"

Eliade's response to Scholem, July 1972	Eliade's response to Ricketts, October 31, 1981
I do not recall having written a single page of legionary doctrine or propaganda.	At first he denied having written anything for *Buna vestire*.
	Then I mentioned the article on General Cantacuzino[a] and he said he could have done *that*.
But Sebastian cites several lines from a text that appeared in the daily of the Iron Guard, *Buna Vestire* (14 December 1937) titled: "Why I Believe in the Victory of the Legionary Movement." I never collaborated on this newspaper. However, this text exists, since Sebastian cites it.	But the one on "Why I believe in the triumph of the Legion" he denied.
Probably it was the oral response made to an inquiry, which was then "edited" by the editor.	He said he *refused* to give an answer and M. Polihroniade wrote one in his name.
	Then, because he didn't wish to embarrass his friend, Eliade did not deny he had written it or disown it.
It is impossible for me to be more precise.	

Sources: Eliade to Scholem, letter dated July 3, 1972; Ricketts's notes on the interview, as cited in Bordaş, "On the *Ḥadīth* Corpus of Mircea Eliade," p. 17. Ricketts summarized what Eliade had told him in his letter of November 7, 1981, to Theodor Lavi (quoted in Gligor and Caloianu, *Theodor Lavi în corespondenţă*, pp. 326–28); *Mircea Eliade*, pp. 928–29; and an interview broadcast on the Voice of America, September 15, 1988 (transcript in the Mircea Eliade Archive of the University of Chicago's Regenstein Library, Box 139, Folder 2).
[a] Eliade, "Mitul Generalului."

articles from the 1930s, while parallels to the two expressions can be found in "Democracy and the Problem of Romania," "Blind Pilots," and "'If You Should Come to Maramureş . . .'"[82] Even were such arguments convincing, relatively little would be gained since—as the same scholars who advance them acknowledge—there is virtually nothing in the "Why I Believe" article that Eliade had not said in his other legionary pieces.[83]

VI

The last point on which Eliade gave Scholem a detailed response was his failure to contact Mihail Sebastian during his last visit to Bucharest.

> It is true that in August 1942, during the few days I passed in Bucharest, I did not try to see him—but for entirely different reasons than those invoked [in Lavi's dossier], i.e. "being a diplomat, I knew the fate being prepared for the Jews." I would never have deigned to respond to that insult, if it were not the case that you, dear colleague, had read it. The fact is that I came to Bucharest following a long interview with Salazar, about which I still cannot give the details—but that one will read in my *Journal.* I had requested an audience with the chief of the National Peasant Party, Iuliu Maniu (then in the opposition), but while heading toward his house, I noticed that I was being followed by an agent of the secret police and I had to make several detours. I thus arrived late and Maniu had left; I could talk only to his secretary. During the few days I passed in Bucharest, I was constantly watched, and that is the reason I sought out neither Sebastian, nor [Alexandru] Rosetti, nor other friends and colleagues, for I could have compromised them. (The secret police, informed by the SS, knew that "overtures" for an armistice had taken place or were in preparation in Lisbon, Stockholm, and Ankara.)[84]

Although this "ambiguous and unconvincing" narrative (as Marta Petreu described it) does include a few truths, comparison to the account of these events in Eliade's posthumously published *Portugal Journal* shows that what he told Scholem was largely fiction.[85] Eliade did return to Bucharest after a meeting with Salazar on July 7, 1942, in which the Portuguese dictator expressed his view that Romania needed to preserve a battle-hardened elite—what he calls "an *esprit de front* group"—capable of rebuilding the country once the war was over. Eliade also reports that during a Berlin stopover, colleagues warned him that the Romanian secret service was aggressively tracking down legionaries.

Arriving in Bucharest on July 13, 1942 (not August, as he later remembered), Eliade relayed Salazar's advice to Mihail Antonescu, Romania's deputy prime minister, who cursorily dismissed it (and not Iuliu Maniu or his secretary). Eliade was disappointed, as were his legionary comrades, who had hoped his efforts would produce a rapprochement with the government. For Eliade clearly believed—and meant to persuade Antonescu—that the Legion was the elite group that could remake Romania on the model of Portuguese fascism, consistent with Salazar's counsel. Nowhere in his contemporary account did Eliade report that he felt himself under surveillance. Further, he described visits with numerous friends, including legionaries who ought to have been at particular risk. Indeed, he claimed to have seen "all my friends from the Criterion group"—a group in which Sebastian had once been central, but clearly no longer was. Table 3.3 compares Eliade's contemporary account of these events to what he told Scholem, showing how much he changed the story.

In his autobiography, Eliade made further changes still, including a different account of Salazar's message. There, he says the Portuguese dictator advised him that Marshal Antonescu ought to keep the Romanian army close to home, rather than putting it at risk on the eastern front. Had such advice actually been given—and taken—the effects would have been enormous. The disaster of Stalingrad, where the Romanian Third and Fourth Armies were annihilated with a loss of 160,000 men, could have been avoided. And had that been so, the Romanian military might even have been able to resist the Red Army's subsequent advance. In effect, this variant of the story transforms Eliade from a low-level diplomat who tried—and failed—to secure rehabilitation for the Legion into a tragic Cassandra, whose dire warnings were misunderstood and ignored, with disastrous consequences.

VII

Early in February 1973, Eliade received a letter from Burton Feldman, a former student of his then living in Israel, informing him that Scholem had engaged Lavi in an inconclusive conversation and that Eliade's responses had not completely satisfied him.[86]

> I gather that Scholem is still puzzled on that especially agonizing charge about anti-Semitism. And here again, I will only try to faithfully report Scholem's feelings, since he was very frank. He seems to be puzzled by what he feels is a certain "reticence" in your letter, about the anti-Semitism charges. That the question he was trying to ask you (and he wonders if he was clear) was really a question that only a friend could ask a friend—in other words, what you felt or might have said (to Sebastian, say) completely privately about this matter, what it amounted to personally, beyond all question of public writings, or such, during the pre-war

Table 3.3 Eliade's shifting account of why he failed to contact Mihail Sebastian in July 1942 during his last visit to Bucharest

Portugal Journal 1942 (published 2010)	Scholem letter 1972
7 July. Yesterday evening António Ferro called to inform me that I would be received in audience today by Salazar. . . .	I came to Bucharest following a long interview with Salazar,
Salazar asks me if there exists in Romania an *esprit de front* group that alone would be able to save the country after the war, because it would be the only spontaneous, total, suprapolitical organization. . . . He believes very strongly in the elite. It isn't necessary that a revolution be understood and supported by the masses. An elite suffices to transform a country.	about which I still cannot give the details—but that one will read in my *Journal*.
Bucharest. Hardly arrived, I am summoned into audience with Mihail Antonescu . . .	I had requested an audience with the chief of the National Peasant Party, Iuliu Maniu (then in the opposition), but while heading toward his house, I noticed that I was being followed by an agent of the secret police and I had to make several detours. I thus arrived late and Maniu had left; I could talk only to his secretary.
I realized that Salazar's idea—an *esprit de corps* group composed of men returned from the front—did not convince him, because he said: "I know what military men are like, they have a pragmatic spirit and they can't lead a country."	
	During the few days I passed in Bucharest, I was constantly watched

Table 3.3 Continued

Portugal Journal 1942 (published 2010)	Scholem letter 1972
At home, several friends were waiting for me; they were amused at the interview, but also disappointed: they had hoped that the audience would have a political meaning (that Ică [Mihail Antonescu's nickname] would attempt, through me, to reach an understanding with the Legion). . . . At Mircea Vulcănescu's, at Mitu Georgescu's, and then, invited by Paul Sterian, at P. Grant's villa at Snagov—I see all my friends from Criterion.	and that is the reason I sought out neither Sebastian, nor Rosetti, nor other friends and colleagues, for I could have compromised them.

Sources: Eliade, *Portugal Journal*, pp. 26–30; Eliade to Scholem, letter dated July 3, 1972.

years. He said that in your letter you said your autobiography and diaries would tell the whole story; but that these would be published probably not in your lifetime. If I can put this painful matter in a nutshell, I think Scholem is puzzled why you just don't tell him *now*, in a completely private letter, as friend to friend. You know his incredibly expressive face and gestures. He spread his arms, and said "After all, I'm 75! I'll never live to read those diaries."[87]

Shortly thereafter, Eliade renewed his efforts to persuade Scholem, focusing exclusively on the accusation of anti-Semitism and asserting his absolute innocence: "I have never been an anti-Semite. (In Romania, I published more than two thousand articles between 1925 and 1940 and there is not a single anti-Semitic page.)"[88] In response, Scholem repeated what he had told Feldman, that is, that he had met with Theodor Lavi and had a long conversation with him, after which he honestly did not know what to think. Scholem's tone remained friendly. He expressed the hope that his colleague would soon visit Israel so they could discuss things further, possibly together with Lavi. That never happened, and there, for the moment, things rested.[89]

Scholem, however, was not the only scholar who became aware of Lavi's dossier. Israeli colleagues also sent a copy to the Italian historian of religions

Alfonso Di Nola, who published a fierce denunciation of Eliade based on it. Building on Sebastian's testimony and Lavi's polemic, Di Nola went further, accusing Eliade of having "erased his real ideological roots" from his recently published *Fragments d'un journal* and having concealed his "real anti-Semitic, fascist, and pro-Nazi aspects." Di Nola further charged that in his scholarly work (particularly his 1947 *Myth of the Eternal Return*) Eliade sought to transform history of religions into "a mystified vehicle of salvation" that would restore the sacred sense of the cosmos, thereby reversing "the corruptive capacity of the Semitic view of the world" and "the disintegrative, worldly force of Semitism."[90]

Further criticism followed in Italy, most quickly from Ambrogio Donini and Furio Jesi, who were less concerned with anti-Semitism than with Eliade's fascism and, in the case of Jesi, the way Eliade's thought on such topics as sacrificial death, mythic models of heroism, the debased nature of modernity, and the need for its salvation drew on and provided support for what he termed the "culture of the right."[91] While a handful of Italians rallied to Eliade's defense, that task largely fell to his fellow countryman, student, and disciple, Ioan Petru Culianu.[92]

4

A Hidden Past

Part III (1972–1985)

I

Few of Eliade's works were available in Romania in the decades after the war, the Communist regime having suppressed them as a result of his legionary past. Although he published seven new books with Romanian publishers between 1939 and 1944, and saw six of his older novels appear in new editions, for a quarter century thereafter all his writings were published abroad—save for two seemingly inoffensive works of fiction.[1] After 1968, however, when Nicolae Ceaușescu refused to participate in the Soviet invasion of Czechoslovakia, his regime cultivated an image of Romania as the most liberal of the Eastern bloc states. In the relatively brief ideological thaw that followed, two of Eliade's novels and a play were published in rapid succession.[2] More important still was *De la Zalmoxis la Genghis-Han* ("From Zalmoxis to Genghis Khan," 1970), a collection of essays treating—and celebrating—Romanian prehistory, folklore, and religion.[3] Here Eliade built on his prewar research and that of authors like Vasile Pârvan and Lucian Blaga, who took such materials as a source of Romanian pride. Legionary ideals, including the supremely creative power of sacrifice, the value of ascetic withdrawal, and the sacred nature of martial virility figure prominently in this volume, which tested and took advantage of such opportunities as were emerging in Romania.[4]

FIGURE 4.1 Ioan Petru Culianu, circa 1970

It was in this context that Ioan Culianu, then in his junior year at the University of Bucharest (Figure 4.1), got his first serious exposure to Eliade's work.[5] Reacting with immediate enthusiasm, he identified strongly with Eliade on intellectual, personal, and probably also political grounds, given his own anticommunism.[6] In order to study the history of religions, a subject then unavailable in Romania, he began with languages (Greek, Hebrew, Sanskrit, Arabic), while reading independently on "anthropology and ethnography, the psychoanalysis of myth and symbols, Gnosticism, Orientalism, the Italian Renaissance, and especially its Platonic and Kabbalistic sources."[7] In 1971, he wrote to Eliade, who encouraged him to continue his studies and keep in touch.

Deciding that his best option was to study abroad, Culianu sought and received a fellowship for summer coursework in Italy, along with the requisite exit visa (the latter obtained with some difficulty, his first application having been unsuccessful). In July 1972, he left Romania, never to return, after having been granted political asylum by the Italian authorities. Once settled, he began formal work in history of religions at the Università Cattolica del Sacro Cuore of Milan. At the same time, he maintained epistolary contact with Eliade and traveled to Paris in September 1974 to meet him.[8] The next year, at Eliade's invitation, Culianu spent a term in Chicago, where he took courses with Eliade and Carsten Colpe. It was in their seminars that we first met. I remember him from that period as an eager, intense, and intelligent young man, but lonely, guarded, and somewhat awkward as he felt his way into a situation he found inviting in many respects, bewildering and off-putting in others. Working hard to find his way, both intellectually and personally, he was particularly eager to establish good relations with Eliade.

Toward that end, he devoted his first book to Eliade. It was scheduled to be published in Italy just as Di Nola's article appeared, as well as Ambrogio Donini's scathing characterization of Eliade as "anti-Semitic and pro-Nazi."[9] Although the bulk of Culianu's book was organized thematically, its first chapter treated Eliade's Romanian period as foundational for his later work.[10] This let Culianu claim privileged access to important material (by virtue of his ability to read the Romanian texts), but it also obliged him to touch on the positions Eliade took in the late 1930s, which he described as a mix of nationalism, traditionalism, vitalism, antirationalism, and "philosophy of crisis." All these came via Nae Ionescu's influence, which, Culianu rightly observed, led rasher members of Eliade's generation to dubious commitments and bloody deeds. On the crucial point, however, he asserted firmly and confidently, if incorrectly: "Any direct connection of Eliade with the legionary movement of Corneliu Codreanu is to be rejected."[11]

II

Culianu wrote that sentence in 1976 or early 1977, as news of Lavi's dossier was just reaching Italy. In doing so, Culianu relied heavily on what Eliade had told him and on a single, unpublished source: the *tesi di laurea* of Roberto Scagno, which he cited prominently and described as "indispensable for a historical framing of Eliade's formation."[12] Drawing on archives established by diasporic legionaries at Freiburg's Biblioteca Română, Scagno had recognized commonalities between Eliade's ideas and those of the Legion. Rather than construing this as evidence of legionary commitment on Eliade's part, he interpreted the overlap as a consequence of the fact that they drew on many of the same sources—native folklore, mystic strains of Orthodox Christianity, and the philosophy of Nae Ionescu—in their (rather different) attempts to reverse the corrosive effects of a "modernity" they considered antithetical to proper Romanian traditions and interests.[13]

Even this was enough to irritate Eliade, as it focused attention on matters he preferred not to discuss or acknowledge. In September 1974, he met with Scagno and tried to steer his interest in other directions.[14] And in January 1978, just as Culianu's book was nearing publication and Di Nola's article had begun making waves, he warned Culianu against following Scagno's lead.[15] This created real difficulties for Culianu, who realized he was putting his reputation and career prospects at risk by entering an increasingly fierce controversy in relatively uninformed and uncritical fashion. And so, in the closing weeks of 1977, he hastily prepared two drafts he thought might serve as an appendix to his book, in which he hoped to address the question of Eliade's politics during the late 1930s more directly and successfully.

Both versions show Culianu struggling with the impossible task of being both loyal and honest—pleasing Eliade while also satisfying the critics. His first draft thus began with a double admission: "His [Eliade's] relations with the movement of C. Z. Codreanu, which I decisively rejected, require a more nuanced judgment. Let me specify that until reading Scagno's thesis, I knew nothing precise concerning the ideological content of the legionary movement." The accompanying note describes what he did to rectify that situation: "For all the information in this appendix, I have consulted the multiauthored volume *Corneliu Codreanu Prezent* (Madrid, 1966)."[16]

Although this book gave Culianu a deeper and more detailed sense of the Legion's history, personnel, and self-understanding, the choice was still unfortunate. Quite simply, it is one of the worst possible sources for a balanced, let alone a critical, account of the Legion, being a hagiographic anthology celebrating the movement and its founder, as is made clear in the book's introductory essay.

> Now, twenty-five years after his assassination in 1938 and in light of political events that have happened since, one can place the immense personality of Corneliu Zelea Codreanu in historical perspective. Political thinker, social reformer, fighter, and unsurpassed organizer, he succeeded in the short span of a decade (1927–37) to stir the depths of a people's soul and to create auspicious conditions for a spiritual adventure such as was never encountered over the course of the Romanian nation's history. . . . At a time when Hitler emphasized the patrimony of "flesh and blood," that is, race, and Mussolini, the "state" and its rich people, Corneliu Codreanu emphasized a third entity: the *spiritual* patrimony

that must dominate and coordinate the other two. In this sense, he gave a superior sense to the notion of politics: *the realization of a vision* in accordance with the supreme laws of creation.[17]

Its limitations notwithstanding, this book helped Culianu to understand what Eliade found attractive in the Legion and also to recognize the "explicit proximity" of Eliade's views to Codreanu's. He used the term "proximity," moreover, to frame both the problem and its solution in much the same way that Scagno had; that is, Eliade was *close to*, but not "of" the Legion.[18] In his first draft, Culianu conceded more than Eliade would have liked, acknowledging legionary violence and anti-Semitism, while attempting to mitigate both by portraying the violence as conducted with a sense of righteous honor and the anti-Semitism as little different from what one found in Romanian political parties of right and left alike. Beyond that, his description of Codreanu's movement was remarkably positive, reflecting Eliade's views and those of the legionary sources he drew on.

> The Legion or Iron Guard was a mystical organization. It considered itself called to liberate society from oppression and the exploitation of man by man, but asserted that, whereas the left cultivates hatred between classes, it had been destined to accomplish a "revolution of love." Therefore, it did not hesitate to suppress personalities that were considered corrupt. Its goal was social justice and, as I already mentioned, its means were, in the first place, "the inner renewal of man" through legionary education and a contempt for death. . . . Until 1938, although anticommunist, the Legion was not of the Right, because it was against exploitation and social injustice, also because large finance did not accept the idea of social class, believing that a "revolution" could be realized without unleashing hatred between classes. And, surely, neither its anti-Semitism nor its nationalism differentiated it neatly from the Left, nor, in other ways, from bourgeois society of the time, in which anti-Semitic movements prospered.[19]

Culianu points to the night of November 29–30, 1938, when Codreanu and thirteen others were murdered on orders of King Carol, as a turning point in the Legion's nature and history.

> What it became thereafter—that is, a follower of National Socialism abroad—was not foreseen in the plans of C. Z. Codreanu. If history will be impartial (as it ought to be), it would have to distinguish clearly

between the National Peasant, proletarian character of the Iron Guard before 1938 and its pro-Nazi character from 1938 onward.[20]

The implications and motives for drawing this exaggerated contrast are clear. If Eliade was actively involved (something neither he nor Culianu would explicitly grant), it was a forgivable lapse limited to the time when the Legion was relatively admirable, even if marred by anti-Semitism and violence—features that, in Culianu's account, Eliade did not endorse.

On December 19, 1977, Culianu sent these drafts to Eliade, asking if he thought they should be included in the forthcoming book. Twelve days later, having received no response, he reconsidered and wrote again: "I have troubled you with reading this appendix to the book on Mircea Eliade. I have reread it with more detachment and I have the sense that it may be discordant with the general tone of the book and the time has still not come for me to write on this that which I wrote, since I know very little and I do not believe I understand things very well."[21]

Apparently Eliade was relieved. In a letter of January 17, 1978, he instructed Culianu why the topic ought not be broached.

> I have to admit: the reference to CZC [= Corneliu Zelea Codreanu] doesn't delight me, because it can give way to "confusions." (I also reproached Scagno for this: my sympathy for the Legion was indirect, via Nae Ionescu, and it had no influence on my thought and writings; it was only the pretext for the loss of my lectures at the University of Bucharest and further, for my being vilified between 1944 and 1968, in Romania and abroad . . .). With regard to Codreanu, I do not know what to believe: he was surely *honorable* and he succeeded in awakening a whole generation, but lacking a political spirit, he provoked a cascade of repressions (Carol II, Antonescu, the Communists), which decapitated the whole generation he had "awakened." . . . I don't believe one can write an objective history of the legionary movement, nor a portrait of Codreanu. The available documents are insufficient. In addition, an "objective" attitude to him could be fatal for the author.[22]

Note the tightly circumscribed lines of defense. Although Eliade concedes he had "sympathy" for the Legion, he characterizes this as "indirect"—mediated by Nae Ionescu—while insisting it had no influence on his work and thought. And he paints himself as the victim of injustice at the hands of maliciously misguided critics.

His remarks about Codreanu are also carefully framed, with praise and criticism in equal measure, at least on the surface. But the main critique—the Captain's lack of "political spirit"—is actually praise, given Eliade's own disdain for the political. From Eliade's perspective, the sole problem is that the Legion's admirable rejection of conventional politics provoked counterattacks by the unscrupulous politicians whose interests it threatened: King Carol, Marshal Antonescu, and the Communists, all of whom emerge as the villains of a story in which Codreanu is the tragic hero. Only slightly less noble is Eliade himself, whose "sympathy" for this "honorable" man cost him his job and exposed him to enemies who specialize in character assassination.

The text also hints darkly at present dangers, suggesting that any attempt to produce an objective account of Codreanu and the Legion could prove "fatal for the author" (*fatală autorului*). Is this metaphor? Hyperbole? Clearly, Eliade meant to discourage his young admirer from further research on the topic.[23] But how serious was the implicit threat? In retrospect, his words hang heavy.

III

Hoping to put the matter to rest, Eliade asked the legionary poet Horia Stamatu to provide Culianu with copies of Codreanu's *For My Legionaries* and other key movement texts, imagining these would help his protégé understand the Legion's "honorable" nature.[24] On January 10, 1978, however, Culianu recorded in his journal: "I am reading *For My Legionaries* with despair, exasperated by its delirious anti-Semitism.... Legionary ideology is as foreign to me as Communism. They are very similar.... The surprise that Mircea Eliade was the partisan of a totalitarian movement and that he remained for all his life a believer in its mythology fills me with bitterness."[25]

In subsequent correspondence, Culianu sought more information from Eliade, only to be rebuffed again. "As I have often told you," Eliade wrote him on February 13, 1978, "I don't take pleasure in 'discussion' of my political positions (or lack of positions)—because to do that properly and exhaustively would take tens, if not hundreds of pages—and I do not have the time, nor heart for that."[26] Then again, on March 1:

> I was neither an anti-Semite nor pro-Nazi. In a polemic with Gh. Racoveanu, à propos of *For Two Thousand Years*, I wrote two articles in *Vremea* on "Judaism and Christianity." Etc., Etc. But I can no longer resist reminding myself what bad blood these stupidities have produced for me (*calomniez, calomniez, il en restera toujours [quelque] chose!* . . .). I have not responded and will never respond.[27]

Consistent with his response to Scholem, Eliade categorically rejected accusations of anti-Semitism and Nazism while ignoring others more difficult to dismiss, including his support for fascism, the Legion, and right-wing "Romanianism"; his attacks on democracy and liberal institutions; his public silence and occasional private enthusiasm regarding legionary violence.

Some have charged Eliade with opportunistically concealing his legionary involvement, lest any hint spoil his reputation. He certainly did, but it is also likely that his denials and evasions helped him manage repressed feelings of guilt, fear, and shame. Over the years he labored, never with more than partial success, to persuade himself and others of two propositions: first, he had done nothing wrong, since he was not really a Nazi or anti-Semite; second, that those who said otherwise did so out of envy, malice, and unprincipled ideological commitments. Beyond that, he was caught in a bind. Were he to acknowledge his past support for the Legion, strong condemnation would follow from many quarters, regardless of whatever mitigating explanations he might offer. And were he to express any regrets, make any apologies, or distance himself in any way, legionaries would likely see him as a traitor and could well take vengeance on him.

One gets a sense of Eliade's troubled conscience, persistent fears, and capacity for self-pity from a September 1973 entry in his journal, where he repeated a story he had read in the émigré press. Of dubious authenticity, it describes the fate of an English tourist, with whom he clearly identified.

> Popular demonstrations in Milan upon the death of Allende. Some demonstrators notice an English tourist raising his arm. The fascist salute! The demonstrators rush over to him. He is beaten, covered with punches, his body is trampled. It would not have taken much for him to

have lost his life there, which would surely have happened if the police hadn't pulled him out at the last minute. While he is being taken by ambulance to the hospital, a nurse is surprised by his thoughtlessness: How could he have displayed the fascist salute at a communist demonstration!

"But I wasn't giving the fascist salute," cried the wounded man, "I was hailing a taxi."[28]

Like the poor Englishman of this story, Eliade apparently saw himself—and very much wanted to see himself—not only an innocent naif, but the victim of a terrible misunderstanding fostered by dangerous leftists.

IV

Unsatisfied with Eliade's responses, Culianu began reading more about interwar Romania and the legionary movement. According to Gianpaolo Romanato, a church historian who became a close friend when the two studied together in Milan, "Culianu carried out lengthy investigations on Romania in the 1930s and 1940s, as well as Eliade's position regarding fascism and Nazism. The numerous letters in which he conveyed to me the results of his researches . . . show how painstaking, troubled, and sincere was his search for the truth. The signs of Eliade's distrust in their encounters (cf. Culianu's letters of October 22 and November 9, 1978), although quickly cleared, were a consequence of all that."[29] Since my own research indicates that Culianu's work on the legionary question was less thorough—and certainly less critical—than Romanato suggests, I wrote to him in January 2019 and asked if I could see the letters to which he referred. Initially, he agreed, but he subsequently changed his mind.[30] The explanation he offered is worth citing, as it reinforces my impression.

I have reread the letters that could interest you and I am finally convinced they are not suited to be made public. I do not wish to seem rude. It is not a question of rudeness or lack of faith with regard to him, believe me. Quite simply, these are confused letters, written by a youth who grew up in the constraining culture of Communist Romania, who began only then, after his flight to the West, to open his eyes and mind to the past of his country, that is, to the years of fascism and the Iron Guard before the Second World War. In the moment he wrote to me, he knew and understood little of those years, and in fact, Eliade was angry at him for these naive researches. I think that today, Culianu would be the first to smile if he could reread what he wrote to me then. To make known his lucubrations of that time would add nothing of importance to our understanding of Culianu and even less to our understanding of Eliade.[31]

On the contrary: the letters would surely add to our understanding of the young Culianu and his shifting relations with the defensive Eliade. They would, however, detract from the idealized picture of his attempt to "get at the truth," which was hardly neutral, objective, or disinterested. Indeed, whatever moral qualms he may have had about Eliade's past coexisted with worries about the loss of his benefactor's support at a precarious time when he had just completed his studies in Italy and assumed his first teaching position.[32] Upon learning that Eliade would not arrange for a French translation of his book, as he had been led to expect, Culianu took this as a direct consequence of and implicit rebuke for "my foolish inquiries on interwar Romania."[33] In a letter of November 9, 1978, to Romanato, he explained the situation.

Now, you asked me what happened with the anticipated translation of my book on Eliade: a real mess, for which I'm to blame (or, better yet: the truth is to blame). Because my inquiries regarding Eliade's past and that of Romania displeased him greatly, he therefore did not recommend my book to his editor (even though I did not include that research in my book). He preferred the book of an American, whose information is shaky. Surely, you will say I was a fool to make Eliade unhappy with all my research. I could say to you: *Amicus Plato, sed magis amica veritas* ["Plato is a friend, but the truth is a better one"] and that's true. But things are more complicated: in reality, this past winter I noticed I'm getting older and the whole system of vague values in which I believed and to which I was accustomed from reading Eliade is a completely false system with regard to the structures of life itself, not to mention those of society. Therefore I have to tell you that in that moment, I saw how naive, but harmful it is in every way, and I bitterly regretted the errors of my whole past, in which I revered the doctrine of this idol. Surely, I can't attribute these errors to him, but I still owe them largely to my interpretations of his writings. Essentially, this happened this winter and he became conscious of this change (expressed in terms no more gentle than those above). Clearly, it was naive. But the same is true of the affection I bore—and always bear—for him. Still, it doesn't seem to me he took it well, coming at the very moment when the world was rushing to give him medals and distinction upon distinction. Because obviously, my function in this world was that of the idiot disciple (*discepolo cretino*) who faced every sort of danger in order to meet him but is permitted no space to criticize him. This was the situation until September, when I saw him again. Now I believe the affectionate ties that previously existed have been reestablished, and for my part, I have come to understand how much depends on him (from every point of view), for which reason I have adopted a prudent, more obsequious attitude.[34]

Evident in this letter is Culianu's deep ambivalence regarding his mentor and patron, whom he simultaneously loved, feared, admired, and resented, and whose favor he sought and needed. In later years, he would insist that the sole motive for his research into Eliade's involvement with the Legion was a principled determination to find the truth and that—fortunately, if implausibly—his painstaking research quelled his earlier doubts. For example, in a letter dated roughly one year after Eliade's death, he wrote as follows.

I spent two years of research trying to understand what was true in the allegations of Jesi and Di Nola. During that time, my relationship with Mr. Eliade was impaired by suspicion. Ultimately, I came to the conclusion that Eliade was *never* an anti-Semite and was never a *member* of the Iron Guard, though ambiguities of the years 1938–39 might wrongly suggest such an affiliation. Furthermore, he was an *anti-Nazi*, insofar as he was a Salazarian.[35]

As the nature of the conclusions announced here suggests, Culianu seems to have conducted his research with apologetic more than forensic goals. Acting much like a counsel for the defense, he sought exculpatory pieces of evidence, lines of argument, and turns of phrase with which he could justify—to himself and others—dismissing the charges against his client. Having found a few such rationales (e.g., Eliade's support for Mihail Sebastian proved he was no anti-Semite, while his admiration for Antonio Salazar supposedly proved he was anti-Nazi), he repeatedly deployed these arguments in subsequent years, as if they were sufficient to settle the question (see the Appendix).

Culianu seems to have regarded his period of doubt as the liminal phase in a rite of passage, during which he endured painful trials but proved himself fearless and resourceful, emerging from the process wiser, more mature, and more confident. Although he modified his position slightly as new evidence came to light in the years after Eliade's death, for the most part he adhered to the broad lines his mentor established: (1) the Legion under Codreanu was largely admirable, not the evil thing it became after the Captain's death; (2) Eliade never joined the movement, although he sympathized with the religious aspirations and hopes for the Romanian nation that Codreanu embodied; (3) he himself was never an anti-Semite, legionary, or Nazi; (4) those who make stronger accusations do so out of ignorance, envy, and/or malice. They are not to be trusted.

V

In the period between 1978 and 1984, consistent with his decision to be "more obsequious,"[36] Culianu avoided discussion of Eliade's past and his politics, while championing his academic and literary accomplishments.[37] Thus, in a volume dedicated to Eliade by a French right-wing journal, he praised his mentor for having raised an inspirational edifice on the ruins left by Nietzsche.[38] Again, in a volume edited by his friend Scagno, he portrayed Eliade as "one of the most noteworthy and influential" critics of European colonialism and racism, possessed of a sympathy for the Other like that of the best Franciscan missionaries and a man whose scholarly research "was for him, as he himself confesses, a form of ascesis or religion, a way of making spiritual progress, an *imitatio Christi*."[39]

Around the same time, Hans-Peter Duerr invited Culianu to contribute to a "critical Festschrift" he was organizing, in which he expected a wide range of scholars to debate Eliade's work from varied positions.[40] Culianu's contribution was a long, complicated piece titled "Mircea Eliade and the Blind Tortoises," which opened by comparing his mentor's general project to the salvific efforts of Taoist sages and Zen masters.[41] Subsequent sections discussed Eliade's relation to earlier Romanian scholars, styling Nae Ionescu as the Socrates to Eliade's Plato.[42] Culianu then took up the question of Eliade's early political commitments.

As far as I can see, it was Italian scholars who were most passionate in the debate about Eliade's activities in prewar Romania. However, they have not yet been able to obtain more than a general understanding of the subject. And in this case, generalization is, perhaps, particularly dangerous since it could cause confusion. And it has done so. That is the reason why many people encouraged me to express my opinion on the question. I did so only reluctantly since my previous statements regarding Eliade's relation to the Romanian *intelligentsia* of 1925–1945 have been misunderstood. Moreover, while Eliade did not actually distance himself from my account, he at least seemed disconcerted by its clumsiness. That led me to further investigations that, although far from thorough, were nevertheless impartial and based on information gathered at first hand.[43]

To judge from his footnotes, Culianu's description of his investigations as "impartial" is less justified than his acknowledgment they were "far from thorough." Although he cited four standard works on interwar Romania, he summarily dismissed them all for presenting what he considered a prejudicial caricature of his country.[44] In contrast, he insisted that Romania in the 1930s was a democracy much like those of Western Europe; that the Legion was a brand of fascism markedly different from all others, being religious as well as political; that legionary anti-Semitism was rooted in economic concerns, not racism; and that Codreanu "did not want any special measures to be taken against Jews." The latter points reflect the self-justifying position taken by legionaries in the wake of the Holocaust. As Horia Sima himself maintained:

> Let us make clear that the anti-Jewishness of the Romanian people *never had a religious or racial foundation.* From the religious point of view, the Romanian people are the most tolerant in the world. There is no case whatsoever of religious persecution in Romania throughout its history. The cause of Romanian anti-Jewishness was *social and economic.*[45]

The set of works Culianu relied on and cited with approval consisted of three books by prominent legionary commanders and two narrowly specialized monographs.[46] All of these helped him attempt to destigmatize his country and its most infamous movement. These volumes, however, were not his chief source. More important was the information he describes as having been "gathered at first hand." Matei Călinescu gave an indication of what that entailed.

> In Italy first, then in France and other countries, Culianu came in contact with diasporic Romanians who were former legionaries, from whom he learned many details—including anecdotes, gossip, past rumors, etc.—about the Movement and those who gravitated around it. This type of imprecise knowledge was not without value for a discriminating mind.[47]

In other words, Culianu absorbed the self-serving views of old legionaries, which he found preferable to the standard scholarly accounts, particularly as they let him "understand" Eliade's position and minimize his errors, offenses, and responsibility. The same uncritical credulity let him accept what Eliade—his most privileged informant—told him: the great historian of religions was not an anti-Semite (as proved by his defense of Mihail Sebastian). He was not pro-Nazi (as shown by his diplomatic appointment to London by an anti-German government). He was never a member of the Legion (in the sense of formal adherence). And he never published in *Buna Vestire* (since the disputed article was, in Culianu's view "easily recognized as a bad forgery").[48]

Shifting from defense to offense, Culianu reframed the question. Why was it, he asked, that "some ill-informed people" keep insisting on Eliade's legionary involvement, even though "these rumors are easily refuted." To resolve that, he proposed "to follow the tracks of this absurd 'black legend' concerning Eliade back to its beginnings."[49]

VI

In Culianu's account, the problems began in the mid-1930s, when the Romanian security forces (Siguranța) "began to keep a vigilant eye on Eliade." The reason, Culianu suggests, following Eliade, was simply that Eliade was Nae Ionescu's closest disciple, whose views and commitments—the security services wrongly believed—could not differ from those of his teacher. Securitate, the postwar successor service, inherited these suspicions along with the files. The postwar Communist regime amplified and widely disseminated these falsehoods in its eagerness to discredit legionaries, émigrés, bourgeois intellectuals, and enemies of the state.[50]

In his 1978 monograph, Culianu briefly mentioned an episode from the late 1940s when Einaudi, the foremost publisher on the Italian left,

FIGURE 4.2 Ambrogio Donini speaking at the World Congress of Intellectuals for Peace, August 1948

Photo from Alamy Ltd.

considered placing the first translations of Eliade's work in a prestigious series directed by Ernesto De Martino and Cesare Pavese. At first, De Martino was hesitant and the project went nowhere. But a compromise was reached and two translations were published, bearing critical introductions by De Martino.[51] Although Culianu did not initially draw strong conclusions from this incident, he later gained information that led him to see deeper significance in it.[52] Specifically, he learned that a third party had been involved in the discussions: Ambrogio Donini, a respected historian of Christianity and high-ranking member of the Italian Communist Party (Figure 4.2).[53] In 1949, acting on information he received from a Romanian colleague while serving as Italy's ambassador to Poland, Donini pressured Einaudi not to publish a "counterrevolutionary writer" and "an enemy of popular democracy, who is active among the counterrevolutionary émigrés in Paris."[54] In response, Pavese observed, "It did not occur to us to examine the author's criminal record, since this is not a question of a political or journalistic work. Whatever Eliade may have done in exile cannot injure the scientific value of his work."[55]

Donini's view did not change over the years, and when he described Eliade as "an anti-Semite and pro-Nazi" in his 1977 *Encyclopedia of Religions*, Culianu considered this part of a long-standing, well-orchestrated Communist campaign of defamation.[56] In a letter of April 10, 1978, to Romanato, Culianu fumed: "Given that we no longer live in that type of regime built by Donini and people like him, *you could ask what is the source of his information*? I would be most grateful if he would cite it, because I too would cite it the next time I write about Eliade and would be indebted to him. But if, on the other hand, he cannot cite it, perhaps he could reflect a bit on the fact that no good comes to anyone from gratuitous calumny."[57]

Culianu went further, describing Donini as "a powerful Communist, loyal to Moscow . . . who lost his position within the Communist Party because of his incurable Stalinist obduracy."[58] Culianu also saw "Communist tendencies" at work in Theodor Lavi's "Eliade Dossier," even though Lavi had been imprisoned by the Communist regime and forced to leave Romania. In his 1984 "Blind Tortoises" article, Culianu was content to issue hyperbolically exaggerated denunciations, as in his unsupported—and unsupportable—assertion: "It is easy to show that more than 90% of [Lavi's] information is false, and the rest highly improbable."[59] Four years later, in a radio broadcast for the Romanian section of the BBC, he ramped up the attack. Having noticed that Lavi began his dossier by citing two Romanian Communists who knew Eliade in the 1930s and testified to his involvement with the Iron Guard, Culianu seized on this to discredit Lavi, while also taking an ugly swipe at Mihail Sebastian.[60]

> Mihail Sebastian, Eliade's best friend, kept a journal, unfortunately venomous (but can we really blame him?) and full of inexactitudes, which clandestinely arrived in Israel, where fragments from it were published in 1972 in a ghostly Romanian-language bulletin (*Toladot*, i.e., "History"). That bulletin, which has Communist tendencies (it ceremoniously cites the academician Miron Constantinescu!), obviously wants to defame Eliade. It promises a sequel that never appeared, but the polemic became particularly heated in Italy, where even today a campaign full of surprises is taking place. This is not the place to give details, but they are not lacking in interest.[61]

Having written off Donini as a Communist and Lavi as a dupe, here Culianu depicts Sebastian as a bitter, misguided Jew, whose hypersensitivity to anti-Semitism led him to a "venomous" attitude and countless unspecified "inexactitudes." In the course of this article, he went on to dismiss other critics in similar fashion, with little pretense of serious engagement. Thus, he observed that Di Nola turned hostile to Eliade (whom he earlier admired) only under Lavi's influence, after which Jesi amplified what he found in Di Nola to produce what Culianu termed "a brilliant example of paranoid 'science.' "[62] "The calumnies continue," he wrote in 1987, as the critique was spreading to other countries, "fed by the Stalinist sources of Italy."[63] That the critics were Marxists (Donini), Jews (Sebastian, Lavi), or both (Di Nola, Jesi) was not something he needed to make explicit. Those among his readers who considered such information important could infer that for themselves.

VII

If Culianu thought his intervention would quell the critics or convince anyone not already in Eliade's corner, such hopes were disappointed. In rapid succession, a series of Italian scholars, some on the left and some on the far right, responded to his "Blind Tortoises" article, pointing out its evasions, embellishments, and errors of fact, while describing its author as less than objective and trustworthy. Crescenzo Fiore, for example, advised readers to exercise "the necessary caution that imposes itself regarding the assertions of an author whom Eliade himself defines as 'Eliadean.' "[64]

Even so, the piece had its desired effect on the one reader for whom it was most intended. In a letter of February 24, 1984, Eliade thanked and reassured his defender: "I am in perfect agreement with what you have written in reference to my 'critics.' "[65] This followed other signs that Culianu had regained Eliade's trust and favor. Early in 1983, Eliade had written to his French publishers, naming Culianu "my universal legatee" who would see to "the future development of all my writings, published and unpublished."[66] Around the same time, Paul Goma, a Romanian dissident living in Paris, asked Eliade and Culianu to develop a jointly authored book for a series he was organizing.[67] Both men liked the idea, and over the next several years they discussed how they could bring it to fruition.

Eliade suggested that the book include three sections: one in which he spelled out his "ideas and beliefs," one in which Culianu did the same, and a concluding dialogue "on the themes you [i.e., Culianu] consider interesting."[68] This notwithstanding, he tried to steer Culianu away from politics, while proposing procedures that would give him control of the questions put to him.

> In June, we will discuss the book. I believe that you have insisted too much on the political moment, which only interested me for two to three years, exclusively owing to my affection for Nae Ionescu. Again, you have said very little about literature (i.e., in comparison to "politics"). I imagine this solution: (1) in May, I will reread and annotate the text; (2) I will propose to you a number of questions to which I will respond "concisely" (with references to some texts from my *Journal*), responses that you can develop at will (in dialogue with them, etc.) because you are largely familiar with them.[69]

Contracts were signed in May 1984, and on September 18 of that year, Culianu described his preference for a book that would focus primarily on Eliade's literary contributions.[70] Apparently reassured, Eliade proposed "a provisional solution" that would let Culianu generate the questions.

> Even if you will not be able to come to Paris, send me a first series of questions. I can sketch responses, either here or (more probably) in Chicago. Succinct responses, with reference to our past discussions or certain published texts (interviews, *Journal*, Autobiography, etc.). In any case, in Chicago I can dictate longer responses to Christinel [Eliade's wife], following my notes, or suggestions for further questions.[71]

In the following months, Culianu produced a long introductory essay for the projected volume, which he now titled *The Unknown Mircea Eliade*, along with twenty-one questions, as per Eliade's suggestion. As its foreword explained, the book would present two aspects of Eliade that had received insufficient attention. Culianu's essay would address "his *historic* existence and his *Sitz im Leben* in Romanian political and intellectual life between 1921–43," while the interview would present "Eliade as *alive*, expressing himself with a strong voice to a sometimes-ignorant youth, but always considerate of someone he permitted to call himself his *disciple*."[72]

Culianu's text contains much of interest, particularly regarding Eliade's literary work. But his treatment of the 1930s, which includes some detailed information, is defensive and highly credulous.[73] Beyond insisting on the familiar points—Eliade was not a member of the Legion, anti-Semitic, or pro-Nazi—he now portrayed him as a man of "democratic conscience," "democratic belief," and "fundamentally democratic spirit," flatly contradicting what he said in the final paragraph of his "Blind Tortoises" article just a few years before: "He was no anti-Semite, no legionary, no Nazi or pro-Nazi, *and also no democrat.*"[74]

A statement in the concluding section of the unpublished manuscript provides insight into the nature and extent of Culianu's understanding, as well as the perspective, motives, sources, and limitations of which it was the product.

> Only through and for Eliade did I learn anything about Romania. In Romania, I learned nothing about Romania.[75]

The two prepositions are precise and revealing. The first—Romanian *prin,* "through, by way of"—indicates that Culianu's knowledge of his homeland's history was mostly gained from and steered by his mentor, who was hardly a disinterested party and for whom the "terror of history" was a virtual leitmotif. The second is even more instructive, disclosing the apologetic motives guiding Culianu's research, for beyond its most basic sense of "for, with a view to," Romanian *pentru* also means "in defense of, on behalf of, for the sake of."[76]

Consistent with this, Culianu relied heavily on Eliade's memoirs, journals, interviews, and fiction for his discussion of interwar Romania. He cited few unbiased sources and made no effort to account for Eliade's self-interest. Conceivably his own loyalty, admiration, and gratitude were sufficiently great that he could not imagine this good and brilliant man might behave in a self-servingly dishonest fashion. But given the extent to which his own career and reputation were now irrevocably linked to Eliade's, he surely understood that it was in his interest to assume the best of his mentor and patron.

That Culianu's research was neither disinterested nor thorough is consistent with the nature of his project. The task he set himself was not to write history with a dispassionate concern for thoroughness, accuracy, and objective truth, but simply to defend his champion. More precisely, as he put it, he aimed "to dispel the rumors assiduously propagated by circles on the left and, after 1946, by the Romanian government installed by the Soviet army, according to which Eliade had been part of the Iron Guard."[77]

To this end, he returned to the familiar lines of defense, while adding a few new wrinkles. In addition to depicting Eliade as having always been a democrat at heart, Culianu maintained that he was admired by figures on the left as late as 1936, that his attitude toward Codreanu was coolly reserved, and that his interest in the Legion was "professional and detached," largely academic in nature. Most astounding, perhaps, was his attempt to identify Eliade with Bérenger, the protagonist of Eugène Ionesco's play *Rhinoceros*, who resisted the fascist herd-instinct of "rhinocerization" longest of all the characters.[78] Surely, Culianu knew that the play reflected Ionesco's own experience in Bucharest of the 1930s, where he—as represented by Bérenger—was one of the few holdouts while others of his "generation" rushed to embrace the Legion. Far from seeing Eliade's role as heroic, Ionesco understood things quite differently, as he made clear in an oft-cited letter of September 1945.

> Mircea Eliade arrived or will arrive [in Paris] in a few days. For him, everything is lost, since "Communism won." He is a great culprit (*un mare vinovat*). But he, and Cioran, and that imbecile Noica, and fat Vulcănescu, and so many others (Haig Acterian! Mihail Polihroniade!) are victims of the late Nae Ionescu, that odious man. If there had been no Nae Ionescu (or if he had not quarreled with the king), we would have had, today, a generation of worthy leaders, between thirty-five and forty years old. Because of him, they all became fascists. He created a stupid, awful, reactionary Romania. The second guilty one is Eliade: at a given moment, he was ready to adopt a position on the left. That was fifteen years ago: Haig Acterian and Polihroniade were Communists. They died because of their stupidity and stubbornness. Eliade rallied some of those from his generation and all the young intellectuals. It was horrible to listen to Nae Ionescu and Mircea Eliade. What if these people had been good mentors?[79]

VIII

If Culianu's essay for the unpublished volume adopted a familiar defensive posture, the list of questions he prepared is a more complicated text that poses real problems of interpretation. His admirers see it as an expression of—and instrument for—his courageous pursuit of the truth, challenging Eliade's evasions and resistance. Thus, for instance, Andrei Oişteanu:

Ioan Petru Culianu proposed to write a book of conversations with Mircea Eliade on the limits of his political sympathies during his youth. He had composed dozens of inconvenient questions about "[Eliade's] sympathy for Hitler," "the rhinocerization of Romania in the years 1934–37," the way in which Eliade was "marked by Orthodox ethics," "claims of his anti-Semitism," the extent to which Eliade was "a man of the extreme Right and even pro-Nazi," his relations with Nae Ionescu and Corneliu Zelea Codreanu, "his weakness for Marshal Antonescu," etc. Although Culianu proposed at that time to demonstrate the absurdity of some of the "slanders," Eliade consistently postponed giving a response to the questions and thus, his participation in writing the book. Culianu acted in good faith but—lacking access to the sources—did not know the truth.[80]

Although the issues Oisteanu named figure in the questions, they are not the first thing one notices. Much more prominent—at least on the surface—is the exorbitant flattery Culianu offered, starting with his first query.

1. Mircea Eliade, you are undoubtedly the most extraordinary man I have ever met. You are sly, although that isn't apparent, you have a Mephistophelian intelligence under the appearance of an innocent dove, you do not bite at anyone, and still all that you say is charged with an irony more terrible than genial. You do so with such tact and seriousness that others do not even recognize it. I have known you now for ten years and I believe that I know how to read between the lines, especially when you give them a dissonant appearance (it is a signal!). There are some who attack you, even those who betray you, yet you remain imperturbable, you work not to see anything and you continue to help them (even materially!), according to what is possible for you. You never have any resentment. You are a great mystagogue, you keep silent, you listen, you encourage all possible misunderstandings about yourself, your works, your beliefs and convictions. You have even created the myth of your taking the attitude of a sphinx and letting all the ambiguities pile up on you. But you are always sensitive, farsighted, charitable, beaming love to those close to you, with energy, vivacity, and joy in life. Yet so many catastrophes have crashed over you: your mentor disappeared or was eliminated, your first wife died before you, you were

exiled, an unemployed intellectual, you were hungry in Paris. . . . Just like the Russian novels you admired in lycée. Did you ever *hate* anyone? Not even some teacher at school? Not even someone among those who would curse or attack you in the right- *and* left-wing press in 1935–37? Not even King Carol II?[81]

Similarly obsequious—to use Culianu's term—is the twelfth question, which played to Eliade's vanity and offered a comforting explanation for a serious blow to his pride.

Mircea Eliade, you could be one of the most fascinating people of this century: with you, one encounters stability and adventure, innocence and cunning, emotion and reason, goodness and righteousness. You are probably one of the last people who are also humanists at the same time. You are not only *accepted* as a scholar and author, but you find yourself at the peak of glory. Why have you still not received the Nobel Prize? Has the fact that you are a former political refugee from a country of the East disturbed the consciences of the diplomats who are members of the Swedish Academy? Still, they gave Solzhenitsyn the prize.[82]

The topic was a painful one. In the mid-1970s, Eliade was nominated for the Nobel Prize in Literature, and initially his hopes were high. When those hopes were unrealized by the decade's end, he decided his candidacy had been sabotaged, and in a journal entry of July 23, 1979, he placed blame squarely on Furio Jesi and other Italian critics, whose goal, he now realized, was "to eliminate me from among the favorites for the Nobel prize."[83] Here, Culianu floated a less threatening explanation that might have helped keep hope alive, given that the Nobel committee had continued to signal its interest in dissidents from Eastern Europe, having given awards not just to Solzhenitsyn in 1970, but to Czeslaw Milosz in 1980 and Jaroslav Seifert in 1984.

Other questions asked Eliade to confirm interpretations Culianu advanced in his introductory essay, for example that his ultimate goal was "soteriologic . . . to help people recover the lost meaning of their existence" (Question 2); that he should be identified with Ionesco's Bérenger (Question 7); that being influenced by Orthodox, rather than Protestant, ethics, he had always been opposed to capitalism (Questions 8, 9, and 10). Other questions were anodyne: Did he think magic and shamanism really work? (Question 15). Wouldn't he like to write more literature and less scholarship? (Question 17). What might have been his fate had he returned to Romania? (Question 11). Could he foresee the fall of the Soviet empire? (Question 21).

Some of the questions provided Eliade with defensive arguments Culianu knew he would find attractive, as when he suggested that all the accusations against him began with a misunderstanding of his relation to Nae Ionescu (Question 4). But he also offered a novel defense he hoped his mentor could accept, since it resolved his own lingering doubts: that is although most people locate Eliade on the far right, that is the result of confusion he himself created and encouraged (Question 3). At the same time, the younger scholar projected his own political stance onto his mentor, whom he depicted as being—and always having been—a non-Marxist democrat.

Culianu apparently saw some basis for this last point in Eliade's fiction, referring to "his novel *Forbidden Forest*, in which Ştefan Viziru, a democrat like Eliade, finds himself caught in the hunt of legionaries."[84] The passage in which Viziru most explicitly identifies himself as a democrat, however, represents yet another instance of Eliade's two-sided defense. Within a short passage, the author's alter ego voices admiration for legionaries, distinguishes himself from them, asserts his belief in democracy, and identifies himself as apolitical, while voicing strong criticism of other democrats. Legionaries were free to believe that Eliade was still one of them but had to practice a certain camouflage; antifascists could read the same passage and conclude he was naive, even muddled, but a democrat at heart.

> They [sc. the legionaries imprisoned at Miercurea Ciuc] believe in something and for that they've been confined behind barbed wire. I believe in democracy, but I don't mingle in politics, therefore I don't participate in their conflict. The defenders of democracy are the very ones who arrested them and brought them here. I'm outside their struggle.[85]

Some of the shorter questions were relatively open-ended, gently offering Eliade the opportunity to address some controversial isssues more directly than he had in the past.

> 5. Through Nae Ionescu, you encountered men of the right, for example, Codreanu. What were your relations with them?

13. Did you really have any sympathy for Hitler? Judging from your political gestures one would say not.

18. St. Augustine reproached himself only for having stolen some pears (and for being passionate about spectacles, but it was sufficient to give that up). By that measure, we are lost from the start. For my part, every summer in my childhood, I delighted in the apricots of my neighbors. What are the things for which you would reproach yourself?[86]

Most intriguing, perhaps, is Question 19, where Culianu praised Eliade's exquisite tact and discretion, noting that these qualities must have been useful during his diplomatic service, but wondering if their continued exercise did not cause "some measure of *truth*" to be lost.[87] Clearly, Culianu was gently nudging the older man to drop his customary guard and speak with greater candor.

Divergent interests, goals, and tactics can be discerned in Culianu's questions, making this a difficult text to interpret. Some, like Oişteanu, consider it a courageous attempt to get at the truth. Alternatively, it can be seen as a generous attempt to help Eliade engage his critics more fully and successfully, not just encouraging him to do so, but providing him with scripts—largely recycled from things he had told Culianu in the course of their conversations—that would prove him innocent on all counts (see esp. Questions 3, 4, 6, 7, and 13). Yet again, one can imagine Culianu using flattery (as in Questions 1, 2, 4, 8, 12, and 17) to relax Eliade so that he might open up in response to questions phrased in unthreatening ways, but which probed at difficult issues (such as numbers 5, 6, 7, 13, 14, 18, and 19). Ultimately, I think it best to understand the text's contradictions and ambiguities as reflecting the ambivalence of an author who was admiring of, devoted to, and dependent on his interlocutor, but also envious, ambitious, and tired of being "the idiot disciple who faced every sort of danger in order to meet him but is permitted no space to criticize him."[88]

In any event, nothing came of the venture. Culianu put his list of questions in the mail on February 3, 1985, only to be told a few weeks later: "I still have not read the elements for our dialogue."[89] For whatever reason—caution surely, perhaps also illness—Eliade never answered those questions.[90]

5

An Unsolved Murder

Part I (1986–1991)

I

However troubling he might have found some of Culianu's inquiries, Eliade was extremely fond of his protégé and genuinely impressed by his scholarship. Many of Culianu's interests echoed his own (occultism, shamanism, magic, alchemy, esoteric trends in the Italian Renaissance), while others showed the influence of Ugo Bianchi (Gnosticism, dualism, early Christianity).[1] Through the early and middle 1980s, the two Romanian scholars kept in close touch, and Culianu paid his mentor regular visits, which he described in rapturous terms: "The ten days of my summer trips to Paris had the character of a pilgrimage to Mircea Eliade, the only event of my life whose constant repetition nearly transformed it into a ritual act."[2] On occasion, they also exchanged visits in Chicago and Groningen (Figure 5.1). For his part, Eliade spoke of Culianu as "the hope of our discipline," "the only one of my fellow-countrymen who is an authentic historian of religions," and "an extraordinary scholar."[3] In the mid-1980s, he went further still. On August 1, 1984, shortly after Culianu's "Blind Tortoises" article appeared, he wrote in his journal: "My admiration for Ioan is sincere and unlimited. . . . I hope I shall be able to write someday all that I think about Ioan Culianu."[4]

On several occasions Eliade recommended Culianu for positions at major universities and eventually brought him to Chicago as a visiting

FIGURE 5.1 Ioan Culianu and Mircea Eliade in Groningen, August 1984

professor for the spring term of 1986. They intended to collaborate on a dictionary of religions, but on April 14, shortly after Culianu's arrival, the seventy-nine-year-old Eliade suffered a severe stroke. Rushed to intensive care, he lingered until the twenty-second, during which time Culianu took charge of most practical arrangements, providing support and comfort to Mircea's second wife, Christinel, deciding who was granted access to Eliade's bedside, conferring with doctors, university officials, and others. He then helped organize the memorial service, where he, Saul Bellow, and Paul Ricoeur read from Eliade's work to a crowd that filled the university's capacious Rockefeller Chapel to overflowing.

Many people at Chicago saw Culianu as Eliade's appropriate successor. Mircea had promoted this idea for some time, and Christinel continued the campaign, voicing her personal appreciation as a complement to Mircea's high professional esteem. Chris Gamwell, dean of the Divinity School, came to support the idea, as did Joseph M. Kitagawa, former dean, professor emeritus in the History of Religions, and a close colleague of Eliade's. On the other hand, Frank Reynolds and Wendy Doniger, the senior faculty members in History of Religions, were resistant, believing Culianu's work too Eurocentric for a department that had traditionally focused its attention on non-Western traditions. Rather than mount a normal search and let these differences spawn open conflict, Dean Gamwell chose to bring Culianu back as a visiting professor in spring 1987, locating him in History of Christianity (where there was no opposition) and secondarily in History of Religions. The appointment became permanent a year later. While not unprecedented, the hiring procedures were unusual, and without the strong, persistent support of both Eliades, Culianu may not have been hired.[5]

Culianu, who had been unhappy in the Netherlands, was thrilled. He quickly attracted an enthusiastic group of students, and his research began moving in novel directions. Even so, the responsibility to defend Eliade's reputation weighed heavily on the young scholar installed as his heir.

II

The death of an eminent scholar always triggers obituaries, tributes, and re-evaluations. Among those asked to write about Eliade was Vittorio Lanternari, an eminent Italian historian of religions, who—like Alfonso Di Nola and Furio Jesi—was both Marxist and Jewish. He responded with a long, serious, decidedly mixed review of Eliade's work that appeared in an Italian journal of critical sociology.[6] Upon its publication, Lanternari sent a copy to Culianu, along with a courteous letter, explaining his attempt to find a middle path between Di Nola's accusations and Culianu's defense. As he put it, "I considered Professor Eliade was really involved in Codreanu's movement and ideology; but I did not ascertain any sure testimonies to his 'anti-Semitism.'"[7] After the article was published, however, fuller evidence came to Lanternari's attention and his opinions hardened.

> I have received, in the meantime, a manuscript from a Romanian writer in which the ideological position of Professor Eliade during the time of Codreanu in Romania is extensively documented through a number of articles he wrote for *Buna Vestire* in those years and also by other witnesses. I am bitterly obliged, at present, to declare that your statement concerning the building of a "black legend" on Mircea Eliade is to be considered insubstantial. I am really sorry that I am forced to make this remark, but it is obliged by a concern for the correctness of historical information.[8]

Culianu responded angrily, defending Eliade's reputation and his own. In the course of his article, Lanternari devoted several pages to Culianu's "Blind Tortoises" piece, picking up on the observation of Crescenzo Fiore that the arguments of Eliade's chief apologist ought be handled with caution.[9] "I am nobody's 'apologist,'" Culianu retorted, insisting that his conclusions were based on two years of painstaking research, not blind loyalty.[10] Culianu's protestations notwithstanding, further developments support Lanternari's characterization of the role the young scholar was playing.

In these controversies, the 1937 article "Why I Believe in the Victory of the Legionary Movement" had become a major point of contention. Critics saw it as the smoking gun that proved Eliade a fascist and anti-Semite, while Eliade had parried by denying the piece was his. In his "Blind Tortoises" article, Culianu amplified Eliade's denials, dismissing the article as "a bad forgery."[11] In response to Lanternari and in a separate letter to Arnaldo Momigliano, who was also party to this exchange, he went further still, denying that Eliade ever published in *Buna Vestire* and challenging anyone who thought otherwise to show him a copy.[12]

Within a day, Culianu worried that he had overstated his case. Accordingly, he wrote to Mac Linscott Ricketts, from whom he thought he had obtained his information.[13] Ricketts was among the most devoted of Eliade's American students, having centered his own research on his teacher's life and work, and having served for many years as his chief translator.[14] While researching his massive book on Eliade's Romanian years, Ricketts spent several months at the Library of the Romanian Academy, photocopying hundreds of Eliade's early publications and translating the ones in restricted archives that he was not permitted to copy.[15] In answer to Culianu's query, Ricketts confirmed the existence of the disputed article and sent him a translation of it, along with eight other legionary pieces of Eliade's.[16] In addition, he offered several comments. Although he accepted Eliade's denial of authorship, he saw the disputed article as consistent with what Eliade believed at that time, since "almost every point can be paralleled in something he did write." Even so, he managed to convince himself that the piece contained nothing truly anti-Semitic, since its references to Jews were "only nationalistic."[17] Culianu happily accepted Ricketts's position on the first and third points, while minimizing the importance of the second.

In his letter to Momigliano, Culianu struck a noble posture, proclaiming that if Lanternari—or presumably, anyone else—could produce a copy of the disputed article, "since I am committed to nothing but the truth ... I will make an *amende honorable*."[18] A week later, he had a translation of that article in hand, but felt no need to honor his commitment, as indicated by his subsequent letter to Ricketts.

> Finally, I am in possession of the whole coveted file concerning Mr. Eliade's political sympathies in 1938–1940. Last year I was probably too upset to carefully memorize what we had talked about this; my impression was that you had denied the existence of the *Buna Vestire* article, but

you probably only confirmed my own contention that it was not written by him. Anyway, things are not much changed and I do not feel like I should redefine my position: Mr. Eliade has never been an anti-Semite, a *member* of the Iron Guard, or a pro-Nazi. But I understand anyway that he was closer to the Iron Guard than I might have liked to think. I am sending you Mr. Lanternari's article. Useless to say, I think he does not know anything he's writing on.[19]

Here, as he would do on other occasions, Culianu brushed aside serious criticisms by dismissing the well-informed, principled scholars who advanced them as ignorant, malicious, or—as we will see in the case of Adriana Berger—pathologically deluded.

III

Over the next several years, Culianu and Ricketts communicated frequently. Although there were minor differences between them, they shared many of the same loyalties, opinions, and goals. Ricketts was better informed about Eliade's shifting position in the intellectual culture and politics of interwar Romania as a result of the research for his book.[20] He was also more prudent, thorough, and analytical than Culianu and at times felt that his younger colleague "does not admit enough."[21] Accordingly, he was more willing to acknowledge Eliade's legionary commitments, which he explained (and thus hoped to mitigate) as the result of political naiveté.[22] This difference notwithstanding, the two men cooperated well—complementing, reinforcing, and encouraging each other.

In the immediate aftermath of Eliade's death, three books discussing his past, his politics, and their relation to his scholarship were in preparation. One was Ricketts's own, while the other two—those of Ivan Strenski and Adriana Berger—were expected to be sharply critical. The three authors were also scheduled to appear on a panel discussing "Eliade in Romania" at the annual meetings of the American Academy of Religion (AAR) in December 1987, where they would make their case before a large, influential, and keenly interested audience.[23] Upon learning of the panel, Culianu was anxious, fearing what "some fools" might say.[24] Ricketts reassured him that he would make a strong case and asked for a copy of Culianu's "Blind Tortoises" article to help him prepare.[25]

Strenski's position was known from an article he published in 1982, the first in English to discuss Eliade's legionary past.[26] Since then, he had pressed his critique further, but found it difficult to locate a publisher for his book on the subject. In the course of their correspondence, Berger informed Strenski of an episode that suggested some reasons why he had encountered difficulties.

> I remember that I was working for Eliade, it must have been between January 84 and May 84, if I am not mistaken, when Eliade received the manuscript of a book by *Ivan Strenski* (I never saw the book; it must have been the *Four Theories*) to review, and he told me: "I hate that man. I'll send the manuscript to Ricketts to review it." Could it be that he (Eliade) asked Ricketts to write a bad review to your ms.? Did you submit it to Chapel Hill first?[27]

The manuscript was, in fact, being considered at the University of North Carolina Press at the time Berger indicated. As it happens, Charles Long, a former student, colleague, and strong supporter of Eliade's, was then teaching at the University of North Carolina and the press asked him to review the manuscript. Eliade's letter of June 5, 1984, to Mac Ricketts shows that Long was consulted, reacted negatively, and relayed his concerns to Eliade, who shared them in turn with Ricketts. After being rejected by thirty different publishers, the book finally found a home and came out just in time to win the AAR's 1987 Award for Excellence in Theory.[28] Once available, it provoked heated debate, but was sufficiently well informed and judiciously argued that it could not be ignored or easily dismissed.

As dangerous as Strenski was, Berger (Figure 5.2) was possibly more so, while also being more vulnerable. In short, she was a traitor and not just an enemy, to use the legionary categories. Romanian and Jewish by birth, she received a doctorate from the Sorbonne in 1983, having written a dissertation on Eliade's fiction, the "Conclusion Générale" of which voiced not just admiration, but adulation.

> Mircea Eliade's literature has renewed the genre of the fantastic, bringing to it not only optimism and the hope of salvation in an era of terror and violence, but also by speaking a universal language based on this spiritual synthesis and the response of knowledge in a world that will thereby be better.... We consider the work of Mircea Eliade as a grand provocation that can only renew our cultural universe.... Eliade is the first (and in this sense, the greatest) Romanian writer who, while preserving his

FIGURE 5.2 Adriana Berger and Mircea Eliade, 1985
Photo from the Mircea Eliade archive of Regenstein Library, Box 167.

original tradition, has made a great contribution to universal culture. . . .
For all these reasons, it was necessary for us to write this study, which
thereby finds its justification. It was an immense privilege for us and
above all, an unforgettable adventure, a very special experience to share
and discover *reading with love*.[29]

Eager to know the man himself, Berger made her way to Chicago, where
Eliade received her warmly and hired her to help organize his private papers. From 1984 to 1985, she worked in that capacity and at first all went
well.[30] Star-struck, she published two laudatory articles about Eliade, and
he helped her obtain a contract from Harper & Row for a book that would
build on her dissertation.[31]

At some point, however, Berger discovered evidence of her idol's legionary past.[32] After several sharp confrontations with Mircea and
Christinel Eliade, Berger ceased working for him, then reached out to
Strenski and other critics, while undertaking a radical revision of her book
project.[33] As she wrote to Strenski on April 17, 1987:

I was completely fooled by Eliade and I didn't try at all to be "historical." I believed everything he told me—and now I realize how false his

statements were—He wanted me to write an *hommage* book, and this is how my book on him began. Fortunately, this is not how it will come out . . . probably it will cost me all chances to ever get a teaching position. But I don't think that I have much choice. I thought of giving it up (for many reasons), but I don't.[34]

Like Culianu, Berger was torn by competing demands. On the one hand, she owed some loyalty to a man she admired, who had shown her kindness and generosity, and whose support was crucial for her career ambitions. On the other, when confronted with evidence of his hidden past, intellectual and moral integrity demanded that she change her view. Culianu, who identified more closely with Eliade and was more deeply beholden to him, resolved this dilemma by insisting—first to himself, then to others—that the evidence he gathered during his period of doubt proved exculpatory. Berger, whose gender and religious identity placed her at a greater remove, took the opposite tack. Whereas Culianu's loyalty led him to reach the desired conclusions and pronounce his inquiry finished, Berger continued to dig relentlessly, interpreting whatever she found with prosecutorial zeal.

In preparing her paper for the AAR, Berger sought to marshal as much data as possible. Thus, in the spring of 1987, she asked Ricketts for copies of the articles he had collected in Romania, and he generously shared these with her. A bit later, she obtained the critical books and articles then appearing in Italy.[35] At the same time, she sensed that Christinel and Eliade's loyalists—whom she termed "the Chicago mafia"—were seeking to block her book's publication.[36] She also worried that Christinel and Culianu were destroying crucial pieces of evidence.[37] The latter fear was shared by Alexander Ronnett, the Eliades' physician and dentist, who wrote as follows:

I know that Master Eliade wrote a journal. He also had a notebook with strongly personal notes and political notations. I know no details. He told me that these short notes will only see light of day after his death. Where are these notes? In my discussions with Prof. Ricketts, who is working on Eliade's journals, I mentioned these special notes and he knows nothing about them. It could be that they burned in the fire in his office or possibly Christinel destroyed them out of personal motives.[38]

Although Berger could read the Romanian sources and knew her country's political history reasonably well, she was not always as attentive to detail or measured in her tone as might have been ideal. She got the big issues right, however, understanding that (1) Eliade was an enthusiastic supporter of the Legion in the late 1930s and retained some sympathy for the movement; (2) he systematically hid that commitment after the war; and (3) many of the same values that led him to support the movement also informed his scholarship. Her observations regarding Eliade's relations with old legionaries in Chicago and Paris are also interesting:

> Eliade tried to keep a distance from the Iron Guard people. In other words, not to cut himself off completely from them, but not to be too close either, in order not to risk his position at Chicago. Therefore, some Iron Guard people criticized him that "he wasn't the Iron Guard member, the legionary from the concentration camp of Ciuc any longer, but the coward from Lisbon."[39]

At certain points, Berger overstated her case, particularly on the charge of anti-Semitism, much as Lavi had done. And like him, she made several errors of fact that let her adversaries impugn her credibility.

Culianu went further still. Rather than engage the evidence and arguments Berger brought forward, he represented her in stereotypically misogynist fashion as a foolish, hysterical woman whose ravings should be ignored. Thus, in his first letter to Ricketts after the AAR meetings, he characterized Berger as "clinically crazy . . . scholarly irresponsible . . . [practicing] a method called paranoiac history."[40] Ricketts quickly joined in, describing her as "an unstable personality" given to "paranoid fantasies relative to Mircea."[41] Slander of this sort circulated widely among Eliade's supporters, providing them with a rationale for dismissing her altogether. Although Berger did manage to publish two powerful, widely read papers, her book never made its way into print.[42] Harper & Row canceled her contract toward the end of 1990, after which Paragon Press, St. Martin's, and Hill & Wang contracted to publish the book, then backed away from their commitments, offering little explanation for their decisions to do so. Upon learning of its rejection, Culianu heaved a sigh of relief and shrugged off her articles as "Adriana's new mischiefs."[43]

IV

For her part, Berger saw Culianu as an extension of Christinel Eliade (Figure 5.3), whom she understood as her chief adversary, consistent with the description of Mrs. Eliade as a "volcanic personality" and "a lioness

FIGURE 5.3 Christinel Eliade, circa 1980

Photo from the Mircea Eliade archive of Regenstein Library, Box 166, Folder 3.

in her husband's defense" by Stelian Pleşoiu, a Romanian graduate student whom the Eliades befriended and took into their home during the
mid-1980s.[44]

The Eliades' relation was a complex one, which began in 1948, when
Mircea was struggling to make his way in Paris, four years after his first
wife had died of cancer. They married in 1950 and from the start, she—a
beautiful, cultured Romanian expatriate of aristocratic descent—was in
awe of her husband's genius and heroic stature (Figure 5.4). Throughout
his life, she doted on him, typed all his manuscripts, managed most of

FIGURE 5.4 Mircea and Christinel Eliade in Paris, early 1950s
Photo from the Mircea Eliade archive of Regenstein Library, Box 167.

his practical affairs, and did everything she could to support his work (Figure 5.5). After his death, she was fiercely determined to honor his memory and defend his reputation against the emerging threats. According to Kenneth Zysk, Berger's husband at the time, "Adriana had strong suspicions that [Christinel] was out to finish her off and do all in her power to prevent Adriana's work from seeing the light of day. I seem to remember an actual threat to that effect, after Adriana made a visit to Chicago or had a phone conversation with her."[45]

Berger got a full blast of Mrs. Eliade's anger on several occasions and saw Mac Ricketts receive similar treatment. Enraged at Ricketts's discussion of Mircea's involvement with the Legion, Mrs. Eliade vowed to block publication of his book and prevailed on Macmillan to reject it, possibly with threats of legal action.[46] In December 1986, Ricketts tried to explain his position and assuage her anger.

> I am very sorry and distressed that you are worried about what I may have said in my book on Mircea about certain articles he wrote in 1936–38 which were, in some respects favorable to the Legion and Captain Codreanu. *Surely* you do not think that I would try to defame Mircea's memory! However, it would be a grave mistake to ignore these things in a book about his life at that time, because the articles have been read

FIGURE 5.5 Mircea and Christinel Eliade at home in Chicago, shortly before Mircea's death in April 1986

Photo from the Mircea Eliade archive of Regenstein Library, Box 166, Folder 4.

by others and bad things have been published about Mircea (in Israel, Italy, etc.) on the basis of *fragments* taken from those articles. These slanders, moreover, are known to some people in America, and it is *to put a stop to them* that I have tried to write fully and openly about what he *really* said. . . . I believe you know I would not write anything harmful to Mircea. But if I were to say nothing about these things, people would accuse me of trying to "cover up" something, and they would continue to spread their lies.[47]

As this letter indicates, the debate was evolving, new evidence was coming to light, and Eliade's supporters felt the need to adjust their defense. Although the concessions they were prepared to make went well beyond what Mrs. Eliade could tolerate, they were still relatively modest, like Ricketts's acknowledgment that a few of Mircea's articles "were, in some respects favorable to the Legion." Adriana Berger also perceived the shift in defensive tactics, which she attributed to Culianu and Ricketts.

Culianu will write and publish now an article or two using new material. If you consider what [David] Tracy said, namely that 1) the articles [i.e.,

Eliade's legionary articles] have been forged by the Communists (I saw the originals) and 2) there are different ways of interpreting this issue, I conclude that the Chicago group now wants to make this appear as if Eliade was a little involved (as Ricketts admits, and to the extent that he admits it) but not really as an active member and this type of patriotic involvement was the cause of misinterpretations. These arguments are obviously strained but when one has to deal with them it is quite difficult.[48]

Ricketts's explanations notwithstanding, Mrs. Eliade was not placated. Some months later, she demanded that Ricketts soften his translation of the passages in Mircea's *Autobiography* that were favorable to Codreanu and excise mention of them from his preface. After initial resistance, Ricketts yielded, signaling this discreetly in an "Acknowledgment" he added to his text, thanking Christinel, who "read the entire manuscript with loving care and offered numerous suggestions for corrections and improvements."[49]

Based on decades of life with her husband and what he had told her concerning his past, Mrs. Eliade dismissed the charges against him as "absolutely untrue and unfounded," insisting that Mircea "never joined any Fascist party or supported anyone with anti-Semitic views."[50] All that he told her, she took as gospel, including his tortured defense of Nae Ionescu and his account of his "wrongful" imprisonment at Miercurea Ciuc.[51] And when she felt others failed to defend her husband in the same wholehearted fashion, she responded with tears, threats, a prosecutorial tone, and/or harsh reproaches. Monica Lovinescu, a leading figure among the Romanian émigrés of Paris and a close friend of the Eliades, recorded numerous incidents in which she and others felt Christinel's wrath.[52] Following Mircea's death, Lovinescu described Christinel as "confused. . . . She cries and is super-nervous." A year later, "She cries constantly and believes that the articles in question can only be fakes." And later still, "Nervous, irritable, borderline aggressive."[53] Throughout, Mrs. Eliade's faith in her husband's absolute innocence was unshakable, sustained by the fact that—as she confided to Lovinescu—"Mircea swore to her that he was never a legionary."[54]

Given Mrs. Eliade's certainty of her husband's innocence, his legionary articles posed a real problem for her—as we can see in an episode Lovinescu recorded. In August 1991, Norman Manea published a sweeping indictment of Eliade in the *New Republic*, which was subsequently republished in Romania and attracted considerable attention.[55] Manea drew heavily from Ricketts's book and Eliade's legionary articles, including some items Ricketts had left unmentioned. After quoting from "Why I Believe in the Victory of the Legionary Movement" and "Vampires," Manea continued: "And still more citations from Eliade's writings of the 1930s can be adduced, about the 'terrifying murders' of which the weak, corrupt, powerless, and still youthful Romanian democracy was guilty; about 'the advance of the Slavic element from the Danubian and Bessarabian regions,' or the fact that 'Jews have overrun the villages of Maramureş and Bucovina, and have achieved an absolute majority in all the cities of Bessarabia.' In sum, there are countless such pronouncements, some even more ridiculous and even more disgusting."[56]

Earlier, Manea had asked Lovinescu whether he should write about Eliade's past, and she did her best to dissuade him, insisting there was "nothing legionary" in the vast bulk of Eliade's work, and promising, "we will defend him in public, if there is need."[57] When Manea's article did ultimately appear, she rushed to make good on that pledge, treating his accusations as exaggerated, prejudicial, and unbalanced, rather than simply false.

> Norman Manea, like other detractors of Mircea Eliade, engages only two or three years (beginning in 1937) and some articles favorable to the Romanian extreme right—all extracted from the study published in the US by Mac Ricketts—out of Eliade's seventy-nine years of existence, his nearly sixty years as a scholar and author, with dozens of books of history of religions, fiction (novels and novellas). Although these articles are surely regrettable, Ricketts circumscribes them in time, while Manea treats them as a black stain on all Eliade's subsequent activity. . . . Yet there are no works of a totalitarian tonality in Mircea Eliade's work, unless it is a sign of inherent fascism when he insists on every human society's need for the sacred and reveals the "camouflage adopted by the sacred in a desacralized world."[58]

Although Lovinescu found the legionary articles troubling, she was prepared to consider them a brief and unfortunate aberration. In her journal, she put matters bluntly: "Even if they are weighty, they occupy a year or two in the life of a man who over the span of his more than sixty volumes preached only tolerance."[59] Christinel, however, was committed to a very different position, consistently maintaining—as Mircea had apparently told her—that the legionary articles were scurrilous forgeries produced for a Communist campaign of disinformation. To quote from Lovinescu's journal again:

> When I see the incredible articles Mircea wrote in his short legionary period (1937–38), I remind myself how he told us that he never wrote such things and (much more serious) how he swore to her that he was never a legionary. I tell myself it is unjust that everything now falls on her head. She understands nothing and maintains only that it is a campaign against Mircea. . . . Christinel believes in Mircea, not in texts. She was displeased by the response I gave to Norman Manea, which probably seemed very weak to her: I acknowledged that some "regrettable" articles existed. But how can Christinel "regret" anything about Mircea when she regrets only his loss and has faith only in him. An atrocious injustice is being done to him *post mortem*, she knows as much. . . . But how do you console Christinel with theories? Better if you avoid keeping her current, you make sure she doesn't know and doesn't learn.[60]

Like Culianu—and to a lesser extent Ricketts—Lovinescu thought it best to keep Mrs. Eliade in the dark, hoping to spare her some pain.[61] Well intentioned as such attempts may have been, they left the widow distrustful and angry, believing that no one else was properly defending the accomplishments and honor of the man she continued to love and to whose memory she remained devoted. In another journal entry, Lovinescu reflected further on her friend's problem and anguish.

> Instead of telling her that I cannot change the reality of the "legionary" quotations of Mircea's (she would swear to me that they are forgeries), I remind her that I did once defend him—against Norman Manea—but I know that she found my response unsatisfactory. What she would like, poor thing, is for me to affirm, just as Mircea swore to her, that he was never a legionary or a supporter and the articles quoted by his enemies are apocryphal. The enemies exist, their campaign is infamous, but the quoted articles are real. Whenever I asked Mircea if compromising articles exist, he denied it. Even when we were alone. . . . He cannot be defended by pretending that nothing among the things from that brief, circumscribed era for which they reproach him is true and that his own texts are really forgeries. That is exactly what Christinel would like. And she cannot obtain it.[62]

The portrait Lovinescu drew is incredibly poignant. Sad, lonely, angry, and defiant, Mrs. Eliade agonized not just over the critics' attacks, but what she came to see as the inadequate efforts of unreliable friends and wavering allies.

V

Ultimately, Culianu himself provoked Mrs. Eliade's distrust and anger. As we saw, in May 1987 Mac Ricketts sent Culianu his translations of Mircea's legionary articles, whose importance Culianu minimized. As he told Ricketts: "things are not much changed and I do not feel like I should redefine my position."[63] Later that year, however, Culianu heard that translations of these articles were circulating in Italy and might soon be published. Under these circumstances, Culianu decided that the best way to control the damage would be to publish an English translation of the articles in an edition where he, Ricketts, and Roberto Scagno could "provide explanations."[64]

Apparently Culianu came to think that if the full texts were made available and given a proper introduction, readers could be made to understand that although Eliade found the Legion's religious aspects attractive, he never formally affiliated with the movement or endorsed its violence and, further, that the anti-Semitism he voiced on a very few occasions was but a regrettable lapse. To help make that point, Culianu planned to include several articles in which Eliade expressed support and admiration for Jewish friends and colleagues. But in thinking this material would satisfy critics, clear Eliade's name, and end the debate, Culianu was at least as naive as the man he sought to defend.

One can see what kind of "explanation" Culianu intended to provide from a letter he wrote to Adrian Marino ten days before floating his proposal to Ricketts. Here, as elsewhere, he sought to represent himself as a principled, conscientious scholar, rethinking a familiar question in light of new evidence. Indeed, he probably saw himself that way. But the outcome of his ruminations was predetermined by his long-standing commitments. Caught in an impossible situation, he struggled to cede the least possible ground while retreating from lines of defense that were fast becoming untenable.

I have obtained the articles. Hard to say if "it is true" or not. It is a problem of hermeneutics. But undoubtedly, there remains an article in *Buna Vestire* (which Mircea Eliade says he did not write, that was an interview twisted by others) and two ambiguous ones in *Vremea*. Hard to say what is right *after* putting in a certain hermeneutic effort. I have discussed what is to be done with one person and another. I believe we have to make hermeneutic efforts that admit a *contiguity* (but *not* an identity!) that is hard to deny. Certainly, some phrases with chauvinistic nuances are regrettable. But they don't seem disastrous. Again, it depends on hermeneutics.[65]

Initially, Ricketts showed no interest in publishing an edition of the legionary articles.[66] Culianu waited a year, then renewed his efforts. In November 1988, they discussed the project once more and Ricketts took notes on the conversation.

Culianu called Nov. 6 about plans for a book in defense of Eliade, to include all allegedly incriminating articles of 1937–38. I would translate these and write a commentary article. Wendy D O'F [= Doniger O'Flaherty] to be the editor. Culianu and Călinescu silent editors. Ask for all critics and supporters who are knowledgeable to write articles. Wants me to help pick contributors. Christinel *not* to know about it.[67]

As this memo makes clear, Culianu intended this to be a book "in defense of Eliade," which would serve that cause by representing the legionary articles as "allegedly," but not truly incriminating. The memo's last point, couched in the imperative, is also significant: Christinel *not* to know. Previously, Culianu withheld information in order to protect Mrs. Eliade from unnecessary pain. Now he did so to protect himself from her wrath, knowing she would oppose his plan and consider it a grievous betrayal.

Within days of the phone call, Ricketts went to work, translating some additional articles he believed ought to be included. On January 29, 1989, he transmitted "many more" than he initially anticipated.[68] From these, Culianu assembled the final set, which included most of the legionary articles, along with Eliade's interventions on behalf of Mihail Sebastian and Moses Gaster, intended as evidence of his philo-Semitism.[69]

Culianu was eager to see these translations published in a format that would let loyalists control their interpretation, without doing so in obvious fashion. He thus meant to serve as the book's "silent editor," along with Matei Călinescu, a Romanian-American literary critic who was a friend of Eliade's, admired his fiction, and reacted to the legionary articles in ways similar to Culianu.[70] Ricketts would handle the translations and contribute an interpretive essay, while Wendy Doniger was to be listed as nominal editor. Although Doniger had been close to Eliade, her relations with Culianu were not good, and when I asked her about this project, she said she had had no part in it, adding that Culianu would not have been so foolish as to involve her.[71] Matei Călinescu's account helps make sense of this discrepancy, for he reported that after he and Culianu agreed to collaborate on the project, "We paid a call to meet with Wendy Doniger, current occupant of Eliade's chair and a good friend of Christinel's, to get her opinion. She thought the idea excellent and she offered her support, but she foresaw difficulties that quickly proved insurmountable (Christinel categorically opposed it)."[72] Upon being informed of that passage, Professor Doniger said she trusted Călinescu and therefore it must have been so, but her involvement was sufficiently slight to leave no trace in her memory.[73]

In any event, Doniger's prediction proved accurate and Culianu's plans soon came to naught. Once Christinel learned of the project, she was well positioned to block it, since Mircea's will named her executor of his estate, whose decisions about his literary and other properties "shall be final, conclusive, and binding."[74] The situation was complicated, however, since Eliade had previously named Culianu as his literary executor and "universal legatee," to whom he consigned "the future development of all my writings, published and unpublished."[75] Initially, Culianu understood his role in modest terms, stating at one point: "All the decisions will belong to Mrs. Eliade herself. My function will be that of an adviser."[76] There were, however, certain projects Eliade had entrusted to him, as recognized in a codicil added to the will on June 6, 1986, recognizing that "Mr. Culianu will take over the following unpublished notes of the late Professor Mircea ELIADE and will make them available for publication." Nine items were listed, the first of which was volume 4 of Eliade's *History of Religious Ideas*. Second was "a collection of newspaper articles in Roumanian, meant to be published in Roumanian and/or in translation."[77] Conceivably Culianu came to believe this gave him the right to publish Eliade's articles of the 1930s, with or without Christinel's consent.

Notwithstanding Culianu's and Ricketts's preference for keeping Christinel in the dark, she quickly learned of their efforts. Determined to stop them, she had her lawyer file an affidavit on February 28, 1989, asserting her full control.

CALVIN SAWYIER, having been first duly sworn, on oath deposes and says that:

I am an attorney and counsellor at law, a member of the bar of the Supreme Court of the United States, and counsel to the estate of Mircea Eliade, deceased.

The entire estate and property of Mircea Eliade, *including the right to authorize publication of his works* and the rights to royalties on his publications, has passed to his wife, Georgette (Christinel) Eliade, his sole heir and legatee, under Article II of the Last Will and Testament of Mircea Eliade, which has been admitted to probate in the Circuit Court of Cook County, Illinois, U.S.A. *She and she alone is fully entitled, just as was Mircea Eliade when he was alive, to authorize publication* and to receive or to direct who should receive the payment of royalties and other property which now belong to her.[78]

From Mrs. Eliade's perspective, that should have settled things. But it did not.

VI

Relations between Eliade's widow and his successor deteriorated further in the months that followed. In March, Culianu published an article in an Italian journal ceding more ground than he had in the past. No longer worried about Eliade's response, he took several relatively modest steps toward showing himself to be a responsible scholar as well as a loyal disciple. The article thus includes four points Culianu never previously conceded:

(1) The "Blind Pilots" article, indisputably of Eliade's authorship, included "a relatively harsh attack on the disproportionate economic and political strength of minorities, including the Jews."

(2) The contested article "Why I Believe in the Victory of the Legionary Movement" contained ideas that were Eliade's, even if the language was not his.

(3) Eliade wrote "six or seven" articles in support of the Legion, "two or three" of which now seemed "disconcerting."

(4) Eliade actively campaigned on behalf of the Legion in the national elections of December 1937.[79]

Other firsts included his description of Nae Ionescu, Eliade's revered mentor, as "the demon [who] lay in ambush" and his reference to the Legion as "a terrorist organization." Even so, Culianu's hedges and circumlocutions were as significant as his concessions. Unable to acknowledge Ionescu's

Table 5.1 Culianu's recycling of Eliade's contention that the anti-Semitism of Codreanu and his movement was not racist

Source	Statement
Eliade to Culianu, June 24, 1978, cited in *The Unknown Mircea Eliade*	Codreanu . . . rejected Nazi racism, promising to continue the "assimilation" of minorities and he strictly forbade legionaries, as well as himself, to participate in irresponsible actions of wild anti-Semitism.
"Mircea Eliade and the Blind Tortoises" 1984	Although Codreanu was a strong anti-Semite, he never tired of stating that his anti-Semitism had *economic* sources. According to M. Nagy-Talavera, at no time did he support German racist ideology. At least in theory, he did not want any special measures to be taken against Jews.
The Unknown Mircea Eliade, 1985	Codreanu . . . specified that his anti-Semitism was limited to economics, in contrast to Nazi racism.
"The Tree of Knowledge," 1989	The Iron Guard [was] a terrorist organization that professed a form of autochthonous quasi-mystical fascism and strongly anti-Semitic, although seemingly not racist.

Note: The first statement is quoted directly from Eliade, the others from Culianu. Italics and quotation marks in the original.

anti-Semitism more directly, he preferred to say that the odious preface to Mihail Sebastian's novel only "reinforced the impression" of Ionescu's having advocated a "vague," strictly theological form of such prejudice. And if Culianu now denounced the Legion as terrorist, he continued to repeat Eliade's assertion that in its Codrenist phase, the movement's anti-Semitism wasn't racist, as if that made it any less bigoted, violent, or dangerous (see Table 5.1).

Apparently Culianu felt the need to address increasingly well-informed critiques. Although he continued to insist that Eliade was never an anti-Semite, a Nazi, or a member of the Legion, he now had to grant that his mentor's legionary articles were real and included some troubling content.[80] To Mrs. Eliade, these were unthinkable concessions. Upon reading the article, she made her displeasure abundantly clear, with consequences Culianu relayed to Ricketts.

> Everything we talked about last November and even more than that is completely blocked. Mrs. Eliade strongly disliked my Italian article

(which I sent you) in which I was largely referring to your book in order to present Mr. Eliade's evolution between 1934 and 1937. As a result, nothing is going on, and in order not to make her suffer (since she obviously *does not understand* the situation), I even had to withdraw my review of your book from the press.[81]

Although Culianu sincerely believed Christinel "did not understand the situation," it is more accurate to observe that he and she understood different parts of a complex whole in ways conditioned by their divergent interests and perspectives. Culianu saw new information coming to light that threatened to discredit some of Eliade's customary denials and obfuscations. In order to stave off the critics without sacrificing his own credibility and self-respect, he wanted to fall back and reorganize the defense. Given that he, Ricketts, and others had shielded Mrs. Eliade from the most threatening attacks, he felt that she could not appreciate how quickly circumstances were changing.

Be that as it may, Christinel knew that her husband firmly—and rightly—believed he had nothing to gain and much to lose from open discussion of this painful topic. She further understood that Culianu owed his present position and stature to the unstinting support she and Mircea had given him over many years, in light of which she considered his conduct shockingly ungrateful. According to T. David Brent, who became Eliade's literary executor after Culianu's death, Mrs. Eliade was determined to protect her husband's reputation against all challenges, and thus "she always opposed any translations or compilations of these so-called anti-Semitic/pro-fascist writings. . . . Culianu had to ask permission from Christinel, which she consistently refused to grant."[82]

It is also possible Mrs. Eliade perceived signs of ambivalence, resentment, and repressed hostility in Culianu. Many years later, Gregory Spinner, one of Culianu's most devoted students, noted:

Culianu maintained an almost total silence about Eliade both in the classroom and out. . . . I would characterize Culianu's attitude towards Eliade as Janus-faced. As his only Romanian student and his literary executor, Culianu could not completely distance himself from Eliade. Yet he was clearly uncomfortable with the legacy he was charged with perpetuating, in part because he was repulsed by the political views which Eliade professed in his youth and never publicly disavowed. The dilemma for Culianu was how he might disengage those politics without drawing further attention to them or to himself, without producing a furor which would sweep up him and his colleagues at Chicago and swirl among the Romanian intelligentsia.[83]

Such ambivalence would have been anathema to Christinel, who could accept nothing less than a full-throated defense of her late husband.

VII

Christinel's opposition forced Culianu to set aside his plans to publish the legionary articles, but not to abandon them altogether. It may be that fuller reflection led him to think his position as literary executor held more power than he initially believed, permitting him to advance the project without Mrs. Eliade's consent. Alternatively, he may have concluded that articles published more than fifty years prior in now-defunct Romanian newspapers were no longer protected by copyright and had entered the public domain. Whatever his rationale may have been, less than a year after telling Ricketts their initiative was "completely blocked," he renewed his efforts.

Thus, at some point in 1990, he approached the Romanian publisher Humanitas about an edition of the original articles, for which he would provide an appropriate introduction. As Humanitas was actively promoting Eliade's work in the post-Ceauşescu era, there was good reason to think the press might be interested, but the proposal went unanswered.[84] These setbacks notwithstanding, Culianu continued to look for ways to make the evidence available and shape the way it was understood. His sister described his last efforts toward that end.

In 1991, he sketched the plan for another book project, with a more complex structure: the documents were to be sent to many personalities of the contemporary cultural and academic world, some already in-volved in the discussion of the "Eliade question," some not yet (among others: Vittorio Lanternari, Bruce Lincoln, Matei Călinescu, Ivan Strenski, Jonathan Z. Smith, Radu Ioanid, Paul Ricoeur, Moshe Idel, Gherardo Gnoli, Wendy Doniger, Mac Linscott Ricketts), who would be asked to give their opinion in a set number of pages. This last volume was to be submitted to Macmillan. In May 1991, a few days before his death, he had received various letters and materials pertaining to the issue (inter alia, from Professors Nathan A. Scott, Mac Linscott Ricketts, and Bryan Rennie) of the proposed book, which remained at an embryonic stage. After the tragedy, the presence of these papers on Culianu's desk acquires somber meanings.[85]

Of the scholars named here, eight—including the three who apparently responded to Culianu's invitation—could be counted on to defend Eliade (Călinescu, Ricoeur, Gnoli, Doniger, Ricketts, Scott, Rennie, and Culianu himself). Three were likely to be critical (Lanternari, Strenski, Ioanid). Two were sufficiently independent to make their position more difficult to predict (Smith, Idel). The last, of course, was me, but I do not recall ever having received an invitation to contribute.

6

An Unsolved Murder

Part II (1991–)

I

The last class Professor Culianu taught ended at 11:30 a.m. on May 21, 1991. Afterward, he talked with several students, visited a book sale then underway in Swift Hall (home to the University of Chicago's Divinity School), and returned to his office on the building's third floor. Around 12:45, he went to the coffee shop in the basement, chatted some more, and returned to his office, collecting his mail along the way. At 1:02 he made a brief phone call, then visited the men's lavatory next to his office.[1] After he entered and seated himself in the fourth of five stalls, his assassin, who had either been waiting or followed him in, climbed on the toilet seat in the fifth stall, peered over the partition, and fired a single .25 caliber bullet through his victim's head. One of the secretaries in the office next to the men's room heard something "like a pop." A minute or two later a student went in to use the facilities, by which time the killer had fled and Culianu lay dying.[2]

As a result of the book sale, Swift Hall was full of visitors, which helped the killer slip in and out unnoticed. Apparently, the killer knew Culianu's habits and selected a predictable time and secluded place that also let him inflict a certain postmortem humiliation. The murder weapon was unusual, but carefully chosen: a small-caliber automatic easy to conceal, but powerful enough to ensure success when used at close range by someone with a skilled, steady hand. The lurid quality of the crime, plus the occult nature of Culianu's research interests, fed all sorts of speculation about the identity and motive of the killer. Some people imagined him—and given that the murder took place in a men's room, we can presume that the killer was male—to have been a disgruntled student, jilted lover, jealous spouse, drug dealer, cult member, or, as one person interviewed by the police put it, one of the "wackos" attracted to Culianu's classes. The details, however, suggest a cool professional who performed the task with precision, then walked away, never to be caught.

Several people told police that Culianu had been receiving threats for some time, which he typically dismissed as unserious.[3] Recently, however, his attitude had changed. One week before his death, he told a friend that he'd installed new locks on his apartment door and purchased some Mace, "as he had fears for his personal safety."[4] A few days later, he gave the translations of Eliade's legionary articles to Mark Krupnick for safekeeping.

II

Although the crime remains unsolved, the most widely accepted theory posits that Culianu was killed by Securitate officers who considered him a threat to their power in the post-Ceauşescu era.[5] Within days of the murder, this theory took shape in a series of telephone conversations among Romanian dissidents including Ioan's sister Tereza Petrescu-Culianu, her husband Dan Petrescu, Dorin Tudoran, Matei Călinescu, and a few others who identified strongly with Culianu, saw the crime as an attempt to intimidate critics, and feared for their own safety.[6] When approached by police, FBI, and the press, they were quick to describe the murder as a political assassination, which in their eyes confirmed the young scholar's exceptional brilliance, courage, and importance.[7]

Proponents of this theory suggest that in the immediate aftermath of Ceauşescu's fall, factions within Securitate felt threatened by Culianu's contributions to *Lumea liberă* ("Free World"), a Romanian expatriate journal with a circulation of ten thousand.[8] Under the general title "Scoptophilia" (i.e., the guilty pleasure of observing lurid things), his earliest columns argued that Romania's "revolution" of 1989 was not the liberatory upheaval it looked like on TV broadcasts, but a carefully orchestrated coup d'état through which masterminds of the KGB replaced Ceauşescu with reliable elements of Securitate.

From January through September 1, 1990, Culianu's articles were satiric and sharply critical, as when he imagined the new president, Ion Iliescu, communing happily with Ceauşescu's ghost, or when he decried Securitate as the world's "Stupidest Intelligence Service."[9] He often drew on ideas from his own scholarly work, invoking cognitive science, information theory, parallel universes, the manipulation of images, and the camouflaged nature of reality. Ultimately, he maintained that Yuri Andropov had KGB supercomputers produce model scenarios through which the crumbling Soviet system might transition to a market economy, then used Eastern bloc countries as laboratories in which to explore these "parallel universes." In Culianu's view, Mikhail Gorbachev continued the experiment through the upheavals of 1989 and all that followed.

While skeptics might dismiss this as "conspiracy theory," Culianu associated it with the Italian genre of "Fantapolitics" (*fantapolitica*), which—as he explained—speaks a hidden, terrifying truth in a manner that leaves the status quo undisturbed, since most people will dismiss the account as too fantastic to be credible. In that spirit, he confidently pointed an accusatory finger at the KGB computers, assuring readers, whom he wished not just to enlighten but to enchant and bedazzle in the mode of a Renaissance magus: "the truth is usually very close to the most fantastic hypothesis."[10]

Some readers found Culianu's columns audacious, captivating, enlightening, or at least delightfully entertaining. Others reacted differently, as the editors of *Lumea liberă* told the FBI.

On June 19, 1991, Dan Costescu and Cornel Dumitrescu, interviewed at 62-49 Adderton Street, Rego Park, New York. Both Costescu and Dumitrescu advised that they are not aware of any threatening letters received by their newspaper or the victim, Culianu. The interviewees advised that Culianu wrote columns for their paper from December 1989 through December 1990 and on numerous occasions they received letters and telephone calls disagreeing with the contents, but to their knowledge no death threats were received.[11]

Earlier, several people interviewed by the FBI said they had heard that *Lumea liberă* received threatening letters that the editors passed along to Culianu, who neither kept the letters, reported them, or paid much attention to them.[12] Whatever the source of this information, the interview with Costescu and Dumitrescu contradicts it.

Whether as the result of threats, complaints, flagging interest, a loss of nerve, or some other reason, the tone and content of Culianu's columns shifted abruptly in the last four months of 1990. After his "Fantapolitics" article of September 1, he no longer discussed Romania's situation openly, engaging it only occasionally and obliquely. In place of topical critique, most of his subsequent articles focused on scholars and cultural figures he admired and whose friendship he was actively courting. Eliade was first in the series, followed by Elie Wiesel, Moshe Idel, Umberto Eco, François Furet, and Grazia Marchianò.[13] He also devoted columns to disparate themes, including the future of feminism in Romania, cognitive science as an improvement on structuralism, and the fascinations of Egyptian history and Cajun culture.[14] While a few articles still had some bite—as when he compared Communist judiciary proceedings unfavorably to the Spanish Inquisition—the column lost its initial focus and intensity.[15]

On December 22, 1990, three days before the first anniversary of Ceauşescu's overthrow, Culianu published his final article in the series, titled "Adio." Both he and *Lumea liberă* 's editors felt the column had run its course, and Culianu said he wanted to concentrate on his research. In parting, he observed that his "Scoptophilia" writings began in jest and had no special goal. He thanked readers for their patience as he ventured far from his initial focus on Romania. He had sought, he explained, to "carry readers to all sorts of places, from Cairo to Rome, from Bucharest to New Orleans," and to "put them in contact with the most striking ideas in the world."[16] Rarefied pleasures of this sort, however, do not figure in his summary of the issues he had consistently wanted to engage: "Now and forever, the shortcomings of Romania."[17]

III

From September 1990 until his death—a full nine months—nearly everything Culianu published was sufficiently unrelated to Romanian current affairs that a close friend told Chicago police the day after the murder: "He did not believe that the victim was shot over Romanian politics. Ioan didn't seem to care anymore."[18] There was, however, one exception. On December 2, 1990, Gabriela Adameşteanu, editor of *22*, one of the liveliest Romanian reviews of the post-Ceauşescu era, visited Culianu in Chicago, interviewed him at length, and recorded their conversation. A portion of the transcript was published in the issue of April 5, 1991.

GABRIELA ADAMEŞTEANU: Have you followed what happened in Romania?
IOAN PETRU CULIANU: I have followed with the greatest sorrow since the
    spring or winter. At the beginning I hadn't the least suspicion. We were

all expertly led by the nose by whoever organized the great scenarios for television, beginning on December 22, 1989. No?

GA: In the first months of the past year, I lived (like so many other people) with the impression that our "good" television went bad after two weeks. Later, I thought it was possible that it all began even with the first images.

IPC: Yes, only this scenario was extremely well prepared. It was said that it was the most successful and spectacular operation of the KGB, after the withdrawal of forces from Afghanistan. Apparently, the KGB has a serious enough tradition of success, especially abroad . . .

GA: I am a little offended when you put all on the sign of the KGB. Wasn't the Romanian Securitate also able to organize the whole thing on its own?

IPC: The idiocy of Romanian Securitate is epic, of an unparalleled depth.

GA: Why did the revolution need so much spectacle, when in all the other countries of the East there was not even one death?

IPC: I don't know how many victims were foreseen, but I believe a certain shedding of blood was foreseen. If you don't have blood, you have to make it flow. The other countries of the East just didn't have a Ceauşescu. Only Romanians were permitted this "luxury."

GA: How great could Ceauşescu's power really have been if, in a single day, an omnipotent dictator became a nobody?

IPC: This shows that the whole Securitate left him in the swamp. He took himself to his redoubt in Tîrgovişte, and there he found the army installed, but no one received him. Probably, at a given moment, the KGB, working by supercomputer (there are some machines that cost tens of millions of dollars and can make you a model of the world for some decades or even more) at the time of Andropov saw that the model no longer led anywhere. And now they understood that without passing to a market economy, the losses would be much greater than the profit. They tore down the wall and they apparently began all the movements in the satellite countries.[19]

IV

Early in April 1991, this interview was published in Bucharest, the first time Culianu's views had seen print in his home country. A few weeks later, he played tour guide for King Michael, who was visiting Chicago and wanted to see the sites associated with Mircea Eliade. At the time, the king, whom the Communists had forced to abdicate in 1947, was building support for restoration of the monarchy. Although unsuccessful, his efforts surely displeased the country's new rulers. It is possible that publication of

Culianu's interview, together with his perceived support for King Michael, so angered powerful figures in the Iliescu regime—including high-ranking officers of Securitate—that they ordered his assassination. Ted Anton and others have ably argued this case, and it cannot be rejected outright. Still, there are reasons I think it unlikely.

Undoubtedly Securitate was capable—technically and morally—of planning and executing an operation of this sort. To do so on the campus of a leading American university, however, would involve enormous risks. Should anything go wrong, there would be serious international consequences for a government still struggling to achieve some measure of recognition and stability. Under such circumstances, it is hard to imagine that well-trained and well-disciplined professionals would accept the risks *unless they considered this mission vitally important*. One thus has to ask: Just how dangerous did they take Culianu to be?

In June 1991 the Romanian journalist Cornel Nistorescu spent four days in Chicago and spoke with Culianu's students, friends, colleagues, police, and others about the murder. Among those he consulted was Liviu Turcu, a former Securitate officer who had defected in January 1989. Turcu's remarks address the crucial question.

> According to my knowledge, in the history of this service, it has not practiced the liquidation of a man of Culianu's stature. He did not fulfill the requirements to be a target. . . . Further, I do not believe this is the work of Securitate, because few secret services would have dared to set such an operation in motion on the territory of the US. What interest would they have to do so? It would have been an enormous political gaffe. Don't forget that in Bucharest, the leadership of the apparatus, the specialists remained the same. Securitate is intact and those at its summit are well-trained people and they do not believe in an undertaking of such stupidity. In my opinion, there is not even a 25% chance that this crime would have been put in motion through the logic of the Securitate system.[20]

Some caution is advisable here, given the possibility that Turcu's remarks might have been strategic disinformation through which a shrewd, still-loyal officer sought to deflect suspicion. The same is not true of Monica Lovinescu, a leading dissident who knew Securitate's methods not from the inside, but as one who had long been on the receiving end of their attention. She also knew Culianu reasonably well, having met him on numerous occasions in Paris. A few days after the murder, her view was consonant with that of Officer Turcu.

> It is correct that I. P. Culianu was a kind of second fiddle. (It is even Tudoran's theory that they made him second fiddle so he could understand the first one.) He published some articles in *Lumea liberă* and an interview in *22*—otherwise disagreeable for the contempt he exhibited toward Romanians in general, his very great delight in being American, and his obsessive admiration for Jews (his chosen people, Christinel told us that he was on the way to converting to Judaism). So, some articles. And the fact of receiving, alongside the dean, King Michael at the University of Chicago. Is that enough to kill him when they only arrested Dumitru Mazilu? When they left Dorin Tudoran and Vladimir Tismăneanu in peace—men who were infinitely more dangerous to them?[21]

Lovinescu was no admirer of Culianu, as evidenced not only by this passage, but by several others where she commented on him unfavorably.[22] The anti-Semitism evident in her reaction to rumors that Culianu was planning to convert to Judaism in anticipation of his marriage to a former student, Hillary Wiesner, may also have figured in her dismissive view of him.[23] Jealousy and wounded pride are also evident, for Lovinescu had been at the center of opposition groups in Paris since the 1950s, made weekly Romanian-language broadcasts for Radio Free Europe, experienced regular harassment from Securitate, and suffered a 1977 attempt on her life that put her in a weeklong coma.[24] Accordingly, she felt Culianu's oppositional activities were too few, too recent, and too inconsequential for him to be the chosen victim of a Securitate assassination. Others, including her husband, herself, and the three figures she mentioned were more deserving of that honor.

If one can suspect Turcu of defending Securitate and Lovinescu of underestimating Culianu, the same cannot be said of Sorin Antohi, a dissident who was active in the same circle as Culianu's sister and brother-in-law and did much to promote Culianu.[25] Even so, he arrived at similar conclusions.

> What Ioan was writing in the Romanian press (in the US and then in Romania as well) was not such a big deal after all. Other Romanian

expatriates would have been killed before Ioan. Some were others were "only" tortured, wounded, beaten up, poisoned, scared. But their public engagement was of a different magnitude. This point has been made by many, including those who thought they deserved Ioan's place on the hit list.[26]

When I lectured in Bucharest in June 2000, most of the colleagues I encountered were eager to discuss Culianu's murder. To my surprise, many expressed views like those of Turcu, Lovinescu, and Antohi, voicing skepticism about Securitate's involvement. No one doubted that the agency and its personnel were capable of such despicable acts. But they felt Culianu was not sufficiently threatening or influential to have justified the risks. "His was not a name you heard at that time," as several people put it. By way of response, others entertained the idea that Culianu's relative unimportance made him an appropriate vehicle for the message that Securitate could still kill *anyone* if it so chose. Their point is intriguing, but the principle of Occam's razor posits that simpler, less baroque, and less ingenious explanations are usually preferable. Given the disproportion between large risks and modest potential gains, I find it unlikely—but not impossible—that Securitate killed Culianu.

V

A second theory, most recently and most powerfully advanced by Moshe Idel, focuses suspicion not on Securitate, but on Chicago's sizable community of former and neo-legionaries.[27] Cornel Nistorescu, the Romanian journalist who visited Chicago shortly after the murder, spoke to several of these men, one of whom offered some telling remarks.

> I talked with many old legionaries from Chicago. They prefer not to give their names. One of them, Eugen Vâlsan, permitted me to give his name and told me: "Culianu arrived in Chicago thanks to Mircea Eliade and Eliade was a legionary, although he didn't engage in legionary politics. I was in the same concentration camp with Eliade. After that, he no longer engaged in legionary politics, but in his essence he remained what he was. From this point of view, *grosso modo*, Culianu being close to Eliade's world, he also belongs to our family. The fact that he was shortly going to marry a Jew was his business. We weren't happy about that, but it did not concern us. It is just another absurd hypothesis. In fact, they

are only looking for a reason to implicate us. The last time I encountered Culianu was in church at Easter. Our relations were more than cordial. All the legionaries, however many there are, called me to hear the news and were pained. We categorically reject any accusation concerning our involvement in the death of this Romanian scholar."[28]

Two points struck Idel as particularly important. First, Vâlsan took pride in claiming Eliade as part of the legionary movement, both in the distant past (as witnessed by his 1938 internment at the Miercurea Ciuc camp) and more recently, even though he had long since ceased openly promoting the cause or acknowledging the connection. This same view of Eliade as intimate with and discreetly sympathetic to the city's legionaries figures in the reminiscences of Dr. Alexander Ronnett, one of the most active legionary leaders in the United States, who was also the Eliades' personal physician and dentist.[29]

Second, Chicago's legionaries considered Culianu a member of their "family." Having been introduced and vouched for by Eliade, he was welcomed as one of their own, for Eliade enjoyed a special position in this tight-knit group. Although Eliade held himself apart to a certain extent, explaining that any sign of public support could cost him his position, they knew his past, valued his ongoing loyalty (even if covert), and were glad to share in his prestige. Accordingly, they cooperated with him in fostering the idea that his support was solid, but a secret, as evidenced in a 1978 banquet at which Dr. Ronnett presented Eliade with an honorific gold medal that bore the emblem of the National Romanian-American Congress on its front and that of the Legion on its back.[30]

Eliade's position was unique. Although marginal in certain ways, he was admired, even idolized: someone whose membership the group desperately wanted to claim. That situation had its complications, however, as Marta Petreu has suggested.

As he would have liked to prevent hostilities from the midst of the Romanian diaspora, Eliade preserved good relations with legionaries. Without denying that he had a certain ideological affinity with them by way of inertia, we cannot exclude his having feared legionary blackmail. . . . As a result of their fame, Eliade and Cioran represented—and continue to represent—a certificate of legitimacy for legionaries, so they were not disposed to give up either one of them. On the other hand, they were disposed to punish them for any betrayal.[31]

If Eliade's situation had its risks, Culianu's was more precarious. Whether a "family" member or not, he had no history with the Legion and had made no commitment to it. How much loyalty the legionaries expected of him—and how much he was prepared to give—was and remains far from clear. In his dealings with them, he was neither a babe in the woods, nor as skillful as he imagined. He had experience dealing with old legionaries from his time in Italy and France, where he played a complicated game, according to Sorin Antohi.

> My sense has been that Ioan at some point accepted to be seen as the continuator of and heir to Eliade's many youthful creeds and endeavors. *Vivere pericolosamente* ["living dangerously"], getting a supreme kick out of it, but also getting to the bottom of things—these seem to be Ioan's maverick/trickster/arriviste strategies before he settled in Chicago. Maybe it was only then that he realized that his approach was going from *iocari serio* ["serious play"] with Iron Guard nostalgics in Paris (mostly intellectuals and artists, I knew some of them in 1990–1992) to facing his death at the hands of the Chicago/US hardened, old and young (ex-Securitate or not) Iron Guardsmen who included or could easily cont(r)act killers. . . . I think the killers (and/or those behind them) wanted to punish someone who may have played along (at least for and/or in their eyes), and only later betrayed them (or seemed likely to do it); someone who had already come too close to being an insider, and only later dropped out.[32]

From the outset, legionary doctrine judged traitors worse than enemies, turncoats being more dishonorable and more dangerous than even the most hostile outsider. As Codreanu instructed his followers, "If I have only one bullet and an enemy and a traitor are in front of me, I would use the bullet on the traitor."[33] The passage with which the Captain closed his memoir-cum-manifesto constitutes a call to arms in similar spirit.

> Do not confuse the Christian obligation to forgive those who have done you wrong with the nation's obligation to punish those who betrayed it and took it upon themselves to oppose it. Do not forget that the swords

with which you are girded are those of the nation. You bear them in its name. In its name, then, you will do vengeance on them: unforgiving and merciless. In this way, and only in this way will you prepare a healthy future for this nation.[34]

Idel was led to ask whether any of Chicago's legionaries considered Culianu's anticipated marriage a betrayal, Vâlsan's protestations notwithstanding. Or were there other offenses—real or imagined—they might have viewed as such? Conceivably, his recent dealings with King Michael might have struck them as traitorous, given the historic antipathy between the Legion and the royal family.[35] In addition, two of Culianu's publications might have prompted questions about his loyalty.

The first was a report, "Free Jormania," written several months after Ceaușescu's overthrow, in which he ridiculed several newly influential nationalist priests as having been clandestine members of the old "Wooden Guard."[36] The second was a jocular account of his troubles with Horia Stamatu, a well-connected legionary poet who took offense at Culianu's unflattering review of his work.[37] It is hard to imagine, however, that even the most thin-skinned legionary would have considered either of these sufficient cause for a murder.

Considerably more provocative was an article in which Culianu voiced blunt criticism of Codreanu, the Legion, and Orthodoxism, which he treated as a specifically Romanian form of "fundamentalism."

> Romanian Orthodoxism, cultivated by Nichifor Crainic and Nae Ionescu and accepted in large measure as the ideology of Corneliu Zelea Codreanu (who, however, acted as the chief of a kind of Orthodox Ku Klux Klan), found that misery had invaded the country, that its institutions were corrupt, that Bolshevism was beating at the door, that foreigners had overrun the country and the good ancestral religion of the people. They demanded the removal of foreign elements from religion (Protestantism and Catholicism) and the removal of the foreign element from the country (this especially in the Iron Guard's ideology) or rather, the conversion of foreigners to the ideal of the "New Man." ... The Iron Guard took its point of departure from this ideology, into which they introduced mystic elements and those of a secret society. The danger of fundamentalism in the breast of Orthodoxy is not extinguished. On the contrary, today it seems more powerful than ever.[38]

Given the Legion's understanding of itself as a crusading order of heroes, steeped in sacrifice and devoted to reconciling the Romanian nation with their Lord and Savior, to be branded "a kind of Orthodox Ku Klux Klan" would be exceptionally offensive: worse still if the insult came from someone inside the "family." Given the content of this article, one can well imagine that some of Chicago's legionaries came to view Culianu as a traitor.

But problems of chronology make it difficult to establish this as the motive for his murder. The "Orthodox Ku Klux Klan" article's date of publication was May–June 1991, just before, or even a bit after, the killing itself. Can we imagine the old legionaries read this piece the moment it came out, reacted with rage, decided to take vengeance, issued threats, and organized a successful assassination that depended on intimate knowledge of the victim's habits and routines, all in a matter of days? Or that Culianu foolishly shared the article with them months before it appeared, giving them adequate time to plot? Or that the editor of the journal in which it was published—Vladimir Tismăneanu, a leading dissident—leaked it to them? Logically, these possibilities exist, but none of them seems likely.

VI

The theories that locate responsibility for Ioan Culianu's murder with Securitate, Chicago's legionaries, or some combination of the two (e.g., a Securitate faction that had assets in Chicago) are particularly attractive for the way they transform a shocking crime into high political drama. Both theories are sufficiently plausible to deserve the serious consideration they have received, but for the reasons explained earlier, I find neither one fully persuasive. There is, moreover, evidence not addressed by either theory that leads me to consider another possible explanation, which—like its predecessors—is suggestive, but hardly conclusive.

The initial point that prompted my inquiry still strikes me as fraught with meaning. When Culianu most acutely feared for his life, he took steps to preserve a sheaf of papers he considered of vital importance, worrying that this material was endangered by the events fast overtaking him. In the folder he entrusted to Mark Krupnick were English translations of articles Mircea Eliade, his friend, mentor, and benefactor, had published in Romanian newspapers of the extreme Right in the late 1930s. Most voiced support for Romania's mystical brand of fascism, the stridently anti-Semitic Legion of the Archangel Michael. Others documented Eliade's support for a Jewish friend and his indignation at the way two Jewish scholars had been driven out of Romania. Notably missing from the file, however, was one of the most damning articles—the February 1937 article in which Eliade effectively defended Nazi aggression against Jews.[39]

The set of materials Culianu assembled could thus support a variety of interpretations. Depending on who was reading these papers, how much they already knew, and what kinds of explanatory material (introduction, footnotes, bibliography, etc.) might accompany the texts, these could be read as damning, moderately incriminating, mitigating, or even exculpatory. In the last year of his life, Culianu made multiple attempts to publish this material, believing the debate over Eliade's past had reached a point where this was necessary. And he believed that he and his collaborators on this project—Mac Ricketts and Matei Călinescu, possibly also Roberto Scagno and Wendy Doniger—could frame the material in ways that would help defend Eliade.[40]

Although this was Culianu's conscious intent, the ambiguous nature of the material also mirrored the ambivalence he occasionally expressed, as when he bridled at being called "the apologist for his 'Master.' "[41] His love and admiration were genuine, as was his appreciation for Eliade's invaluable support and exceptional kindness. But he also harbored resentments, normally unacknowledged and unexpressed, toward a man who had misled and disappointed him at several crucial junctures. And notwithstanding his enduring gratitude, he feared remaining in Eliade's shadow. Whatever else his publication of the legionary articles might accomplish, it would let him establish some critical distance, showing him to be no mere extension of his mentor, but a mature and confident scholar possessed of independence and integrity.

Culianu never abandoned his defense of Eliade—whom he continued to insist was not anti-Semitic, pro-Nazi, or a member of the Legion, but a great-spirited sage devoted to the enlightenment and salvation of the modern world: someone who could be compared, without exaggeration, to Zen masters and Sufi mystics. There is one point, however, on which he felt obliged to modify his position in ways that a critic would consider utterly inadequate, but which those most loyal to Eliade's memory found deeply distressing.

As we saw, before receiving Ricketts's translations of the legionary articles in May 1987, Culianu ignored the importance of those articles and even went so far as to doubt their existence. Upon reading this material for the first time, he reacted defensively, simultaneously acknowledging and denying the problem. "Things are not much changed," he told Ricketts, "and I do not feel like I should redefine my position."[42] His subsequent actions were broadly, but not perfectly consistent with that pronouncement, for he gradually modified his evaluation of those articles in subtle, but significant ways.

Thus, in a 1988 radio broadcast, Culianu publicly acknowledged for the first time that Eliade had indeed written in support of the Legion. On two subsequent occasions, he went further, while struggling to find an impossible point of balance. In these, his last publications on the topic, he acknowledged the authenticity of the articles (whose number he understated) and signaled discomfort with their content (in relatively mild terms). Reading the three pieces in sequence (Table 6.1), one gets the impression he was trying to placate critics, while disarming their core accusations. In the process, he also managed to put more distance between himself and Eliade.

VII

Christinel Eliade remained her husband's staunchest defender. Adamant in her belief that Mircea never supported the Legion, she dismissed the problematic articles as forgeries produced and publicized by his unscrupulous enemies. What is more, when anyone close to her acknowledged the authenticity of these documents, she took offense and judged them disloyal, as ultimately came to pass with Culianu.

We have already seen that in February 1989, not quite three years after Professor Eliade's death, his widow was sufficiently suspicious of Culianu's intentions, commitment, and reliability that she took legal action designed to keep him from publishing any of Mircea's work without her explicit consent.[43] And a few months later (June 1989), upon learning that Culianu—previously her closest, most dependable ally—had conceded Eliade's authorship of the legionary articles and called some of them "disconcerting," he caught a full blast of her anger. The force of her reaction surprised and unsettled Culianu, sufficiently so that he withdrew some articles already in press, while suspending his plans to publish the translations.[44] Others became aware of the mounting tension between the two, as Dorin Tudoran, a leading Romanian-American intellectual, recognized when Mrs. Eliade pointedly asked him, "So, what is going on with Néné [Ioan's nickname]?"

Table 6.1 Concessions made by Culianu regarding Eliade's legionary articles in his later comments on the subject

BBC radio broadcast, 1988[a]	"The Tree of Knowledge," March 1989[b]	Adameșteanu interview, December 1990, published April 1991[c]
Obviously, Mircea Eliade had *legionary sympathies*, which he expressed in articles published in the journal *Vremea*, but also in the legionary dailies *Buna Vestire* and *Sânziana*. From all this literature, however, it does not follow in any way that Mircea Eliade was a *member* of the Iron Guard, as has repeatedly been accused. For him, the legionaries were a nonviolent national movement, which attracted him through its similarity to Gandhi's movement in India, for which he was enthusiastic, and for its "Tolstoyan" spirit.	One cannot say that Eliade would ever have been a *member* of the organization, as various ill-informed articles now pretend, but he did write six or seven articles in favor of the Guard, of which two or three, reread today at a distance of forty years, are disconcerting. If one of these ("Blind Pilots" of September 19, 1937) contains a relatively harsh attack on the disproportionate economic and political strength of minorities, including the Jews, we do not encounter anti-Semitic accents (a *single sentence* in an ocean of articles, numbering more than 1,200!).	It's a question of three articles in which there are serious nuances of xenophobia and chauvinism. . . . There are three articles with a very unpleasant chauvinism. For the rest, some articles in favor of the Iron Guard, of Moța and Marin, and so on, which, you know, can be explained otherwise. Notwithstanding his lapse of 1937, Eliade does not seem like an anti-Semite.

Note: All texts are direct quotations, emphasis and quotation marks reflecting those of the originals.
[a]"Mircea Eliade din 1937 pînă în 1945" ("Mircea Eliade from 1937 until 1945"), typescript of a radio broadcast made through the Romanian section of the BBC, published in Culianu, *Studii Românești II*, p. 164.
[b]Culianu, "L'Albero della conoscenza," pp. 39–40.
[c]Adameșteanu, *Obsesia politicii*, p. 198.

and showed clear skepticism and dissatisfaction when he claimed, "There is nothing going on."[45]

Within a year, however, Culianu renewed his efforts and attempted to interest a Romanian publisher in an edition of the legionary articles. When that failed, he tried to organize a volume in which the articles would be accompanied by interpretive responses from various friends, colleagues, and scholars. In the months immediately preceding his death, he was actively soliciting contributions for such a book, and a few responses were found on his desk immediately after the murder.[46]

Mrs. Eliade had made it abundantly clear that she did not want to see the articles translated or published in any form and, further, that she had full legal rights to control their publication, would never grant permission for such use, and would be troubled by any attempt to do so. Given how close she and her husband had been to Culianu, how much they had done for him, and how much she relied on him at the time of Mircea's death, it is likely she experienced his renewed efforts to publish these articles as a terrible betrayal. Accordingly, relations between the two deteriorated significantly in the years after Culianu assumed his professorship in Chicago. Once there, he grew more confident and independent, developments that prompted a corresponding increase in Mrs. Eliade's suspicions and resentment.

Sensing her agitation, Culianu sought to protect her—and himself—from potential distress by keeping her in the dark about numerous developments. But as word of his initiatives filtered back, she became increasingly antagonistic. A photograph taken on April 27, 1991—less than a month before the murder—shows Christinel holding Ioan at a distance and fixing him with a frosty glare that he meets with apparent discomfort and anxiety, while his fiancée smiles at the camera, oblivious to the underlying tension or the events soon to follow (Figure 6.1).

VIII

Although accounts of Mrs. Eliade differ, certain qualities are regularly mentioned, including aristocratic hauteur, a volatile temper, and absolute devotion to her husband. She was a proud, beautiful woman, accustomed to having people defer to her wishes. To cite one small example, on several occasions in the mid-1970s, I was present when the Eliades entertained a mixed group of students, friends, and colleagues. At some point each evening, Christinel put on dark glasses to signal that she was tired or bored, and the significance of this gesture was common knowledge. Within minutes, all paid their thanks and headed for the door, save for one or two who would help with the cleanup.

In the years following Mircea's death, Mrs. Eliade became increasingly brittle and frustrated as she found herself unable to command the kind of loyalty she felt she and her late husband deserved. Quick to take offense

FIGURE 6.1 Ioan Culianu, Hillary Wiesner, and Christinel Eliade, April 27, 1991

Photo from the Mircea Eliade archive of Regenstein Library, Box 166, Folder 4.

at real or perceived slights, she alternated between anxiety and anger. The most affectionate portrait of her comes from Matei Călinescu:

> Christinel Eliade . . . came from a noble family of Moldova, spoke Romanian with a delightful aristocratic Moldavian accent, and was totally devoted to her husband's memory after whose death she installed, in the apartment on Woodlawn Avenue, an altar with fresh flowers in a corner of the living room, under an enlarged photograph of the young Eliade.[47]

Stelian Pleșoiu gave a fuller and more nuanced picture of Mrs. Eliade in the course of an interview that appeared in the Romanian press.

REPORTER: What was Mrs. Eliade like?

STELIAN PLEȘOIU: Christinel Eliade was the opposite of her husband. She was a very distinguished and very beautiful kind of woman, with remarkable features. She had alabaster eyes, smoked a lot, and was very authoritarian. She was very tough; she always placed herself in the position of the head of the household. Although she erred many times, she was the head of the house. She treated me no different from others, but she treated her husband very differently. With her authoritarian, commanding voice, she put us all in order, she had us all take out the trash . . .

REPORTER: Even the master's colleagues?

STELIAN PLEŞOIU: Yes, yes! She didn't take account of anyone's position and, believe me, people of high positions and titles came to the house. And the greater someone's title was, the more she humiliated him with beautiful, but cutting words: "Please, take the trash out when you leave, please bring me a pack of cigarettes, etc." But in her own way, she had many admirers, and many people wouldn't say a word against her. I believe this whole attitude began from the fact that her husband was a very gentle man and everyone would have taken advantage of him . . .

REPORTER: So she was the master's protector?

STELIAN PLEŞOIU: Exactly! And many did take advantage of him, and she protected him with all her cunning and skill as a woman.[48]

Adriana Berger spoke of Mrs. Eliade as "an extension of the man," who was determined to suppress all potentially damaging information about him. Berger also described episodes in which Christinel browbeat her, Mac Ricketts, and the editors at Harper and Row, when she felt they were disregarding her wishes or disserving her late husband's interests.[49] Most intimate, detailed, and revealing, however, were Monica Lovinescu's descriptions of Christinel in the years after Mircea's death. Within a month of his passing, Lovinescu observed, "she is excessively attentive to what is written about Mircea (Mircea is gone and this obsession remains)."[50] A year later, she described Christinel as "confused, not only as for sleep, but in general. More foolish than last year. . . . She cries and is super-nervous."[51] Lovinescu mentions sporadic outbursts against old friends for imagined slights and betrayals. Thus, to cite a few examples, Mrs. Eliade assailed Emil Cioran in a tone he considered insufferable and threatened to break relations when he chose not to help with a volume in Eliade's honor.[52] Some time later, she berated Alain Besançon for his failure to respond to a critical article and burst into tears when he tried to explain.[53] And when Christinel found Lovinescu's defenses of Mircea inadequate, she upbraided her friend "with the voice of a prosecutor general."[54] Ultimately, Lovinescu came to share Culianu's view that critical articles were best hidden from Mrs. Eliade, which left her all the more isolated, untrusting, and desperate.[55] In June 1987, Lovinescu found her friend "confused . . . foolish . . . super-agitated."[56]

By 1993, she reflected with sadness, "My first impression of Christinel is confirmed. She is different from previous years. Nervous, irritable, border-line aggressive. As if there has been a mutation."[57]

We have seen that Mrs. Eliade directed verbal aggression at Culianu in the later phase of their relationship and took legal action to preempt his publication plans. Is it possible she also contemplated physical aggression or set such acts in motion? Culianu's concern for the safety of the translated legionary articles suggests he connected the threats to his life with her attempts to suppress those articles. Still, it is hard to imagine Mrs. Eliade would have gone so far as to hire a killer in order to keep them from publication. What is easier to imagine is a situation like that in which Henry II thundered, "Will no one rid me of this turbulent priest?" until some among his entourage took it upon themselves to solve the problem of Becket for him.

The Eliades occupied a unique position within Chicago's Romanian-American community. Romanians in general and legionaries in particular were enormously proud of the professor's accomplishments and equally protective of his reputation. Upon his death, much of Chicago's Romanian community swarmed to the Eliades' apartment, where they lamented their loss of "the master," celebrated his remarkable accomplishments, eagerly sought souvenirs, and offered condolences to his widow, whom they addressed in reverential terms as if she were vir-tual royalty.[58]

As keeper of her husband's flame, had Christinel complained loudly and often enough, there were people in a position to take action on her behalf, for the community included a large number of former and neo-legionaries. Some, like Dr. Ronnett, the Eliades' physician and dentist, were actively involved in organizations steeped in conspiracy and open to violence.[59] Upon hearing that Mrs. Eliade experienced Culianu's shifting stance as a betrayal of Mircea's legacy, memory, and cause, there were those who might well conclude the ungrateful upstart deserved the fate the Legion reserved for traitors.

No concrete evidence has emerged that would connect Mrs. Eliade directly to the murder, so this—like the other theories that have been advanced—remains speculative and hypothetical. We do know how she reacted to Culianu's death, however. On the very day after, T. David Brent, senior editor at the University of Chicago Press, had a regularly scheduled meeting with Mrs. Eliade in connection with his work on the posthu-mously published English translations of Eliade's journals. As he recalled many years later, he found her as elegant and charming as ever on that day, showing relatively little emotion when they spoke of Culianu's death. Rather, she proceeded to ask that Mr. Brent assume the position of literary executor for Mr. Eliade's works, while signaling her discomfort with her late husband's wish that Culianu play that role. "I never really liked him," she confided rather offhandedly.[60]

IX

In the summer of 1987, Culianu finished work on *The Emerald Game*, a novel he coauthored with Hillary Wiesner. Loosely styled after Umberto Eco's *The Name of the Rose*, the book traces a series of murders in Renaissance Florence whose motive and significance articulate with the occult iconography of Botticelli's *Birth of Venus*. The novel's setting was familiar territory for Culianu, while its plot drew heavily on his research into astrology, alchemy, sects, heresies, controversies, magic, and the alternative universes that still flourished in the early modern period.[61]

The book's strictly literary qualities are modest, and the agent who handled it—quite coincidentally, my aunt, Ray Lincoln—never found a publisher for it. After her fiancée's murder, Ms. Wiesner showed no further interest in the manuscript, which sat in storage until I asked my cousin Joe Lincoln, a Philadelphia attorney, to look for it. Rescued from his garage, it has now been transferred to the Special Collections of the University of Chicago's Regenstein Library.

One passage in this book strikes me as particularly interesting, both as a general principle and with specific relevance to Culianu's murder. Toward the middle of the action, the protagonist—an English visitor to Florence, who is intelligent and eager, but has only an outsider's imperfect knowledge of the city's intricate lines of conflict—voices his theory that a sinister Savonarolan conspiracy is responsible for the killings. His older, better-informed, and more cautious partner in the inquiry suggests otherwise.

> Surely you have witnessed a small part of the several rivalries and grudges that we sustain among ourselves. And this morning's revelations were only a crumb of the cake, take my word for it. The heretic is more reviled than the distant infidel; that is, it is those with whom we have the smallest disagreements that we hate with the most passion. Your chances, Tommaso, of being killed by a friend and acquaintance far outweigh the likelihood of murder by a stranger.[62]

X

It has never been my intention to play detective and solve the murder of Ioan Petru Culianu. By a circuitous route, a set of documents made its way from his hands to mine. For many years I ignored them, and in a moment of carelessness, I lost them. What I have done since and what I present here is an attempt to atone for my lapses.

In the process, I have learned a great deal about Mircea Eliade and Ioan Culianu, friends and colleagues I thought I knew reasonably well, but about whom I was ignorant or mistaken on a great many points. Along the way, I also learned much about countless people who crossed their paths and about Romania's tortuous history, a topic on which I—like most non-Romanians—previously knew almost nothing. It has been quite an education, if hardly a happy one.

Reading Eliade's articles from the late 1930s with close attention to the context in which they were written, then again from Culianu's perspective, helped me confront some of my fears and resolve some, but not all my doubts concerning my *Doktorvater*. Ultimately, my judgment of the articles and of Eliade's legionary involvement has shifted, becoming more critical and less defensive than Culianu's. While I see no literal blood on Eliade's hands, the nature and goals of the Legion were abundantly clear. Hypernationalist, rabidly anti-Semitic, antidemocratic, antimodern, and anticommunist, it was a militantly aggressive movement, open to—often enough, eager for—violence. As such, the Legion differed little from other fascisms, save for its mystic aura and religious commitments—qualities Eliade found so appealing that he was able to overlook its deeply abhorrent aspects. Careful research can help one comprehend and regret his stance, but not excuse or forgive it. The same holds true for his subsequent evasions and denials.

Working through these materials has not brought me peace. But it has helped me understand a few things. First, I have come to see how a highly intelligent man could come to support a reprehensible cause, then hide his involvement for decades thereafter. Second, it has shown me how another intelligent man could feel so admiring of and so beholden to the first that he would defend him vigorously and tenaciously, in defiance of evidence and logic. Third, I can see how the younger man's attempts to manage the irreconcilable demands of personal loyalty and intellectual integrity led him to acknowledge painful truths in ways he meant to be tactful, sympathetic, and supportive, but which also helped satisfy some of his unconscious envy, resentment, and longing for independence. Finally, I can imagine how others could have understood his actions as a betrayal grievous enough to warrant his death.

The articles that are the impetus for this book remain troubling texts, written in turbulent times, and their troubles continue to reverberate. As a young man full of talent, energy, and ambition, Eliade made a terrible mistake, giving enthusiastic support to a morally repugnant movement. Later, he tried to hide that piece of his past, understanding that were it to become known, it would have serious consequences for his career and reputation. Over time, others got drawn into the vortex his secret created, some of whom struggled to discover the truth and others to obscure it. None was fully successful, but all suffered as a result, often quite badly, including not only Christinel Eliade and Ioan Culianu, but Adriana Berger, Ivan Strenski, Mac Ricketts, Theodore Lavi, Gershom Scholem, Monica Lovinescu, Norman Manea, Alfonso di Nola, Saul Bellow, and a great many others. I have gotten off easier than most, but no one involved has been fully spared.

One cannot help feeling anger, bewilderment, and regret at those who created, prolonged, and exacerbated the vortex, as well as deep sorrow and sympathy for those caught in it. If I had the faith that some of them professed, I would ask God to show them all mercy.

APPENDIX

———◦◦◦———

Continuity and Change in
Culianu's Defenses of Eliade

Table A.1 Responses to the charge of anti-Semitism

	Assertion	Supporting rationale	Responses to critics
1984 "**Mircea Eliade and the Blind Tortoise**"	It was easy to demonstrate that Eliade . . . never expressed anti-Semitic views.	Eliade defended Jews against representatives of the Iron Guard and even against his own teacher, Nae Ionescu.	(a) *Italian critics repeat Communist calumnies.* (b) *The information in* Toladot *is "more than 90% false, and the rest highly improbable."*
1985 *The Unknown Mircea Eliade*	I have myself elsewhere analyzed—in order to reject them categorically—all sorts of strange rumors according to which Eliade would have been "anti-Semitic."	(a) *Eliade defended Mihail Sebastian against Nae Ionescu.* (b) Eliade never made himself an accomplice to the absurd measures of expelling Jews demanded by legionaries.	
1988 "**Mircea Eliade and Nae Ionescu**"	Fundamentally, Nae Ionescu was not anti-Semitic. Even less so was Mircea Eliade, as proved by the polemic of 1934.	He flatly stated that he was not in agreement with the simplistic spirit of a certain Orthodox anti-Semitism exhibited by Ionescu.	(a) *Sebastian's journal is "full of inexactitudes."* (b) Toladot *"has Communist tendencies" and "obviously wants to defame Eliade."*
1988 "**Mircea Eliade from 1937 until 1945**"	Eliade was never an anti-Semite; on the contrary, even the opposite.	(a) *He opposed Nae's "vague theological justification for anti-Semitism."* (b) *"Blind Pilots" voices admiration for Jewish "vitality, tenacity, and genius."*	
1989 "**The Tree of Knowledge**"	Eliade was certainly not anti-Semitic.	*Against Ionescu, "Eliade endeavored to demonstrate theologically that anti-Semitism is an aberration."*	"Blind Pilots" includes "a relatively harsh attack on the disproportionate economic and political strength of minorities, including the Jews."

Note: Passages appearing primarily in roman type are direct quotations from Culianu. The italics there are his. Passages appearing primarily in italics are summations of Culianu's argument, but not his own words. Here direct citations from him are place inside quotation marks.

Table A.2 Treatment of the controversy over Nae Ionescu's preface to Mihail Sebastian's novel

	Description of Ionescu	Assessment of the preface	Description of Eliade's intervention
1984 "Mircea Eliade and the Blind Tortoise"	Up to this time, he was unquestionably a tolerant and generous man and one of the very few Romanians who, out of deep curiosity and respect for the Jewish culture, had learned Hebrew and acquired an extensive knowledge of Hebrew literature.	This rather simplistically religious anti-Semitism corresponds perfectly with the spirit of the Iron Guard.	When Eliade read Ionescu's foreword to Sebastian's novel, he took the part of his friend against his teacher.
1985 *The Unknown Mircea Eliade*	Without himself becoming an anti-Semite in the proper sense of the term, he undertook to develop a new position.	Nae Ionescu, through his malicious gesture, sowed doubt among all parties.	Following [Sebastian's] testimony, when "everything was collapsing around him," he had only one support: Mircea Eliade, [who dared] to enter into public polemic with his mentor and to oppose his bizarre theological arguments.
1988 "Mircea Eliade and Nae Ionescu"		. . . the simplistic spirit of a certain Orthodox anti-Semitism exhibited by Ionescu.	He flatly stated that he was not in agreement with . . . Ionescu.
1989 "The Tree of Knowledge"	The demon, however, lay in ambush. Nae Ionescu, whom Eliade liked to describe as a Socrates, but whom others gladly compared to Mephistopheles.	Nae Ionescu reinforced the impression of advocating a vague theological anti-Semitism in the preface.	Eliade endeavored to demonstrate theologically that anti-Semitism is an aberration.

Note: All passages cited are direct quotations from Culianu.

Table A.3 Explanations of the "smoking gun" article, "Why I Believe in the Victory of the Legionary Movement," published in *Buna Vestire* on December 17, 1937

	Assertion	Reasoning	Concessions
1984 "Mircea Eliade and the Blind Tortoise"	(a) The first assertion in *Toladot* consists of a citation from an article that Eliade never wrote, in a review in which he never published. The quotation sounds so artificial, so far from Eliade's style, that it can easily be recognized as a bad forgery. (b) Eliade . . . never published in *Buna Vestire*.	(a) "How can the Romanian *nation* end its life, infected by *squalor and syphilis* (?), when it is *overrun by Jews and foreigners?* . . . The revolution of the Legion must achieve the highest goal: salvation of the *nation* . . ." I have used italics to identify the words and expressions that do not belong to Eliade's style and vocabulary.	
1988 "Mircea Eliade from 1937 until 1945"	The only pages published under the name of Mircea Eliade that contain *a single dubious phrase* appeared in the issue of *Buna Vestire* dated December 17, 1937, under the title 'Why I Believe in the Victory of the Legionary Movement.'	This is obviously a question of an unrecorded interview (we are in 1937!) that was probably transcribed in haste by some legionary collaborator on a paper that did not often show Eliade's laborious meticulousness in his effort to dissociate himself from the Iron Guard. What appears to be the only regrettable statement regarding the Jews in a vast corpus that is otherwise full of contrary statements is thus a sentence that Eliade did not write himself.	Obviously, Mircea Eliade had legionary *sympathies*, which he expressed in articles published in the journal *Vremea*, but also in the legionary dailies *Buna Vestire* and *Sânziana*.
1989 "The Tree of Knowledge"	We do not encounter anti-Semitic accents (*a single sentence* in an ocean of articles, numbering more than 1200!), except in an interview of December 17, 1937 . . .	. . . which Eliade denied ever having *written*. It is thus probable that the unpleasant phrase did not belong to Eliade himself, but to the legionary editor who had obtained the interview.	As Mac Linscott Ricketts noted, the ideas (but surely not the style!) were his.

Table A.3 Continued

	Assertion	Reasoning	Concessions
December 1990 Interview by Gabriela Adameşteanu	It's a question of three articles in which there are serious nuances of xenophobia and chauvinism. Regarding one of them, Eliade stated in print that it was not his.	... the phraseology is not his.	(a) All those who know Eliade's writings of that period recognize that the interview was based on what Eliade himself said ... (b) That is the only place where there is a direct reference to the Jews. But there are three articles with a very unpleasant chauvinism.

Note: All passages cited are direct quotations from Culianu and the italics are in the original.

Table A.4 Responses to charges of legionary involvement

	Assertion	Supporting rationale	Responses to critics
1984 "Mircea Eliade and the Blind Tortoise"	It was easy to demonstrate that Eliade never was a member of the Iron Guard.	Not only *Toladot* and Co. confused him with his teacher, Nae Ionescu, who *really* was a theorist of religious anti-Semitism and a supporter of Fascism, but the Romanian government made the same error.	(a) *Italian critics repeat Communist calumnies.* (b) *The information in Toladot is "more than 90% false, and the rest highly improbable."*
1984 "Mircea Eliade and the Ideal of the Universal Man"	Eliade always situated himself in democratic positions, refusing to fall into the excesses of his friends on the right or on the Communist left.	Eliade will finish by being abusively considered to be of the right, because of the more and more marked politics of his mentor, Nae Ionescu.	

(*continued*)

Table A.4 Continued

	Assertion	Supporting rationale	Responses to critics
1985 *The Unknown* *Mircea Eliade*	I have myself elsewhere analyzed—in order to reject them categorically—all sorts of strange rumors according to which Eliade would have been . . . "a member of the Iron Guard."	Because those around Nae Ionescu were now of the right, Eliade passed in their eyes as being of the right.	(a) Did Eliade really harbor any admiration for Codreanu? He was probably impressed by the latter's sincere mysticism, which made him inept, however, at politics. His interest must have been somewhat professional and detached. In any case, Codreanu was not Eliade's *friend*. . . . For an intellectual, the Codreanu phenomenon was unique and fascinating. (b) His abusive detention, like his personal connection with Codreanu, gave rise to another legend, assiduously propagated by circles on the left and, after 1946, by the Romanian government installed by the Soviet army, according to which Eliade would have been part of the Iron Guard.
1988 **"Mircea Eliade** **and Nae** **Ionescu"**	One cannot assert that Nae Ionescu was a "member" of the legionary movement. Still less can one say that Mircea Eliade was a member of the Iron Guard.	Nae Ionescu had the function of a Mephistopheles for Eliade, drawing him into a political adventure with very serious consequence.	If in 1938, both Nae Ionescu and Mircea Eliade were interned in the Miercurea Ciuc camp in the context of large anti-legionary actions, they were there in the capacity of sympathizers, not members.

Table A.4 Continued

	Assertion	Supporting rationale	Responses to critics
1988 "Mircea Eliade from 1937 until 1945"	He was not a *member* of the Iron Guard, but a militant sympathizer.	Sebastian does not specifically accuse Eliade of having been a *member* of the legionary movement. That for which he reproaches him is his lack of a firm attitude, i.e., an *opportunism*.	(a) Obviously, Mircea Eliade had legionary *sympathies*, which he expressed in articles published in the journal *Vremea*, but also in the legionary dailies *Buna Vestire* and *Sânziana*. (b) He was surely close to the legionaries, who reminded him of Gandhi and Tolstoy and *because* they reminded him of Gandhi and Tolstoy.
1989 "The Tree of Knowledge"	One cannot say that Eliade was ever a *member* of the organization, as various ill-informed articles now pretend.	What Sebastian charged him with was not so much a pro-fascist attitude as simply political opportunism.	(a) He did write six or seven articles in favor of the Guard, of which two or three, re-read today at a distance of forty years, are disconcerting. (b) Eliade followed Nae Ionescu on the tangled path of ruin. . . . In 1937, during an electoral campaign in which the Iron Guard achieved a disquieting success, Nae Ionescu sided completely with them and Mircea Eliade followed him.

Note: Passages appearing primarily in roman type are direct quotations from Culianu. The italics there are his. Passages appearing primarily in italics are summations of Culianu's argument, but not his own words. Here, direct citations from him are placed inside quotation marks.

Table A.5 Responses to the charge of being pro-Nazi

	Assertion	Supporting rationale
March 1978 Letter to Mircea Eliade	I explain that you were not pro-Nazi	because you were pro-Salazarian.... Salazar was not really what we call a "fascist," that is, he did not have an *ideology*.
1984 "Mircea Eliade and the Blind Tortoise"	Even if he was no democrat, Eliade was ... not a particular friend of the Germans.	He was appointed cultural attaché to London by the only anti-German and pro-English government of the years 1938–44.
1985 *The Unknown Mircea Eliade*	A man of good sense, Eliade had no sympathy for Hitlerist Germany at a time when many lost their head.	(a) In March 1940, the liberal, anglophile government of Gheorghe Tătărescu ... entrusted him with the position of cultural attaché to London, which he took up on April 10, 1940. (b) It is very probable that Salazar's idea of *social reform*, his *anti-plutocratic* attitude, *nationalism*, and the *uplift of the people* with full respect for *national traditions* and the Church found favorable echoes in Eliade.
1988 "Mircea Eliade from 1937 until 1945"	Was he ever pro-Nazi? For those who know a little history, the response will immediately be clear when we say that he was a *Salazarian*.	(a) We know that Salazar, himself of Jewish origin, was nearly as terrified of Hitler as of Stalin and he stated in public that a Nazi conquest of Europe would be the greatest disaster imaginable. (b) In truth, it was the anglophile Tătărescu government that named Eliade cultural attaché to London in 1940.
1989 "The Tree of Knowledge"	Eliade was certainly not ... pro-Nazi.	(a) Eliade had the unexpected, but enviable good fortune to be transferred to Lisbon, where he passed the war years, delighting in the neutrality and shrewdness of Salazar, who hated Hitler as well as Stalin, and to whom he dedicated a book in 1942, with anti-Nazi tendencies.

Note: Passages appearing primarily in roman type are direct quotations from Culianu. The italics there are his. Passages appearing primarily in italics are summations of Culianu's argument, but not his own words. Here, direct citations from him are placed inside quotation marks.

NOTES

<hr/>

Chapter 1

1. Bruce Lincoln, *Priests, Warriors, and Cattle: A Study in the Ecology of Religions* (Berkeley: University of California Press, 1981), p. xi.
2. Thoughtful overviews of the debate and the issues it raises are available in Mihai Dinu Gheorghiu, "Mircea Eliade: Carrière internationale et identité nationale," *Balkan-Arkhiv* 22–23 (1999): 307–18; Natale Spineto, *Mircea Eliade storico delle religioni* (Brescia: Morcelliana, 2006), pp. 25–44; Carlo Ginzburg, "Mircea Eliade's Ambivalent Legacy," in Christian K. Wedemeyer and Wendy Doniger, eds., *Hermeneutics, Politics, and the History of Religions: The Contested Legacies of Joachim Wach & Mircea Eliade* (New York: Oxford University Press, 2010), pp. 307–23; and Philippe Borgeaud, "Un mythe moderne: Mircea Eliade," in Borgeaud, *Exercices de mythologie*, 2nd ed. (Geneva: Labor et Fides, 2015), pp. 179–205. Major interventions include Crescenzo Fiore, *Storia sacra e storia profana in Mircea Eliade* (Rome: Bulzoni, 1986); Ivan Strenski, *Four Theories of Myth in Twentieth-Century History* (Iowa City: University of Iowa Press, 1987), pp. 70–128; Mac Linscott Ricketts, *Mircea Eliade: The Romanian Roots, 1907–1945* (Boulder, CO: East European Monographs, 1988); Claudio Mutti, *Mircea Eliade e la Guardia di Ferro* (Parma: Edizioni all'insegna del Veltro, 1989); Mircea Handoca, *Pro Mircea Eliade* (Cluj-Napoca: Editura Dacia, 2000); Bryan Rennie, *Changing Religious Worlds: The Meaning and End of Mircea Eliade* (Albany: State University of New York Press, 2000); Alexandra Laignel-Lavastine, *Cioran, Eliade, Ionesco: L'oubli du fascisme* (Paris: Presses Universitaires de France, 2002); Hannelore Müller, *Der frühe Mircea Eliade: Sein rumänischer Hintergrund und die Anfänge seiner universalistischen Religionsphilosophie* (Münster: Lit, 2004); Emanuela Costantini, *Nae Ionescu, Mircea Eliade, Emil Cioran: Antiliberalismo nazionalista alla periferia d'Europa* (Perugia: Morlachi Editore, 2005); Daniel Dubuisson, *Impostures et pseudo-science: L'oeuvre de Mircea Eliade* (Villeneuve d'Asq: Presses Universitaires du Septentrion,

2005); Andrei Oişteanu, *Religie, politică şi mit: Texte despre Mircea Eliade şi Ioan Culianu* (Iaşi: Polirom, 2007); Mihaela Gligor, *Mircea Eliade, anii tulburi: 1932–1938* (Bucharest: EuroPress, 2007); Traian Vedinaş, *Bătăliile mistagogului: Mircea Eliade şi politicele anilor '30* (Cluj-Napoca: Editura Grinta, 2008); Marcello De Martino, *Mircea Eliade esoterico: Ioan Petru Culianu e i "non detti"* (Rome: Edizioni Settimo Sigillo, 2008); Wedemeyer and Doniger, *Hermeneutics, Politics*; Mihaela Gligor, ed., *Mircea Eliade between the History of Religions and the Fall into History* (Cluj-Napoca: Presa Universitara Clujeana, 2012); and Moshe Idel, *Mircea Eliade: From Magic to Myth* (New York: Peter Lang, 2014). Article-length contributions are too numerous to mention and will be found in the bibliographies of the above volumes.

3. Cf. Mircea Eliade, *Journal III: 1970–1978*, trans. Teresa Lavender Fagan (Chicago: University of Chicago Press, 1989), pp. 194–95 (entry of May 25, 1975).

4. Martha Lincoln and Bruce Lincoln, "Toward a Critical Hauntology: Bare Afterlife and the Ghosts of Ba Chuc," *Comparative Studies in Society and History* 57 (2015): 191–220.

5. Mircea Eliade, "Lucruri de taină . . ." ("Secret things"), one of the "Fragmente" published in *Vremea* 8, no. 401 (1935): 9, which he republished in *Fragmentarium* (Bucharest: Humanitas, 1994; orig. 1939), p. 63 and saw a French translation appear in a volume devoted to him: "Les Secrets," *Cahiers de l'Herne* 33 (1978): 61–62. The Romanian original has been reprinted many times and is readily available on the internet.

6. Ted Anton, *Eros, Magic, and the Murder of Professor Culianu* (Evanston, IL: Northwestern University Press, 1996).

7. Mircea Eliade, *Textele "legionare" şi despre "românism"* (*"Legionary" Texts and those on "Romanianism"*), ed. Mircea Handoca (Cluj-Napoca: Editura Dacia, 2001).

Chapter 2

1. Most broadly on this period, see Irina Livezeanu, *Cultural Politics in Greater Romania: Regionalism, Nation Building and Ethnic Struggle, 1918–1930* (Ithaca, NY: Cornell University Press, 1995).

2. On the nature of this seemingly interminable debate, see Keith Hitchins, *Rumania: 1866–1947* (Oxford: Clarendon Press, 1994), pp. 292–334; Katherine Verdery, "National Ideology and National Character in Interwar Romania," in Ivo Banac and Katherine Verdery, eds., *National Character and National Ideology in Interwar Eastern Europe* (New Haven: Yale Center for International and Area Studies, 1995), pp. 103–33; and Marius Turda, "Conservative Palingenesis and Cultural Modernism in Early Twentieth-Century Romania," *Totalitarian Movements and Political Religion* 9 (2008): 437–53.

3. Much has been written on Romanian anti-Semitism in this period. Inter alia, see Leon Volovici, *Nationalist Ideology and Antisemitism: The Case of Romanian Intellectuals in the 1930s* (Oxford: Pergamon Press, 1991); William Brustein and Amy Ronnkvist, "The Roots of Anti-Semitism: Romania before the Holocaust," *Journal of Genocide Research 4* (2002): 211–35; Mihai Vişan, *Naţionalism şi antisemitism interbelic românesc* (Bucharest: Paco, 2003); Raul Cârstocea, "A Marginal Group on Europe's Margin? Anti-Semitism in Romania from the Congress of Berlin to the Legion of the Archangel Michael," in Silviu Miloiu et al., eds., *Europe as Viewed from the Margins* (Târgovişte: Cetatea de Scaun, 2007), pp. 189–201; Raul Cârstocea, "The Path to the Holocaust: Fascism and Antisemitism in Interwar Romania," *Shoah: Intervention, Methods, Documentation 1* (2014): 43–52; and Henry Eaton, *The Origins and Onset of the Romanian Holocaust* (Detroit: Wayne State University Press, 2013).

4. Among Eliade's fellow students at Spiru Haret were Constantin Noica, Haig Acterian, Mihail Polihroniade, Ion Victor Vojen, and Petre Viforeanu. In his last year of lycée, Eliade also participated in a literary circle that included several university students, including Vasile Marin and Petru Comarnescu, all of whom would play significant roles in later history. Biographies of Eliade that include substantive discussion of his Romanian years include Ioan Culianu, *Mircea Eliade* (Assisi: Cittadella, 1978); Ricketts, *Mircea Eliade*; and Florin Ţurcanu, *Mircea Eliade: Le prisonnier de l'histoire* (Paris: La Découverte, 2003).

5. Cited by Liviu Bordaş, "Between the Devil's Waters and the Fall into History, or: An Alternate Account of Mircea Eliade's Diopteries," trans. Mac Linscott Ricketts, *International Journal on Humanistic Ideology 4* (2011): 54.

6. Ibid., pp. 63–68. Eliade discussed his friendship with Mărculescu in his *Autobiography*, vol. *1: Journey East, Journey West*, trans. Mac Linscott Ricketts (New York: Harper & Row, 1981), pp. 54, 69, 74–76, and 95–97.

7. On Eliade's antipathy to Western modernity, see Pedro Jesús Pérez Zafrilla, "El nacionalismo rumeno en la obra de Mircea Eliade," *Thémata 39* (2007): 309–13; Radu Vancu, "The Counter-modern Eliade: *Widerverzauberung der Welt* in the Life and Work of Mircea Eliade," *World Literature Studies 2* (2015): 23–35; and Sandra Cibicenco, "Archaic Elements in Mircea Eliade's 'Legionary' Writings," *Studia Universitatis Babes-Bolyai, Philosophia 37* (2016): 37–51.

8. On the group variously termed the "Young Generation," "New Generation," "Generation of 1927," and "Criterion Group" (after a lecture series Eliade helped organize), see Matei Călinescu, "The 1927 Generation in Romania: Friendships and Ideological Choices," *East European Politics and Societies 15* (2001): 649–77; Cristina Bejan, "The Paradox of the Young Generation in Inter-war Romania," *Slovo 18* (2006): 115–28; Iulian Boldea, "Generaţia '27: Itinerarii identitare," *Communication interculturelle et litteraire 22* (2015): 113–32; and Marta Petreu, *Generaţia '27 între Holocaust şi Gulag* (Iaşi: Polirom, 2016). On the Criterion group more specifically,

Mac Linscott Ricketts, "Criterion," in Hans-Peter Duerr, ed., *Die Mitte der Welt: Aufsätze zu Mircea Eliade* (Frankfurt am Main: Suhrkamp, 1984), pp. 192–215, and the exceptionally rich discussion of Cristina Bejan, *Intellectuals and Fascism in Interwar Romania: The Criterion Association* (Cham, Switzerland: Palgrave Macmillan, 2019).

9. On Nae Ionescu, see Tatiana Niculescu, *Nae Ionescu, il seduttore di una generazione* (Rome: Castelvecchi, 2021). Also useful are Florin Müller, "Nae Ionescu: Repere ale gândirii politice antidemocratice," *Studii și materiale de istorie contemporana 9* (2010): 202–16; Florin Müller, "Nae Ionescu, ideologia totalitară și mișcarea legionară, 1934–1940," *Revista istorică 8* (1997): 119–23; Costantini, *Nae Ionescu*; Romina Surugiu, "Nae Ionescu on Democracy, Individuality, Leadership and Nation: Philosophical (Re)sources for a Right-Wing Ideology," *Journal for the Study of Religions and Ideologies 8* (2009): 68–81; and Marta Petreu, *Diavolul și ucenicul său: Nae Ionescu—Mihail Sebastian*, 3rd ed. (Iași: Polirom, 2016), esp. pp. 19–32 and 224–25. For Eliade's relation to his mentor, see Mircea Eliade, "Professor Nae Ionescu," editor's afterword to Nae Ionescu, *Roza vînturilor* (Bucharest: Editura Cultura Naționala, 1937), reprinted in Eliade, *Profetism românesc*, vol. 2: *România în eternitate* (*Romanian Prophetics: Romania in Eternity*) (Bucharest: Editura Roza Vînturilor, 1990), pp. 178–89; and Hannah Müller, "Mircea Eliade und Nae Ionescu: Der Schüler und sein Meister," *Zeitschrift für Religionswissenschaft 12* (2004): 79–98.

10. Mircea Eliade, "Itinerariu spiritual" ("Spiritual Itinerary"), serialized in *Cuvântul* between September 6 and November 16, 1927, republished in Eliade, *Profetism românesc*, vol. 2, pp. 19–61, on which see Crina Poenariu, "Eliade and the Prophetic Allotropy in the Articles of Youth," *Globalization, Intercultural Dialogue and National Identity 2* (2015): 685–90. Eliade pursued many of the same themes in other articles of the late 1920s and early 1930s that have been reprinted in Eliade, *Virilitate și ascezǎ: Scrieri de tinerețe, 1928* (*Virility and Ascesis: Writings of Youth*), ed. Mircea Handoca (Bucharest: Humanitas, 2008).

11. In usage of the time, the semantics of Romanian *experiență* encompassed both "experience" and "experiment." On the importance of this concept for Nae Ionescu, Eliade, and others of the Young Generation, see Philip Vanhaelemeersch, *A Generation "Without Beliefs" and the Idea of Experience in Romania (1927–1934)* (Boulder, CO: East European Monographs, 2006).

12. Mircea Eliade, "România în eternitate" ("Romania in Eternity"), *Vremea 8*, no. 409 (October 13, 1935): 3, reprinted in Eliade, *Profetism românesc*, vol. 2, pp. 127–29.

13. Ibid.

14. Mircea Eliade, "Democrație și problema României" ("Democracy and the Problem of Romania"), *Vremea 9*, no. 468 (December 18, 1936): 3.

15. On the various currents within the Romanian Right, see Zigu Ornea, *The Romanian Extreme Right: The Nineteen Thirties*, trans. Eugenia Maria Popescu (Boulder, CO: East European Monographs, 1999). More specifically on Cuza

and his party, Marius Turda, "Fantasies of Degeneration: Some Remarks on
Racial Anti-Semitism in Interwar Romania," *Studia Hebraica 13* (2003): 336–
48; Marius Turda, "New Perspectives on Romanian Fascism: Themes and
Options," *Totalitarian Movements and Political Religions 6* (2005): 143–50;
and Horia Bozdoghină, "A.C. Cuza—politicianul antisemit," *Archiva
Moldaviae 9* (2017): 139–60.

16. On Codreanu, see Oliver Jens Schmitt, *Căpitan Codreanu: Aufstieg und Fall
des Rumänischen Faschistenführers* (Vienna: Paul Zsolnay Verlag, 2016). On
Codreanu's relation to and differences with Cuza, see Valentin Săndulescu,
"Note privind extremismul de dreapta în România Mare: Clarificări
doctrinare şi practice politice," *Studii şi materiale de istorie contemporană 1*
(2013): 171–83.

17. Book-length treatments of the Legion include Armin Heinen, *Die Legion
"Erzengel Michael" in Rumänien* (Munich: Oldenbourg Verlag, 1986);
Radu Ioanid, *The Sword of the Archangel: Fascist Ideology in Romania*
(Boulder, CO: East European Monographs, 1990); Constantin Iordachi,
*Charisma, Politics and Violence: The Legion of the "Archangel Michael" in
Inter-war Romania* (Trondheim: Norwegian University of Science and
Technology, 2004); Armin Heinen and Oliver Jens Schmitt, eds., *Inszenierte
Gegenmacht von rechts: Die "Legion Erzengel Michael" in Rumänien 1918–
1938* (Munich: Oldenbourg Verlag, 2013); Radu Dinu, *Faschismus, Religion
und Gewalt in Südosteuropa: Die Legion Erzengel Michael und die Ustaša
im historischen Vergleich* (Wiesbaden: Otto Harrassowitz, 2013); and Traian
Sandu, *Un fascisme roumain: Histoire de la Garde de fer* (Paris: Perrin, 2014).
The works that give fullest attention to religious aspects of the movement are
Roland Clark, *Holy Legionary Youth: Fascist Activism in Interwar Romania*
(Ithaca, NY: Cornell University Press, 2015), and Constantin Iordachi, *Fascist
Faith of the Legion Archangel Michael in Romania, 1927–1941: Martyrdom and
National Politics* (New York: Routledge, 2022).

18. Inter alia, see Emilio Gentile, "Fascism as Political Religion," *Journal
of Contemporary History 25* (1990): 229–51; Roger Griffin, ed., *Fascism,
Totalitarianism and Political Religion* (New York: Routledge, 2005);
Roger Eatwell, "Reflections on Fascism and Religion," *Politics, Religion &
Ideology 4* (2003): 145–66; António Costa Pinto, *Rethinking the Nature of
Fascism: Comparative Perspectives* (New York: Palgrave Macmillan, 2011);
and A. James Gregor, *Totalitarianism and Political Religion: An Intellectual
History* (Stanford: Stanford University Press, 2012). Much of this work
builds on ideas introduced by George L. Mosse in earlier works, including
Nazi Culture: Intellectual, Cultural, and Social Life in the Third Reich
(New York: Grosset and Dunlap, 1966) and *Masses and Man: Nationalist and
Fascist Perceptions of Reality* (New York: H. Fertig, 1980).

19. On the central importance of Orthodoxy for the legionary movement,
Radu Ioanid, "Sacralised Politics of the Romanian Iron Guard," *Totalitarian
Movements and Political Religions 5* (2004): 419–53; Keith Hitchins, "Religion
and Identity in Interwar Romania: Orthodoxism," *Plural 29* (2007): 25–44;

Paul A. Shapiro, "Faith, Murder, Resurrection: The Iron Guard and the Romanian Orthodox Church," in Kevin P. Spicer, ed., *Antisemitism, Christian Ambivalence, and the Holocaust* (Bloomington: Indiana University Press, 2007), pp. 136–70; Roland Clark, "Nationalism, Ethnotheology, and Mysticism in Interwar Romania," Carl Beck Papers in Russian and East European Studies, no. 2002 (2009); and Ionuț Florin Biliuță, "The Archangel's Consecrated Servants: An Inquiry in the Relationship between the Romanian Orthodox Church and the Iron Guard (1930–1941)" (PhD dissertation, Central European University Budapest, Department of History, 2013).

20. Cf. Traian Sandu, "Le fascisme, révolution spatio-temporelle chez les Roumains," in *Vers un profil convergent des fascismes?* (Paris: L'Harmattan, 2010), pp. 217–30, and Mihai Chioveanu, "La liturgie apocalyptique d'un mouvement politique séculaire: Déchifrer l'idéologie de la garde de fer," *Analele Universității de București, Seria științe politice 2* (2012): 47–62. Specifically on anti-Semitism as a touchstone of Legionary ideology, see Volovici, *Nationalist Ideology and Antisemitism*, esp. pp. 61–70; R. M. Cârstocea, "The Role of Anti-Semitism in the Ideology of the 'Legion of the Archangel Michael' (1927–1938)" (PhD dissertation, University College London, 2011); Radu Dinu, "Antisemitismus als soziale Praxis," in Heinen and Schmitt, *Inszenierte Gegenmacht von rechts*, pp. 113–29; and Milad Doroudian, "The Romanian Intellectual, Christian Orthodoxy, and Identity in Connection to Iron Guardism," *Romanian Journal of History and International Studies 4* (2017): 7–34.

21. On legionary militarism, see Mihai Chioveanu, "Religious Politics and Politics of Religion in 1930s Romania: The 'Redemptive' Hyper-nationalism of the Legion of 'Archangel Michael,'" *Studia Hebraica 6* (2006): 163–78, and Constantin Iordachi, "God's Chosen Warriors: Romantic Palingenesis, Militarism and Fascism in Modern Romania," in Constantin Iordachi, ed., *Comparative Fascist Studies: New Perspectives* (New York: Routledge, 2010), pp. 326–56. On oaths and rituals, Radu Dinu, "The Legionary Movement between 'Political Religion' and 'Collective Effervescence,'" *Arhivele totalitarismului 3–4* (2008): 16–25, and Mihai Chioveanu, "'Glaubenseiferer': Die Erneuerung der Nation und die Verzauberung der Politik im Rumänien der Zwischenkriegszeit," in Heinen and Schmitt, *Inszenierte Gegenmacht von Rechts*, pp. 69–88. On the theme of national rebirth, Raul Cârstocea, "Approaching Generic Fascism from the Margins: On the Uses of 'Palingenesis' in the Romanian Context," in Constantin Iordachi and Aristotle Kallis, eds., *Beyond the Fascist Century: Essays in Honour of Roger Griffin* (Cham, Switzerland: Palgrave Macmillan, 2020), pp. 153–76.

22. Corneliu Zelea Codreanu, *Cărticica șefului de cuib* (Madrid: Colecția "Omul Nou," 1952), pp. 115–25, emphasis added. Like all legionary discourse, this passage uses the disparaging term *jidani* ("Yids") to speak of Jews, instead of the more polite and neutral *evrei* ("Hebrews").

23. Corneliu Zelea Codreanu, *Pentru legionari* (Delhi: Facsimile Publisher, 2013; orig. Sibiu: Editura "Totul Pentru Țara," 1936), pp. 119–20. An English

translation of this book was published under the title *For My Legionaries: The Iron Guard* (Madrid: Editura "Libertatea," 1976), with frequent republications in England, the United States, and India.

24. On the student protests of 1922–23, which sought to limit Jewish university enrollment (the so-called *Numerus clausus* controversy), see Raul Cârstocea, "Students Don the Green Shirt: The Roots of Romanian Fascism in the Antisemitic Student Movements of the 1920s," in *Alma Mater Antisemitica: Akademisches Milieu, Juden und Antisemitismus an den Universitäten Europas zwischen 1918 und 1939* (Vienna: New Academic Press, 2016), pp. 39–66, and Ana-Maria Stan, "The 1922–1923 Student Revolts at the University of Cluj, Romania: From Local Anti-Semitic Academic Protests to National Events," in Pieter Dhondt and Elizabethanne Boran, eds., *Student Revolt, City, and Society in Europe* (New York: Routledge, 2018), pp. 286–303.

25. Codreanu, *Pentru legionari*, p. 112.

26. Ibid., pp. 112–13.

27. Codreanu treats his murder of Constantin Manciu and subsequent trial in *Pentru legionari*, pp. 149–65. See also Clark, *Holy Legionary Youth*, pp. 49–55, and Sandu, *Un fascisme roumain*, pp. 49–54.

28. Most fully on these and other legionary murders, see Cristian Manolachi, "Political Assassination in Romanian Interwar Society. Case Study: The Legionary Movement" (PhD dissertation, University of Cluj-Napoca, Faculty of History and Philosophy, 2018); Clark, *Holy Legionary Youth*, pp. 99–111; Ilarion Țiu, "Terrorism as Political Tool: The Assassination of Prime Minister Armand Călinescu by Legionnaires, 21st of September 1939," *Cogito 9* (2013): 61–69; and Iordachi, *Fascist Faith*, pp. 201–12.

29. On Stelescu and his murder, see Ioanid, *Sword of the Archangel*, pp. 87–89; Clark, *Holy Legionary Youth*, pp. 108–9; and Sandu, *Un fascisme roumain*, pp. 117–20.

30. On the legionary pogroms, see Radu Ioanid, "The Pogrom of Bucharest 21–23 January 1941," *Holocaust and Genocide Studies 6* (1992): 373–82; Cristian Alexandru Groza, "The Fascist Phenomenon: National Legionary State between Laws, Journals, Memoirs, and the Jewish Repression between 20–23 January 1941," *Journal of Education, Culture and Society 1* (2014): 61–78; and Carmen Țăgșorean, "The Assault on the Bucharest Jewish Community during the Legionary Rebellion, as Seen by the Press," *Holocaust: Studii și cercetări 7* (2015): 43–56.

31. Mircea Eliade, *Contribuții la filosofia renașterii* (*Contributions to the Philosophy of the Renaissance*), published in an edition edited by Constantin Popescu-Cadem (Bucharest: Academia de Științe Sociale și Politice a R.S. România, 1984) and in a French translation: *Contributions à la philosophie de la Renaissance: Suivi de itinéraire italien*, trans. Alain Paruit (Paris: Gallimard, 1992).

32. When *Cuvântul* was available, it remained Eliade's favorite outlet; when it was closed, he shifted primarily to *Vremea*, which was equally right wing in

orientation. He also occasionally published in *Axa*, *Buna Vestire*, *Iconar*, and *Sânziana*, official publications of the Legion.

33. A French translation was subsequently published, which established Eliade's scholarly reputation beyond his native country: Mircea Eliade, *Yoga: Essai sur les origines de la mystique indienne* (Paris: Paul Geuthner, and Bucharest: Fundația pentru Literatura și Arta "Regele Carol II," 1936).

34. Some critics denounced the frank treatment of sexual themes in Eliade's novels as "pornographic," which made him sufficiently controversial that university administrators would not grant him a salaried position. On this episode, see Ricketts, *Mircea Eliade*, pp. 779–88.

35. Details of these publications from the 1930s can be found in Douglas Allen and Dennis Doeing, *Mircea Eliade: An Annotated Bibliography* (New York: Garland Publishing, 1980), and Mircea Handoca, *Mircea Eliade: Biobibliografie*, 5 vols. (Bucharest: Editura "Jurnalul Literar," 1997–2010). The monographs (whose content he recycled in numerous subsequent publications) were *Alchimia asiatica*, vol. 1: *Alchimia Chineza și Indiana* (*Asiatic Alchemy*, 1935), *Cosmologie și alchimie babiloniana* (*Babylonian Cosmology and Alchemy*, 1937), and *Mitul reintegrarii* (*The Myth of Reintegration*, 1939); the collections he edited were Bogdan Petriceicu Hasdeu, *Scrieri literare, morale și politice* (*Literary, Moral, and Political Writings*), 2 vols. (1937) and Nae Ionescu, *Roza vânturilor 1926–1933* (1937).

36. On Crainic, see Dumitru Micu, *"Gândirea" și Gândirismul* (Bucharest: Editura Minerva, 1975); Keith Hitchins, "Orthodoxism: Polemics over Ethnicity and Religion in Interwar Romania," in Banac and Verdery, *National Character and National Ideology*, pp. 135–56; Roland Clark, "Nationalism and Orthodoxy: Nichifor Crainic and the Political Culture of the Extreme Right in 1930s Romania," *Nationalities Papers 40* (2012): 107–26; and Iuliu-Marius Morariu, "Aspects of the Anti-Semitic Views of Nichifor Crainic Reflected in *Gândirea* Journal," *Research and Science Today 1* (2019): 110–18.

37. *Axa* began publication in October 1932 and ceased in December 1933. On the journal and its leading figures, see Paula Mureșan, "Mișcarea Legionară—De la precursorul Mișcarii la ideologii revistei Axa," *Hiperborea 6* (2013): 50–52, and Valentin Săndulescu, "Generation, Regeneration, and Discourses of Identity in the Intellectual Foundations of Romanian Fascism: The Case of the *Axa* Group," in Diana Mishkova, Balázs Trencsényi, and Marija Jalava, eds., *Régimes of Historicity in Southeastern and Northern Europe, 1890–1945* (London: Palgrave Macmillan, 2014), pp. 210–29. On Eugen Ionescu's withdrawal from the journal, see Maria Lupas, "Early Resistance to Fascism: Eugène Ionesco's Interwar Romanian Journalism," *Journal of Modern Literature 37* (2014): 74–91.

38. Mihail Polihroniade, "Convertirea d-lui Mircea Eliade la românism" ("Mircea Eliade's Conversion to Romanianism"), *Axa 2*, no. 18 (September 19, 1933): 5. The articles Polihroniade reprinted in *Axa* were Mircea Eliade, "A nu mai fi Român" ("To No Longer Be Romanian"), *Vremea 6*, no. 304 (September 10,

1933): 6, and "Studenţii români cer revizuirea tratatelor" ("Romanian Students Protest the Revision of Treaties"), *Cuvântul 9*, no. 3015 (1933): 1.

39. Mircea Eliade, "O convertire la românism" ("A Conversion to Romanianism"), *Cuvântul 9*, no. 3021 (September 22, 1933): 1, reprinted in Eliade, *Textele "legionare"*, pp. 93–94. Polihroniade had the final word in this exchange, "Românismul dlui Mircea Eliade" ("Mircea Eliade's Romanianism"), *Axa 1*, no. 19 (October 1, 1933): 7, reprinted in Mircea Handoca, *"Dosarele" Eliade*, *vol. 1: Pro şi contra (1926–1938)* (Bucharest: Editura Curtea Veche, 1998), pp. 56–59.

40. Mircea Eliade, "Dizolvarea Garzii de Fier" ("Dissolution of the Iron Guard"), *Axa 2* (December 25, 1933): 1. Shortly before the national elections of 1933, the government formally dissolved the Legion's status as a political party, with the result that it was barred from competing. At Polihroniade's invitation, a number of influential people were asked to comment on this action, and their responses, including that of Eliade, were published on *Axa's* front page.

41. Mircea Eliade, "Contra dreptei şi stângii" ("Against Right and Left"), *Credinţa 2*, no. 59 (February 14, 1934): 2, reprinted in Eliade, *Textele "legionare"*, pp. 95–97.

42. See further Oana Soare, "Ce fel de revoluţie dorea Eliade?," *Diacronia* (2013): 371–80, reprinted in Luminiţa Botoşineanu, Daniela Butnaru, and Ofelia Ichim, eds., *Metafore ale devenirii din perspectiva migraţiei contemporane* (Iaşi: Alfa, 2013), pp. 371–80.

43. Most fully and perceptively, see Raul Cărstocea, "Breaking the Teeth of Time: Mythical Time and the 'Terror of History' in the Rhetoric of the Legionary Movement in Interwar Romania," *Journal of Modern European History* 13 (2015): 79–97.

44. On fascist discourse regarding the "new man," see Jorge Dagnino, Matthew Feldman, and Paul Stocker, eds., *The "New Man" in Radical Right Ideology and Practice, 1919–1945* (London: Bloomsbury Academic, 2018). On its prominence within the Legion, Valentin Săndulescu, "Fascism and Its Quest for the 'New Man': The Case of the Romanian Legionary Movement," *Studia Hebraica 4* (2004): 349–61; Cecilie Endresen, "Romania's Saving Angels. 'New Men,' Orthodoxy, and Blood Mysticism in the Legionary Movement," *Bulletin for the Study of Religion 41* (2012): 16–22; Rebecca Haynes, "Die Ritualisierung des 'Neuen Menschen'—Zwischen Orthodoxie und Alltagskultur," in Heinen and Schmitt, *Inszenierte Gegenmacht von Rechts*, pp. 89–112; and Ronald Clark, "Salience of 'New Man' Rhetoric in Romanian Fascist Movements," in Dagnino et al., *The "New Man"*, pp. 275–95. On Eliade's enthusiasm for this notion, see Michel Gardaz, "Mircea Eliade et le 'nouvel homme' à la chemise verte," *Numen 59* (2012): 68–92.

45. Mircea Eliade, "Câteva cuvinte mari" ("Some Big Words"), *Vremea 7*, no. 341 (June 10, 1934): 3, reprinted in Alexandru Florian and Constantin Petculescu, eds., *Ideea care ucide: Dimensiunile ideologiei legionare* (Bucharest: Editura Noua Alternativă, 1994), pp. 218–20. In several articles of 1935, Eliade continued to advocate revolution, denouncing the major political parties

while remaining noncommittal about what sort of movement he could support. Cf. "Cum încep revoluțiile" ("How Revolutions Begin"), *Vremea 8*, no. 380 (March 17, 1935): 3, reprinted in Eliade, *Profetism românesc*, vol. 2, pp. 69–72; "Demagogie prerevoluționară" ("Pre-revolutionary Demagoguery"), *Vremea 8*, no. 413 (November 10, 1935): 3, reprinted in *Profetism românesc*, vol. 2, pp. 133–35; and "Democrație și problema României." In subsequent years, he would articulate a clearer view of the antidemocratic, antimodern, spiritual, and antipolitical revolution he favored, which he ultimately identified with the legionary movement. For a fuller discussion of this development in his position, see Soare, "Ce fel de revoluție?"

46. Mircea Eliade, "De ce sînt intelectualii lași?" ("Why Are Intellectuals Cowards?"), *Criterion 1*, no. 2 (November 1934): 2, reprinted in Eliade, *Profetism românesc*, vol. 2, pp. 31–33.

47. Mircea Eliade, "Criza românismului?" ("Romanianism's Crisis?"), *Vremea 8*, no. 375 (February 10, 1935): 3, reprinted in Eliade, *Profetism românesc*, vol. 2, pp. 60–62.

48. Mircea Eliade, "Românismul și complexele de inferioritate" ("Romanianism and Inferiority Complexes"), *Vremea 8*, no. 386 (May 5, 1935): 7. The verb here translated as "extract," Romanian *scoate*, is significant, but less than precise; inter alia, it can mean "to extract, to pull or draw out," "to remove," "to tear or pluck out," "to evict, drive away, banish," and "to dismiss, fire."

49. Mircea Eliade, "Popor fără misiune?!..." ("People without a mission?!..."), *Vremea 8*, no. 416 (December 1, 1935): 3, republished in Eliade, *Profetism românesc*, vol. 2, pp. 135–38.

50. Eliade denounced "politicianism" in numerous articles, including "Cum încep revoluțiile," "Elogiu Transilvaniei" ("In Praise of Transylvania"), *Vremea 8*, no. 386 (May 5, 1935): 3, reprinted in Eliade, *Textele "legionare"*, pp. 124–26, and many thereafter. The term was coined in 1904 by Constantin Rădulescu-Motru, "Cultura română și politicianismul," reprinted in Constantin Vlad, ed., *Conservatismul românesc: Concepte, idei, programe* (Bucharest: Nemira, 2006), pp. 49–53. On its currency in the discourse of the extreme Right, see Roland Clark, "The Romanian Right: Images of Crisis, the Press, and the Rise of Fascism," in Marco Bresciani, ed., *Conservatives and Right Radicals in Interwar Europe* (New York: Routledge, 2021), pp. 196–97, 206 and n. 24.

51. Codreanu, *Pentru legionari*, p. 124.

52. Eliade, "Democrație și problema României."

53. Eliade, "Popor fără misiune?!"

54. Ibid.

55. Ibid.

56. For the earlier date, see Laignel-Lavastine, *Cioran, Eliade, Ionesco*, pp. 173–79, and Adriana Berger, "Mysticism and Politics in Mircea Eliade's Writings" (paper presented at the American Academy of Religion, December 7, 1987). The Siguranța report of July 3, 1943 (reproduced in Dora Mezdrea, ed., *Nae Ionescu și discipolii săi în arhiva Securității, vol. 2: Mircea Eliade* [Bucharest: Editura "Mica Valahie," 2008]), pp. 42–45), states that Eliade

enrolled in the legionary nest for writers led by Radu Gyr, the movement's foremost poet, in 1935.

57. Mircea Eliade, "Ion Moța și Vasile Marin" ("Ion Moța and Vasile Marin"), *Vremea 10*, no. 472 (January 24, 1937): 3.

58. See the testament Moța left with Nae Ionescu upon his departure, explaining his intent: Ion I. Moța, *Testamentul lui Ion Moța* (Bucharest: n.p., 1937). German and Spanish translations are also available (and frequently reprinted).

59. On Moța and Marin, see Mircea Platon, "The Iron Guard and the 'Modern State': Iron Guard Leaders Vasile Marin and Ion I. Moța, and the 'New European Order,'" *Fascism 1* (2012): 65–90; Răzvan Ciobanu, "Legionarismul și 'noua ordine' fascistă în gândirea lui Ion I. Moța," *Astra salvensis 4* (2016): 161–76; and Raul Cârstocea, "Native Fascists, Transnational Anti-Semites: The International Activity of Legionary Leader Ion I. Moța," in Amd Bauerkämpfer and Grzegorz Rossolinski-Liebe, eds., *Fascism without Borders: Transnational Connections and Cooperation between Movements and Régimes in Europe from 1918 to 1945* (New York: Berghahn, 2017), pp. 216–42. Moța's collected articles were published under the title *Cranii de lemn: Articole 1922–1936* (Sibiu: Editura "Totul Pentru Țară," 1936). Marin's include *Fascismul: Organizarea constituțională a statului corporativ italian* (Bucharest: Editura Colportajului Legionar, 1932); *Crez de generație* (Bucharest: Tiparul Cartea Românesca, 1937); and *Cuvînte pentru studenți* (Bucharest: I. Copuzeanu, 1937).

60. "Mota și Marin, jur în fața lui Dumnezeu, în fața jertfei voastre sfințe, pentru Hristos și Legiune, să rup din mine bucuriile pământești, să mă smulg din dragostea omenească și, pentru învierea Neamului meu, în orice clipă să stau gata de moarte!"

61. Most extensively on the funeral, see Valentin Săndulescu, "Sacralised Politics in Action: The February 1937 Burial of the Romanian Legionary Leaders Ion Moța and Vasile Marin," *Totalitarian Movements and Political Religions 8* (2007): 259–69, and Raul Cărstocea, "Bringing Out the Dead: Mass Funerals, Cult of Death and the Emotional Dimension of Nationhood in Romanian Interwar Fascism," in Andreas Stynen et al., *Emotions and Everyday Nationalism in Modern European History* (London: Taylor & Francis, 2020), pp. 134–63. More broadly on the movement's celebration of martyrdom, Rebecca Ann Haynes, "The Romanian Legionary Movement, Popular Orthodoxy and the Cult of Death," in Mioara Anton, Florin Anghel, and Cosmin Popa, eds., *Hegemoniile trecutului: Evoluții românești și europene* (Bucharest: Curtea Veche, 2006), pp. 113–25; Mihai Stelian Rusu, "The Sacralization of Martyric Death in Romanian Legionary Movement: Self-Sacrificial Patriotism, Vicarious Atonement, and Thanatic Nationalism," *Politics, Religion & Ideology* 17 (2016): 249–73; and Mihai Stelian Rusu, "Staging Death: Christofascist Necropolitics during the National Legionary State in Romania, 1940–1941," *Nationalities Papers* 49 (2020): 576–89. On similar practices and ideology among other fascist movements, see Sabine Behrenbeck, *Die Kult um die toten Helden. Nationalsozialistische Mythen,*

Riten, und Symbole 1923–1945 (Greifswald: Vierow, 1996), Mark Neocleous, "Long Live Death! Fascism, Resurrection, Immortality," *Journal of Political Ideologies* 10 (2005): 31–49, and Valerio S. Severino, "Reconfiguring Nationalism: The Roll Call of the Fallen Soldiers (1800–2001)," *Journal of Religion in Europe* 10 (2017): 16–43.

62. Eliade, "Ion Moţa şi Vasile Marin."

63. Mircea Eliade, "Comentarii la un jurământ" ("Commentaries on an Oath"), *Vremea 10*, no. 476 (February 21, 1937): 2.

64. Mircea Eliade, letter of July 24, 1936, to Emil Cioran, cited by Laignel-Lavastine, *Cioran, Eliade, Ionesco*, p. 118.

65. Entry of March 2, 1937, in Mihail Sebastian, *Journal, 1935–1944: The Fascist Years*, trans. Patrick Camiller (London: Rowman & Littlefield, 2012), p. 114.

66. Eliade, "De unde începe misiunea României?" ("Whence Begins Romania's Mission?"), *Vremea 10*, no. 477 (February 28, 1937): 3.

67. Mircea Eliade, "O Revoluţie creştină" ("A Christian Revolution"), *Buna Vestire 1*, no. 100 (June 27, 1937): 3.

68. Mircea Eliade, "Noua aristocraţie legionară" ("The New Legionary Aristocracy"), *Vremea 11*, no. 522 (January 23, 1938): 2. The comparison to Gandhi's movement also appears in "Comentarii la un jurământ." On Eliade's sympathy for Gandhi and the way it influenced his view of Codreanu's Legion, see the sensitive discussion of Raul Cârstocea, "The Unbearable Virtues of Backwardness: Mircea Eliade's Conceptualisation of Colonialism and His Attraction to Romania's Interwar Fascist Movement," in Dorota Kołodziejczyk and Siegfried Huigen, eds., *Central Europe between the Colonial and the Postcolonial* (Basingstoke: Palgrave Macmillan, 2023), pp. 113–40.

69. Mircea Eliade, "Piloţii orbii" ("Blind Pilots"), *Vremea 10*, no. 505 (September 19, 1937): 3. Several other articles included similar, if less sustained xenophobic outbursts. Cf. "Românismul şi complexele de inferioritate"; "Democraţie şi problema României"; "'Să veniţi odată în Maramureş . . .'" ("'If you should come to Maramureş . . .'"), *Vremea 10*, no. 516 (December 5, 1937): 2; and "De ce cred în bîruinţa mişcării legionare" ("Why I Believe in the Victory of the Legionary Movement"), *Buna Vestire 1*, no. 244 (December 17, 1937): 1.

70. Eliade, "Piloţii orbii."

71. Petreu, *Generaţia '27*, p. 148.

72. Eliade, "Piloţii orbii."

73. Eliade, "Să veniţi odată în Maramureş."

74. Eliade, "De ce cred în bîruinţa mişcării legionare."

75. Eliade gave fullest expression to this vision in the programmatic article he contributed to the first issue of the journal he founded shortly after assuming his chair at the University of Chicago: Mircea Eliade, "History of Religions and a New Humanism," *History of Religions 1* (1961): 1–8, reprinted as Chapter 1 of *The Quest: History and Meaning in Religion* (Chicago: University of Chicago Press, 1969). On the nature of the mission he envisioned for his discipline and its relation to his own life and values, see Russell McCutcheon, *Manufacturing Religion: The Discourse of Sui Generis Religion and the Politics*

of Nostalgia (New York: Oxford University Press, 1997); Steven Wasserstrom, *Religion after Religion: Gershom Scholem, Mircea Eliade, and Henry Corbin at Eranos* (Princeton: Princeton University Press, 1999); and Idel, *Mircea Eliade*.

Chapter 3

1. Sebastian, *Journal, 1935–1944*, p. 132 (entry of December 7, 1937), reported that Eliade was actively campaigning for the Legion in a team with Mihail Polihroniade, Haig Acterian, Marietta Sadova (Acterian's wife), and others. His account was confirmed in all details by the oral testimony of legionary commander Mircea Nicolau in Mariana Conovici, Silvia Iliescu, and Octavian Silivestru, eds., *Țara, Legiunea, Căpitanul: Mişcarea legionară în documente de istorie orală* (Bucharest: Humanitas, 2008), pp. 40 and 120–22.

2. Mircea Eliade, letter to Cezar Petrescu, May 1938, in Mircea Eliade, *Europa, Asia, America . . . Corespondența*, ed. Mircea Handoca (Bucharest: Humanitas, 2004), vol. 2, pp. 467–69.

3. Archives of the National Council for the Study of Securitate Archives, Marietta Sadova file, Fond I 209489, vol. 2, f. 2 and reverse. Sadova ("the Romanian Leni Riefenstahl") was a leading actress at the Romanian National Theater, where her husband, Haig Acterian, a friend of Eliade's and Polihroniade's from their school days, was director. Both spouses became staunch legionary activists and converted the theater into an instrument of legionary recruitment and propaganda during the National Legionary State. Most fully on Sadova, see Bejan, *Intellectuals and Fascism*, pp. 35–36, 228–38, 267–71, and Octaviana Jianu, "Marietta Sadova (1897–1981)," *Arhivele Totalitarismului 1–2* (2018): 265–68. Sadova's account of Eliade having participated in a legionary nest with herself, Polihroniade, and other Bucharest intellectuals was confirmed by Alexander Ronnett, Eliade's personal physician and leader of Chicago's legionary community. Cf. Mac Linscott Ricketts, "An Afternoon with Mircea Eliade's Doctor, Dentist, and Confidant," in Ricketts, *Former Friends and Forgotten Facts* (Norcross, GA: Criterion Publishing, 2003), pp. 99–100.

4. Siguranța report on Eliade, April 19, 1938, in Mezdrea, *Nae Ionescu şi disipolii săi*, vol. 2, p. 22. Cf. the reports of April 29 and May 13 on pp. 23 and 26, respectively.

5. Mezdrea, *Nae Ionescu şi discipolii săi*, vol. 2, pp. 22, 23, and 25.

6. On Nicolescu, see Mihai Stelian Rusu, "Domesticating Viragos: The Politics of Womanhood in the Romanian Legionary Movement," *Fascism 5* (2016): 167–69.

7. Mezdrea, *Nae Ionescu şi discipolii săi*, vol. 2, pp. 22, 26, and 27 (Siguranța reports of April 19, May 13, and May 16, 1938). Regarding Codreanu's call for his supporters to remain calm and avoid provoking further repressive action, see Ştefan Palaghiță, *Garda de Fier spre reînvierea României* (Bucharest: Editura Roza Vînturilor, 1993), pp. 112–13, 115, and 117, and Ilarion

Țiu, *The Legionary Movement after Corneliu Codreanu* (Boulder, CO: East European Monographs, 2009), pp. 20–21, 28–29, and 31.

8. Cf. Mircea Eliade, *Autobiography, vol. 1*, pp. 280–92; *vol. 2: 1937–1960: Exile's Odyssey*, trans. Mac Linscott Ricketts (Chicago: University of Chicago Press, 1988), pp. 4–15, 62–73, and 84–85; and *Journal*, vol. 3, pp. 161–62.

9. Mircea Eliade, letter to Cezar Petrescu, May 1938, in Eliade, *Europa, Asia, America*, vol. 2, pp. 467–69.

10. Nicolae Matei Condeescu (sometimes spelled Condiescu) was brigadier general in the Romanian army reserves, an aide and close confidant to King Carol. From 1936 to 1939 he also served as president of the Romanian Writers' Society, a position that put him in touch with the country's foremost intellectuals. Eliade's account of being arrested appears in his *Autobiography*, vol. 2, pp. 14–15.

11. Nina Eliade, letter of August 1, 1938, to Constantin Rădulescu-Motru, in Eliade, *Europa, Asia, America*, vol. 3, pp. 14–15. Rădulescu-Motru was professor of philosophy at the University of Bucharest, president of the Romanian Academy and a politician of the nonlegionary Right, who had been a teacher of Eliade's and was sympathetic to him.

12. Eliade, *Autobiography*, vol. 2, p. 63.

13. Ibid., p. 66.

14. Mircea Eliade, *The Forbidden Forest*, trans. Mac Linscott Ricketts (Notre Dame: University of Notre Dame Press, 1978; originally published in French, 1955 and in Romanian, 1970–71), pp. 148–49. Further assertions of Viziru's opposition to the Legion are found at pp. 161–62 and 165, while he identifies himself as a relatively inactive democrat at p. 171. On the self-serving way Eliade reworked events of his past in this novel, see the critical discussions of Marta Petreu, "Eliade par lui-même," in Petreu, *De la Junimea la Noica: Studii de cultură românească* (Iași: Polirom, 2011), pp. 343–88, and Lioara Coturbaș, "Diary Pages in *The Forbidden Forest*: Mircea Eliade's Detention in Miercurea Ciuc," *Analele Universității Ovidius din Constanța, Seria Filologie 1* (2011): 67–76.

15. In addition to Professor Rădulescu-Motru, General Condeescu, and Minister of the Interior Călinescu, Mrs. Eliade sought support from Mihai Ralea, minister of labor. Cf. the Siguranța report of September 28, 1938, in Mezdrea, *Nae Ionescu și discipolii săi*, vol. 2, pp. 32–33, and Eliade, *Autobiography*, vol. 2, pp. 63, 70, and 73.

16. Eliade was released to a medical facility after he exhibited respiratory problems that authorities typically ignored, but in his case defined (incorrectly, but conveniently and perhaps duplicitously) as symptoms of tuberculosis. After three weeks of recuperation at the Moroeni sanatorium, he was released from state custody. For his account of these events, see Eliade, *Autobiography*, vol. 2, pp. 73–76.

17. Mezdrea, *Nae Ionescu și discipolii săi*, vol. 2, p. 33. The document bears a handwritten note added by Armand Călinescu: "He will be set at liberty."

18. Mezdrea, *Nae Ionescu și discipolii săi*, vol. 2, p. 34. Another copy of the same document was recovered and published by Stelian Tănase, "Mircea Eliade— un episod legionar," *Sfera Politicii 159* (2011): 108–11. Lt.-Col. Gherovici was among the sixty-four political prisoners murdered on November 26, 1940, by authorities of the National Legionary State at the Jilava Prison.

19. Mezdrea, *Nae Ionescu și discipolii săi*, vol. 2, p. 39.

20. Eliade, *Autobiography*, vol. 2, pp. 66–67.

21. On the spiraling violence that followed Codreanu's murder, see Heinen, *Die Legion "Erzengel Michael,"* pp. 374–79; Palaghiță, *Garda de Fier*, pp. 114–25; Sandu, *Un fascisme roumain*, pp. 169–81; Clark, *Holy Legionary Youth*, pp. 219–21; and most extensively Țiu, *Legionary Movement after Codreanu*, pp. 32–109.

22. Among the victims was Mihail Polihroniade, Eliade's schoolmate and friend from childhood. Key efforts to protect Eliade were made by Alexandru Rosetti, professor of linguistics at the University of Bucharest, a confidante of King Carol, and Constantin Giurescu, professor of history and secretary of the King's National Renaissance Front. Cf. Eliade's account in *Autobiography*, vol. 2, pp. 4–5, and Sebastian, *Journal, 1935–1944*, pp. 240–43 (entries of September 23 and 25, 1939).

23. On the troubles Eliade encountered in England, see Bryan Rennie, "The Diplomatic Career of Mircea Eliade: A Response to Adriana Berger," *Religion 22* (1992): 375–92. Rennie's presentation of the surviving documentary evidence is thorough, but his discussion is consistently defensive and at times naive.

24. On the National Legionary State and its abuses, see Ilarion Țiu, "Romanian Fascism during World War II. The National-Legionary Government (September 1940–January 1941)," *Cogito 8* (2016): 34–49, and Groza, "The Fascist Phenomenon."

25. On the legionary rebellion, see Palaghiță, *Garda de Fier*, pp. 147–55; Clark, *Holy Legionary Youth*, pp. 229–32; Sandu, *Un fascisme roumain*, pp. 353–57; and Țiu, *Legionary Movement after Codreanu*, pp. 176–84. On the Bucharest pogrom, Radu Ioanid, "The Pogrom of Bucharest," and Țâgșorean, "The Assault on the Bucharest Jewish Community."

26. See Palaghiță, *Garda de Fier*, pp. 155–59; Ilarion Țiu, "Legionary Movement's Exile in Nazi Germany (1941–1944)," *Cogito 2* (2014): 109–19; Țiu, *Legionary Movement after Codreanu*, pp. 184–90.

27. Mircea Eliade, *Portugal Journal*, trans. Mac Linscott Ricketts (Albany: State University of New York Press, 2010), pp. 30, 48, and 86 (entries of July 1942, November 9, 1942, and June 7, 1943, respectively). On Eliade's time in Portugal, see Sergiu Miculescu, "Mircea Eliade, under the Terror of History (1941–1945)," *Analele Universității Ovidius din Constanța, Seria Filologie 1* (2012): 329–40, and Sorin Alexandrescu, *Mircea Eliade, dinspre Portugalia* (Bucharest: Humanitas, 2006).

28. Mircea Eliade, *Salazar și revoluția in Portugalia* ("Salazar and the Revolution in Portugal," Bucharest: Editura Gorjan, 1942), esp. pp. 9–10 and 211–12.

29. Eliade, *Portugal Journal*, pp. 31–32. Mircea Vulcănescu and Constantin Noica were philosophers who studied with Nae Ionescu and were deeply

influenced by him, particularly as regards religion, mysticism, existentialist philosophy, and right-wing politics. Both were leading members of the "Young Generation," participants in the Criterion group, and close friends of Eliade's. Noica was a committed legionary and served as editor in chief of *Buna Vestire* during the National Legionary State. Vulcănescu was sympathetic to the movement, but not actively enrolled in it.

30. On this episode, see the discussion of Alexandrescu, *Mircea Eliade, dinspre Portugalia*, pp. 154–58, which is defensive at points and perceptive at others.

31. Eliade, *Autobiography*, vol. 2, p. 65.

32. Eliade, *Autobiography*, vol. 2, p. 85 (emphasis added). The legionary massacre of sixty-four "detainees" to which Eliade refers took place on November 26, 1940 (not the twenty-ninth) at the Jilava Prison (not Văcăreşti).

33. In a 1981 conversation with Mac Linscott Ricketts, Eliade went so far as to describe Sima as "a fanatic, a madman, a fool, perhaps not balanced." The notes Ricketts took during their discussion have been published by Liviu Bordaş, "On the Ḥadīth Corpus of Mircea Eliade: Preliminary Notes and an Open Gloss," *Journal of Romanian Studies* 5 (2023): 73–82, where the phrase quoted appears at p. 78.

34. Mircea Eliade to Brutus and Tantzi Coste, letter dated October 15, 1948, in Eliade, *Europa, Asia, America*, vol. 3, pp. 473–75.

35. Ibid.

36. The cleavage within the later Legion is discussed at greatest length by Palaghiţă, who was a leading figure in the Codrenist faction, *Garda de Fier*. It also receives considerable attention in Ţiu, *Legionary Movement after Codreanu*.

37. Testimony given to Securitate by Cristofor Dancu, June 7, 1964, in Mezdrea, *Nae Ionescu şi discipolii săi*, vol. 2, pp. 73–77.

38. Ibid.

39. Ibid.

40. Eliade's four most important books appeared during his Parisian period, building on research he began in Bucharest and continued in Lisbon: *Le mythe de l'éternel retour: Archétypes et répétition* (Paris: Gallimard, 1947), *Traité d'histoire des religions* (Paris: Payot, 1948), *Techniques du yoga* (Paris: Gallimard, 1948), and *Le chamanisme et les techniques archaïques de l'extase* (Paris: Payot, 1950).

41. On these events, see Ţurcanu, *Mircea Eliade*, pp. 345–48, and Laignel-Lavastine, *Cioran, Eliade, Ionesco*, pp. 408–12.

42. By the 1980s, this had begun to change, as witness Saul Bellow's *Ravelstein* (New York: Viking, 2000), where the character based on Eliade, "Radu Grielescu," is suspected of cultivating a friendship with the Jewish narrator (Bellow's equally transparent alter ego) to shield himself against charges of anti-Semitism and help hide his legionary past. See further Philip Ó Ceallaigh, "'The Terror of History': On Saul Bellow and Mircea Eliade," *Los Angeles Review of Books* (August 11, 2018) and the subsequent exchange

between Bryan Rennie and Philip Ó Ceallaigh, *Los Angeles Review of Books* (September 13, 2018).

43. Theodor Lavi, "Dosarul Mircea Eliade," *Toladot 1* (1972): 21–27.
44. For biographical information on Lavi, see Miriam Caloianu, "Biografie Theodor Lavi," in Mihaela Gligor and Miriam Caloianu, eds., *Theodor Lavi în corespondență* (Cluj: Presa Universitară Clujeană, 2012), pp. 403–11. Having long been active in Zionist organizations, he was arrested in 1950, when these were outlawed by the Communist regime. Sentenced to fifteen years in prison, he was released in 1955 and emigrated to Israel shortly thereafter. In 1973, he founded the Hebrew University's Center for Research on Romanian Jewry and from 1972 to 1977 he directed the journal *Toladot*, in which his "Eliade Dossier" appeared.
45. Gershom Scholem, "On Sin and Punishment: Some Remarks Concerning Biblical and Rabbinical Ethics," in Joseph M. Kitagawa and Charles H. Long, eds., *Myths and Symbols: Studies in Honor of Mircea Eliade* (Chicago: University of Chicago Press, 1969), pp. 163–77.
46. Lavi, "Dosarul Mircea Eliade," p. 21.
47. On the friendship between Eliade and Sebastian, see Petreu, *Diavolul și ucenicul său*, pp. 347–70; Mac Linscott Ricketts, "Mircea Eliade and Mihail Sebastian: The Story of a Friendship," in Julien Ries and Natale Spineto, eds., *Deux explorateurs de la pensée humaine: Georges Dumézil et Mircea Eliade* (Turnhout: Brepols, 2003), pp. 229–44; and Andrei Oișteanu, "Mihail Sebastian și Mircea Eliade: Cronica unei prietenii accidentate," *Revista 22* (December 5, 2007), p. 1.
48. Sebastian, *Journal, 1935–1944*. On Sebastian, see Petreu, *Diavolul și ucenicul său*; Irina Livezeanu, "A Jew from the Danube: *Cuvântul*, the Rise of the Right, and Mihail Sebastian," *Shevut 16* (1993): 297–312; and Yehoshofat Pop, "A Journey into the Intellectual World of the Romanian Jew, Mihail Sebastian and His Testimony during the Fascist Years," *Holocaust: Studii și cercetări 6* (2014): 59–92.
49. Corneliu Z. Codreanu, circular of May 30, 1936, in his *Circolări și manifeste* (Munich: Colecția "Europa," 1980). On the mutual hostility of Titulescu and the Legion, see Iordachi, *Fascist Faith*, pp. 82, 204, and 214–15.
50. Lavi, "Dosarul Mircea Eliade," p. 23, citing Sebastian, *Journal, 1935–1944*, pp. 78–79, but conflating this entry with that of November 27, 1935 (Sebastian, *Journal, 1935–1944*, pp. 28–29) and misdating the composite as November 27, 1936.
51. Lavi, "Dosarul Mircea Eliade," citing journal entries of January 15, 1937, February 25, 1937, March 2, 1937, December 7, 1937, December 17, 1937, January 16, 1938, December 10, 1938, February 12, 1941, and March 6, 1941 (Sebastian, *Journal, 1935–1944*, pp. 106, 112–13, 113–14, 132, 133, 146, 192, 322–23, and 328, respectively).
52. Lavi, "Dosarul Mircea Eliade," p. 27. Sebastian's judgment was slightly different: "He's neither a charlatan nor a madman. He's just naïve. But there

are such catastrophic forms of naiveté" (March 2, 1937, *Journal, 1935–1944*, p. 114, a passage cited by Lavi).

53. Sebastian, *Journal, 1935–1944*, p. 133, citing Eliade, "De ce cred în bîruinţa mişcării legionare."

54. Most extensively on Comarnescu, see Bejan, *Intellectuals and Fascism*, pp. 51–55, 116, 179–93, 197–205, 238–40, et passim and Ioan-Emanuel Stavarache, "Petru Comarnescu—A Remarkable Personality of the Romanian Culture," *International Journal of Communication Research 10* (2020): 266–70.

55. Ibid. Lavi seems to have misunderstood the episode, believing that Eliade took exception to an unnamed French play in which he perceived "the Judaic spirit of the French." Sebastian's entry of March 25, 1937 (Sebastian, *Journal, 1935–1944*, pp. 119–20, 133) clearly states it was of the Jooss Ballet. On Jooss, see Suzanne Walther, *The Dance of Death: Kurt Jooss and the Weimar Years* (New York: Routledge, 1994).

56. Sebastian, *Journal, 1935–1944*, pp. 238–39 (entry of September 20, 1939). Lavi quoted Sebastian's text verbatim, although he misdated the entry to September 29.

57. Sebastian, *Journal, 1935–1944*, p. 498. Lavi again miscited the date, which he listed as July 27, 1942, rather than July 23.

58. Lavi, "Dosarul Mircea Eliade," p. 26.

59. Ibid., p. 27. Lavi took the phrase "moral infamy" directly from Sebastian's *Journal, 1935–1944*, p. 490 (entry of May 27, 1942), which has no bearing on the question of anti-Semitism.

60. Gershom Scholem to Theodore Lavi, letter of June 6, 1972, in *Briefe III: 1971–1982*, ed. Itta Shedletzky (Munich: C.H. Beck, 1999), p. 278.

61. Gershom Scholem to Mircea Eliade, letter of June 6, 1972, in ibid., p. 30.

62. Mircea Eliade to Gershom Scholem, letter of July 3, 1972, in ibid., pp. 277–81.

63. Nae Ionescu, "A fi 'bun român,'" *Cuvântul 6*, no. 1987 (November 1, 1930), reprinted in Ionescu, *Roza vînturilor*, pp. 194–98. Most thoroughly on this point, see Ana Bărbulescu, "Nae Ionescu's Impenetrable Boundaries: Romanianness, Otherness, Jewishness," *Holocaust: Studii şi cercetări 11* (2018): 277–310.

64. Ionescu's call for the removal of Jews from politics appeared in his article "Şi un cuvînt de pace," *Cuvântul 9*, no. 3076 (November 17, 1933); his observations on the aggressive nature of philo-Semitism in "Între 'agresivitate' antisemită şi 'pasivitate' filosemită: Răspuns dlui A.L. Zissu," *Cuvântul 9*, no. 3085 (November 26, 1933). The two are reprinted in Nae Ionescu, *Între ziaristică şi filosofie: Texte publicate în ziarul Cuvîntul* (Iaşi: Editura Timpul, 1996), pp. 159–62 and 168–70, respectively.

65. Nae Ionescu, "Prefaţă" to Mihail Sebastian, *De două mii de ani* (Bucharest: Editura Naţionala-Ciorney, 1934 and Braşov: Editura Arania, 1934), reprinted in Mihail Sebastian, *De două mii de ani—Cum am devenit huligan* (Bucharest: Humanitas, 1990), pp. 7–25.

66. Ibid.

67. On this episode, see Matei Călinescu, "Romania's 1930's Revisited," *Salmagundi 97* (Winter 1993): 133–51; Leon Volovici, "Mihail Sebastian: A

Jewish Writer and His (Antisemitic) Master," in Richard Cohen, Jonathan Frankel, and Stefani Hoffman, eds., *Insiders and Outsiders: Dilemmas of East European Jewry* (Portland, OR: Littman Library of Jewish Civilization, 2010), pp. 58–69; Moshe Idel, "A Controversy over a Preface: Mihail Sebastian and Nae Ionescu," *Modern Judaism 35* (2015): 42–65; and Petreu, *Diavolul și ucenicul său*, pp. 205–55.

68. Mircea Eliade to Gershom Scholem, letter of July 3, 1972.

69. Mircea Eliade, "Iudaism și anti-Semitism—preliminarii la o discuție" ("Judaism and Anti-Semitism: Preliminaries to a Discussion"), *Vremea 7*, no. 347 (July 22, 1934): 5.

70. Among the critical responses to Eliade's article, the most important were Gheorghe Racoveanu, "O problemă teologică eronat rezolvată? Sau ce n-a înțeles d. Mircea Eliade," *Credința 2*, no. 195 (July 29, 1934), and Gheorghe Racoveanu, "Creștinism, Iudaism, și . . . îndrăzneală," *Credința 2*, nos. 215, 216, 218, 221 (August 22, 23, 25, 29, 1934).

71. Eliade, "Iudaism și Anti-Semitism" (emphasis in the original).

72. Ibid.

73. Cf. Eliade, "Itinerariu spiritual," where Vico, Montesquieu, and Spengler join Gobineau and Chamberlain, Rosenberg's work not yet having been published; "Cum încep revoluțiile," where Nietzsche joins Gobineau, Chamberlain, and Rosenberg; and his review of Julius Evola's *Rivolta contro il mondo moderno*, *Vremea 8*, no. 382 (March 31, 1935): 6, where Evola and Spengler join Gobineau, Chamberlain, and Rosenberg. Eugène Ionescu, "Mircea Eliade," *Cahiers de l'Herne 33* (1978): 272, also placed Chamberlain, Spengler, and Papini foremost among the authors the young Eliade admired. Nae became particularly enamored of Chamberlain and Gobineau in the course of his graduate studies in Germany (1913–19), as reported by Niculescu, *Nae Ionescu*, pp. 60–70 and 130.

74. Constantin Rădulescu-Motru, "Rassă, cultură, și naționalitatea în filozofia istoriei," *Arhiva pentru știința și reforma sociala 1* (1922): 22.

75. Eliade, "Post-scriptum," *Vlăstarul 4* (February 1928): 4, republished in Eliade, *Virilitate și Asceză*, p. 67.

76. Sebastian, *Journal, 1935–1944*, p. 132. He cites the phrases without comment, perhaps because he was too pained to do so, or because he took their significance to be self-evident.

77. *Adevărul în procesul lui Corneliu Z. Codreanu: Maiu 1938* (Serviciul propagandei Legionare), p. 78.

78. Eliade to Scholem, July 3, 1972, pp. 277–81. Note that Eliade gives an incorrect date for the article (December 14, 1937, instead of December 17), perhaps because he misremembered, but possibly to make it more difficult for Scholem—or anyone else—to track it down.

79. The others are "O Revoluție creștină," "Mitul Generalului," and an untitled piece that appeared on January 14, 1938.

80. Eliade, "De ce cred în bîruința mișcării legionare."

81. Ioan Culianu, "Mircea Eliade und die Blinde Schildkröte," in Hans-Peter Duerr, ed., *Die Mitte der Welt: Aufsätze zu Mircea Eliade* (Frankfurt am Main: Suhrkamp, 1984), pp. 234–35.

82. Eliade, "Democrație și problema României," "Piloții orbii," and 'Să veniți odată în Maramureș.' "

83. Thus, inter alia, Sorin Alexandrescu, *Paradoxul român* (Bucharest: Editura Univers, 1998), p. 227: "If the text as such is not attributable to Eliade, the ideas still repeat those he expressed elsewhere." The same point was made by Ricketts, *Mircea Eliade*, p. 929, and Ioan Culianu, "L'Albero della conoscenza: Invito alla lettura di Mircea Eliade," *Abstracta 4*, no. 35 (March 1989): 40.

84. Eliade to Scholem, July 3, 1972.

85. Petreu, *Diavolul și ucenicul său*, pp. 364–65.

86. Lavi left a detailed account of his discussion with Scholem, which was preserved in his archive at Hebrew University in Jerusalem and published in Mihaela Gligor and Mariam Caloianu, *Intelectuali evrei și presa exilului românesc* (Cluj-Napoca: Presa Universitară Clujeană, 2013), pp. 355–61.

87. Burton Feldman to Mircea Eliade, letter of January 29, 1973, in the Mircea Eliade Archive in the Special Collections of the University of Chicago's Regenstein Library, Box 88, Folder 2.

88. Mircea Eliade to Gershom Scholem, letter of March 10, 1973, in Scholem, *Briefe III*, pp. 316–17. To further support his point, Eliade cited two articles—"Doctorul Gaster" ("Doctor Gaster"), *Vremea*, no. 442 (June 21, 1936): 9, and "Moartea Doctorului Gaster" ("Dr. Gaster's Death"), *Revista Fundațiilor Regale*, no. 5 (May 1939): 395–399—in which he expressed admiration for Moses Gaster and regret at the shameful way Romania had treated one of its greatest Jewish scholars.

89. Gershom Scholem to Mircea Eliade, letter of March 29, 1973, in Scholem, *Briefe III*, p. 63. Negotiations for a visit never got far, since Scholem was unable to extend an official invitation and Eliade had every reason to avoid a discussion with Lavi. See further Laignel-Lavastine, *Cioran, Eliade, Ionescu*, pp. 495–97.

90. "Mircea Eliade e l'antisemitismo," *La Rassegna Mensile di Israel 43*, nos. 1–2 (January–February 1977): 12–15.

91. Furio Jesi, "Un caso imbarazzante: Sconosciuto di Mircea Eliade, un grande studioso di miti," *Tuttolibri 5*, no. 15 (April 21, 1979) : 13, and Furio Jesi, *Cultura di destra: Il linguaggio delle "idee senza parole." Neofascismo sacro e profano: Tecniche, miti e riti di una religione della morte e di una strategia politica* (Milan: Garzanti, 1979), pp. 38–50.

92. On Culianu's life and work, see the account of his sister, Teresa Culianu-Petrescu, "Ioan Petru Culianu: A Biography," in Sorin Antohi, ed., *Religion, Fiction, and History: Essays in Memory of Ioan Petru Culianu* (Bucharest: Editura Nemira, 2001), pp. 25–57; Anton, *Eros, Magic*; Elémire Zolla, *Joan Petru Culianu, 1950–1991* (n.p.: Alberto Tallone, 1994); and Roberta Moretti, *Il sacro, la conoscenza e la morte: Le molte latitudini di Ioan Petru Culianu (Iași 1950–Chicago 1991)* (n.p.: Il Cerchio, 2019), pp. 19–48.

Chapter 4

1. The bibliographical details are available in Allen and Doeing, *Eliade, Annotated Bibliography*, and Handoca, *Mircea Eliade, Biobibliografie*. In the same period, he published Romanian-language works with legionary publishers in Spain, Argentina, and Germany, as well as nineteen books in French, sixteen in English, thirteen in German, twelve in Spanish, nine in Italian, and smaller numbers in Portuguese, Dutch, Danish, Swedish, Greek, Polish, and Japanese.

2. For the details, see Allen and Doeing, *Eliade, Annotated Bibliography* and Handoca, *Mircea Eliade, Biobibliografie*.

3. Mircea Eliade, *De la Zalmoxis la Genghis-Han: Studii comparative despre religiile și folclorul Daciei și Europei Orientale*, trans. Maria Ivanescu and Cezar Ivanescu (Bucharest: Humanitas, 1970). The original French text was published in the same year and an English translation followed quickly: *De Zalmoxis à Gengis-Khan* (Paris: Payot, 1970) and *Zalmoxis, the Vanishing God: Comparative Studies in the Religions and Folklore of Dacia and Eastern Europe*, trans. Willard Trask (Chicago: University of Chicago Press, 1972).

4. Concerning Eliade's interest in Romanian folklore and prehistory, its relation to earlier Romanian scholarship on the topic, and the place of such discourse in the ideology of the Far Right, see Dan Dana, *Métamorphoses de Mircea Eliade: À partir du motif de Zalmoxis* (Paris: J. Vrin, 2012).

5. According to Culianu, he was fifteen when he first heard Eliade's name and seventeen when he first read any of his work. Ioan Petru Culianu, *Mircea Eliade*, 3rd ed., trans. Florin Chirițescu and Dan Petrescu (Iași: Polirom, 2004), p. 295.

6. In the years after Culianu left Romania, "his refusal of Communism was total, absolute," according to Gianpaolo Romanato, "Ricordo di un amico: Ioan Petru Culianu," in Antohi, *Religion, Fiction, and History*, vol. 1, p. 79. Cf. the December 1989 affidavit Culianu filed when applying for American citizenship (available at https://archive.org/stream/IoanCulianu/Ioan Culianu Part 01 of 01_djvu.txt): "Since the date of my escape from Romania, I have been constantly engaged in activities meant to expose the crimes and the failure of the Communist dictatorship in Romania and to denounce the falsehood of Communism in general. . . . My position is clear-cut concerning Romanian communism, which I accused of having destroyed all spiritual values of Romania and having introduced arbitrary values dictated by censors and mendacious politicians."

7. Petrescu-Culianu, "Ioan Petru Culianu," pp. 34–35, citing a description given by Culianu's fellow student Dana Popescu-Șișmanian.

8. Much of Culianu's correspondence with Eliade and Bianchi has been published. See Tereza Culianu-Petrescu, Dan Petrescu, and Matei Călinescu, "The Correspondence between Mircea Eliade and Ioan Petru Culianu," *Archaeus 8* (2004): 341–64; Ioan Petru Culianu, *Dialoguri întrerupte. Corespondență Mircea Eliade-Ioan Petru Culianu*, ed. and annotated by Tereza Culianu-Petrescu and Dan Petrescu (Iași: Polirom, 2013); Daniela

Dumbravă, "The Unpublished Correspondence between Ugo Bianchi
and Ioan Petru Culianu," *Archaeus 14* (2010): 93–120; Daniela Dumbravă,
"Culianu's Shifting Perspectives on the History of Religions: A Preliminary
Analysis of His Correspondence with Ugo Bianchi," *Annali di Scienze
Religiose 6* (2013): 45–91; Liviu Bordaş, "Ioan Petru Culianu, Mircea Eliade
şi *felix culpa*. Supplementa," *Studii de istorie a filosofiei româneşti 18* (2022): 1–
35; Liviu Bordaş, "'Întotdeauna far într-o lume nihilistă': Mircea Eliade şi
Ioan Petru Culianu—completări documentare," *Studii de istorie a filosofiei
româneşti 8* (2012): 303–61, and *"Ca o flacără întunecată" Mircea Eliade
şi Ioan Petru Culianu—noi completări documentare* (Bucharest: Editura
Academiei Române, 2014). The exchange between Eliade and Culianu has
been studied by Georgiana Claudia Mihail, "The Pragmasemantic Analysis
of the Correspondence between Mircea Eliade and Ioan Petru Culianu: The
Proof of Unconditional Devotion and Circularity of Literary and Ontological
Perspectives between the Master and the Disciple," *Acta Universitatis
Danubius 11* (2017): 102–15, with emphasis on the benevolent guidance
and patronage provided by Eliade and Culianu's adoption of his mentor's
initiatory model for self-development.

9. Culianu, *Mircea Eliade*, 3rd ed. Donini's denunciation appeared in his article
"Fenomenologia della religione," in Donini, *Enciclopedia delle religioni*
(Milan: Teti editore, 1977), p. 189.

10. Culianu, *Mircea Eliade*, 3rd ed., pp. 29–68.

11. Ibid., p. 34.

12. Ibid., p. 27.

13. Roberto Scagno, "Religiosità cosmica e cultura tradizionale nel pensiero di
Mircea Eliade" (Tesi di laurea, Università degli Studi di Torino, Facoltà di
Lettere e Filosofia, 1973), a copy of which is available in Box 115, Folder 1
of the Eliade Archive in the Special Collections of University of Chicago's
Regenstein Library. Scagno's later publications on the relation between
Eliade's life and thought are now available in the new edition of *Libertà e
terrore della storia: Con altri studi sull'opera e il pensiero di Mircea Eliade*
(Alessandria: Edizioni dell'Orso, 2022; original publication, 1982).

14. Eliade, *Journal*, vol. 3, pp. 170–71 (entry of September 12, 1974).

15. Cf. Eliade's letter to Culianu of January 17, 1978, in Culianu, *Dialoguri
întrerupte*, pp. 125–26, and Culianu's letters to Eliade dated December 19, 1977,
and January 25, 1978, in Bordaş, *"Ca o Flacără Întunecată"*, pp. 283–84 and
284–86, respectively.

16. Ioan Culianu, "Mircea Eliade între 'burghez' şi 'antiburghez,'" in Culianu,
Mircea Eliade, 3rd ed., p. 320.

17. Ion Protopopescu, "Corneliu Zelea Codreanu," in *Corneliu Codreanu
Prezent!* (Madrid: n.p., 1966), pp. 13 and 18. Protopopescu served as
minister of public works in the National Legionary State. In addition to his
contribution, the volume includes tributes and reminiscences from seven
legionary commanders, five other ministers in the National Legionary

State, three founding members of the movement, and several of its leading ideologists.

18. Culianu, "Mircea Eliade între 'burghez' şi 'antiburghez,'" p. 326.

19. Ibid., p. 325.

20. Ibid. Cf. the very different conclusions of Schmitt, *Căpitan Codreanu*, p. 174: "After 1945, Codreanu's followers shifted all responsibility to Sima and constructed a 'Codrenist' Legion of moral integrity, whose anti-Semitism was denied or relativized. This rehabilitation of Codreanu is refuted by the evidence brought to light through research." On the continued attempts of "Codrenist" legionaries to deny, minimize, or explain away the virulent anti-Semitism that characterized the movement from its very beginnings, see Paul Cosmina, "Antisemitismul Legionarilor Codreniști-Foşti Deținuți Politici," *Anuarul Institutului de Istorie Orală 5* (2004): 232–55.

21. Culianu to Eliade, letters of December 19 and December 31, 1977, in Bordaş, *"Ca o Flacără Întunecată"*, pp. 281–83 and 283–84, respectively.

22. Eliade to Culianu, letter of January 17, 1978, from Culianu, *Dialoguri întrerupte*, pp. 125–26.

23. Although Culianu was eager to make amends, it seems he did not understand that the only way to do so was to avoid the topic. In a letter of March 17, 1978, in Culianu, *Dialoguri întrerupte,* pp. 142–43, he tried to provide reassurance, while inadvertently indicating he was still concerned with the issue:

    A few days ago, very sad that I had distressed you with the whole story of Donini & Co., to whom my replies were very clumsy, I telephoned to retract the final note I had added in extremis. There, I explain that you were not at all anti-Semitic and you were not pro-Nazi, because you were pro-Salazarian. Many people have told me, however, that the last part of the argument does not work. Nevertheless, I do believe the argument is correct. Salazar was not really what we call a "fascist," that is, he did not have an *ideology*. But I may be wrong after all and only speak nonsense.

24. Stamatu was a prize-winning poet whose legionary commitments endured from 1930 to the end of his life. Among the editors of *Buna Vestire*, he took an active part in the Legionary Rebellion of January 1941, after which he fled Romania for Germany. Condemned to death in absentia after the war, he lived in different centers of former-legionary activity (Freiburg, Paris, Madrid) and founded several publications of the extreme Right (*Libertatea românească, Fapta, Forschungstelle für Weltzivilisation*). With Eliade, Cioran, and others, he helped found the Romanian Research Institute in Paris and became head of its literary section.

25. Cited by Tereza Culianu-Petrescu in a note she contributed to Culianu, *Dialoguri întrerupte*, p. 127. Cf. Ioan Culianu to Mac Linscott Ricketts, letter of January 19, 1988, in Liviu Bordaş, "Ioan Petru Culianu–Mac Linscott Ricketts Correspondence," in Mihaela Gligor, ed., *Mircea Eliade between the History of Religions and the Fall into History* (Cluj-Napoca: Presa Universitară Clujeană, 2012), pp. 147–48.

26. Eliade to Culianu, letter of February 13, 1978, in Culianu, *Dialoguri întrerupte*, pp. 135–36.

27. Eliade to Culianu, letter of March 1, 1978, in ibid., p. 140.

28. Eliade, *Journal*, vol. 3, p. 127.

29. Romanato, "Ricordo di un amico," p. 150. Cf. Culianu-Petrescu, "Ioan Petru Culianu," pp. 45–46.

30. Gianpaolo Romanato to Bruce Lincoln, emails dated January 20 and 29, 2019.

31. Gianpaolo Romanato to Bruce Lincoln, email dated April 29, 2019.

32. Culianu finished his work at the Università Cattolica in 1976, with a *tesi di laurea* on "Gnosticism and Contemporary Thought," subsequently published as *Gnosticismo e pensiero moderno: Hans Jonas* (Rome: L'Erma di Bretschneider, 1985). After teaching briefly in Milan, he accepted a position as assistant professor of Romanian language and literature at the University of Groningen in November 1976 and was promoted to associate professor with tenure in 1978.

33. Culianu to Romanato, letter of October 22, 1978, in Romanato, "Ricordo di un amico," p. 116.

34. Culianu to Romanato, letter of November 9, 1978, in ibid., pp. 118–20. The book that was translated in place of Culianu's was Douglas Allen, *Mircea Eliade et le phenomène religieux*, trans. Constantin Grigoresco (Paris: Payot, 1982); English original: *Structure and Creativity in Religion: Hermeneutics in Mircea Eliade's Phenomenology and New Directions* (The Hague: Mouton, 1978).

35. Ioan Culianu to Vittorio Lanternari, letter of April 28, 1987, in Bordaş, "Culianu-Ricketts Correspondence," pp. 175–77. Much the same point recurs in Culianu's letter of January 19, 1988, to Mac Linscott Ricketts in ibid., pp. 147–48.

36. This is precisely what Culianu said when writing to Romanato in Italian. When a Romanian translation of the letter was published, *più ossequioso* became *mai respectuoasă* ("more respectful"), consistent with the desire of Culianu's admirers to minimize any hints of opportunism, sycophancy, or cowardice in his dealings with Eliade. Gianpaolo Romanato, "Amintirea unui prieten: Ioan Petru Culianu," in Sorin Antohi, ed., *Ioan Petru Culianu: Omul şi opera* (Iaşi: Polirom, 2003), p. 135.

37. Romanian versions of these articles were published in Ioan Petru Culianu, *Studii româneşti I: Fantasmele nihilismului şi secretul doctorului Eliade*, trans. Corina Popescu and Dan Petrescu (Bucharest: Neamira, 2000), pp. 211–395; and Ioan Petru Culianu, *Studii româneşti II: Soarele şi luna. Otrăvurile admiraţiei*, trans. Maria-Magdalena Anghelescu, Corina Popescu, and Dan Petrescu (Iaşi: Polirom, 2009), pp. 127–244. In addition to those discussed below, these texts include "Metamorfoza lui Mircea Eliade," *Limite* (Paris) *28–29* (1979): 35–36, "M. Eliade et la pensée moderne sur l'irrationnel," *Dialogue 8* (1983): 39–52, and "Mircea Eliade et son oeuvre," *Aurores 38* (December 1983): pp. 10–12. Slightly later, but similar in character are "Eliade et le refus du symbolisme," *3e Millénaire 13* (1984): 89–93, "Mircea Eliade et l'idéal de

l'homme universel," *Bulletin du Club Français de la médaille 84* (1984): 48–55, and "M. Eliade at the Crossroads of Anthropology," *Neue Zeitschrift für systematische Theologie und Religionsphilosophie 27* (1985): 123–31.

38. Ioan Culianu, "L'anthropologie philosophique," *Cahiers de l'Herne 33* (1978) : 203–11.

39. Ioan Petru Culianu, "Mircea Eliade e la lunga lotta contro il razzismo," in Marin Mincu and Roberto Scagno, eds., *Mircea Eliade e l'Italia* (Milan: Jaca Book, 1986), pp. 9–12.

40. Three volumes resulted from this project, all under Duerr's editorship: *Die Mitte der Welt*; *Alcheringa, oder die beginnende Zeit: Studien zu Mythologie, Schamanismus und Religion* (Frankfurt am Main: Qumran, 1983); and *Sehnsucht nach der Ursprung: zu Mircea Eliade* (Frankfurt am Main: Syndikat, 1983). Although the intention was to include a wide spectrum of opinion, contributors tilted heavily in Eliade's favor. Only Culianu and R. J. Zwi Werblowsky made mention of Eliade's legionary past, speaking emphatically in his defense. The testimony of Werblowsky—who was both a rabbi and a leading Israeli historian of religions—was particularly significant. While acknowledging he had read only part of Eliade's 1934 polemic with Nae Ionescu, he considered these articles sufficient proof that "Eliade was never an anti-Semite." R. J. Zwi Werblowsky, "*In nostro tempore*," in Duerr, *Die Mitte der Welt*, pp. 128–37 (passage quoted at p. 134).

41. Ioan Petru Culianu, "Mircea Eliade und die Blinde Schildkröte."

42. Ibid. The discussion of Nae Ionescu is in Section II ("The Romanian Socrates was Called Nae Ionescu"), while that of earlier influences (Mihail Eminescu, B. P. Hasdeu, Nicolae Iorga, Vasile Pârvan, Nichifor Crainic, and Lucian Blaga) is divided between Section II and III ("Parsifal and Master Manole").

43. Ibid. Section IV of the essay, treating Eliade's political involvement, is titled "An Answer Must Be Found." The passage cited appears at pp. 219–20.

44. Ibid. p. 230. The works he cited were Henry L. Roberts, *Rumania: Political Problems of an Agrarian State* (New Haven: Yale University Press, 1951); Hugh Seton-Watson, *Eastern Europe between the Wars, 1918–1941*, 3rd ed. (New York: Harper & Row, 1967); Eugen Weber, "Romania," in Hans Rogger and Eugen Weber, eds., *The European Right: A Historical Profile* (Berkeley: University of California Press, 1965), pp. 501–74; Nicholas M. Nagy-Talavera, "The Green Shirts and the Others: A History of Fascism in Hungary and Romania" (dissertation, 1967; University Microfilms Int.), pp. 414–602.

45. Horia Sima, *History of the Legionary Movement* (Hampshire, England: Legionary Press, 1995), p. 13.

46. The works in question are Codreanu, *Pentru legionari*; Moța, *L' uomo nuovo*; *Corneliu Codreanu Prezent!*; Dumitru Micu, *Gîndirea şi gîndirismul*; and Stelian Neagoe, *Triumful raţiunii împotriva violenţei: Viaţa universitară ieşană interbelică* (Iaşi: Editura "Junimea," 1977).

47. Matei Călinescu, "Culianu: Eliade: Culianu," in Antohi, *Religion, Fiction, and History*, Vol. I, pp. 235–36.

48. Culianu, "Mircea Eliade und die Blinde Schildkröte," p. 234.

49. Ibid., p. 233.

50. Securitate did, of course, develop—and circulate—its own view of people under surveillance, interpreting almost any evidence as confirmation of its suspicions. On the way the agency's files could produce virtual döppelgängers of the people in question, see Katherine Verdery, *My Life as a Spy: Investigations in a Secret Police File* (Durham, NC: Duke University Press, 2018).

51. Mircea Eliade, *Tecniche dello Yoga*, trans. Anna Macchioro, preface by Ernesto De Martino (Turin: Einaudi, 1952), and Mircea Eliade, *Trattato di storia delle religioni*, trans. Virginia Vacca, preface by Ernesto De Martino (Turin: Einaudi, 1954).

52. Culianu first discussed the incident in *Mircea Eliade*, pp. 170–71, then again in "Mircea Eliade und die Blinde Schildkröte," pp. 233–34, after having read Furio Jesi, "Un caso imbarazzante," p. 13.

53. On Donini, the sole biography is regrettably superficial; Italo Arcuri, *Ambrogio Donini e la storia delle idee: Lo storico delle religioni, l'intelettuale dissidente, il partigiano militante* (Rome: EMIA Edizioni, 2016).

54. See further Luisa Mangoni, *Pensare i libri: La casa editrice Einaudi dagli anni trenta agli anni sessanta* (Turin: Boringhieri, 1999), pp. 533–35 and 562. Regarding the source of Donini's information, Vittorio Lanternari reported: "Ambrogio Donini informs me personally that in the postwar period when he was Italian ambassador to Poland, he received direct reports from the Romanian ambassador there, as well as colleagues in France, regarding Eliade's past as an 'anti-Semite and pro-Nazi.'" Vittorio Lanternari, "Ripensando a Mircea Eliade," *La critica sociologica 79* (1986): 79.

55. Mangoni, *Pensare i libri*, citing Pavese's letter of October 5, 1949, to De Martino.

56. Donini, "Fenomenologia della religione." Culianu was alerted to this text by an article by Gianpaolo Romanato, "I marxisti di fronte al fenomeno religioso: Una posizione rigorosamente atea," *Popolo* (March 11, 1978), p. 3.

57. Ioan Culianu to Gianpaolo Romanato, letter of April 10, 1978, in Bordaş, *"Ca o flacără întunecată"*, pp. 288–89.

58. Ioan Culianu, "Mircea Eliade und die Blinde Schildkröte," p. 234. This characterization is exaggerated, but not without basis. Long a leading figure in the PCI, Donini was unwilling to denounce the Soviet invasion of Czechoslovakia in 1968, in contrast to other leaders of the party. By 1979, he had been removed from all official positions.

59. Ibid.

60. Lavi, "Dosarul Mircea Eliade," 21–22, cited Miron Constantinescu, "Garda de Fier sub judecata istoriei," *Magazin istoric 5*, no. 1 (January 1971): 75, and Lucreţiu Pătrăşcanu, *Sub trei dictaturi* (Bucharest: Editura Politică, 1970), p. 54. Constantinescu was a sociologist who had been a leader of antifascist students in Bucharest during the 1930s. Imprisoned during the war, he became a member of the Communist Party's politburo after 1945 but was

purged when he supported Nikita Khrushchev's efforts at de-Stalinization, after which he worked as a researcher on Romanian history and sociology for roughly a decade. Upon rehabilitation during the 1968 thaw, he served as minister of education, president of the Academy of Social and Political Sciences, and president of the Great National Assembly. Pătrăşcanu was a friend of Constantinescu and had a similar profile but was less fortunate. Having completed a doctorate at the University of Leipzig, he was elected to the Chamber of Deputies and was one of the few Marxists active in Eliade's Criterion group. Imprisoned during the war, he helped engineer the coup that overthrew the Antonescu dictatorship. After the war, he served on the Central Committee of the Communist Party but fell into disfavor for what his colleagues perceived as personal arrogance, excessive intellectualism, and opposition to Stalinist directives. Arrested in 1948, he was executed in 1954, following investigations, interrogations, and two suicide attempts. In April 1968, he was posthumously rehabilitated in the same liberalization campaign that benefited Constantinescu. Although these men were hardly Stalinist hacks, Culianu leaped on the fact that Lavi cited their work as reason to denounce his dossier as propagandistic disinformation.

61. Ioan Culianu, "Mircea Eliade şi Nae Ionescu," in Culianu, *Studii Româneşti II*, pp. 160–63. Lavi was unable to publish the promised sequel when Sebastian's relatives objected to his unauthorized use of passages from their kinsman's still-unpublished journal.

62. Culianu, "Mircea Eliade und die Blinde Schildkröte." p. 236.

63. Ioan Culianu, "Mircea Eliade: À la recherche du Graal," manuscript included in the University of Chicago's Regenstein Library Culianu archive. This phrase was dropped from the version of this article published in *CNAC-Magazine*, Centre Pompidou 39 (May–June 1987): 8–9.

64. Fiore, *Storia sacra e storia profana*, p. 19. Similar remarks can be found in Lanternari, "Ripensando a Mircea Eliade" and Claudio Mutti, *Mircea Eliade e la guardia di ferro*. Harshest of all was the judgment of Alfonso Di Nola, "Mircea Eliade tra scienza delle religioni e ideologia 'guardista,'" *Marxismo Oggi 5–6* (1989): 67, who characterized Culianu as "a direct disciple of Eliade, [who] intervened in the debate with an article sufficiently rough and thoughtless to be placed among those ascribable to 'base polemics.'"

65. Eliade to Culianu, letter of February 24, 1984, in Culianu, *Dialoguri întrerupte*, pp. 251–52.

66. Eliade did not ask if Culianu was willing to assume such responsibilities. Rather, he informed him ex post facto in a letter of March 28, 1983, cited in Culianu, *Dialoguri întrerupte*, p. 244, which included photocopies of the letter he had sent to Payot on February 3. In the latter text, he explained his decision and predicted, "In less than ten years, Prof. I.P. Couliano will be considered one of the most important contemporary historians of religions."

67. The series, provisionally titled "Est-Ouest," was to be published by Hachette. Regarding Goma's plans for this series and the reactions of Eliade and Culianu to his proposal, see Tereza Culianu-Petrescu and

Dan Petrescu's note to Eliade's letter of November 29, 1982, in Culianu, *Dialoguri întrerupte*, pp. 241–42.

68. Eliade to Culianu, letter of November 29, 1982, in ibid., pp. 241–42.
69. Eliade to Culianu, letter of March 28, 1983. in ibid, p. 244.
70. Culianu to Eliade, letters of May 9, 1984, and September 18, 1984, in ibid, pp. 260 and 263, respectively.
71. Eliade to Culianu, September 21, 1984, in ibid., p. 265.
72. Ioan Culianu, "Foreword" to the manuscript titled *The Unknown Mircea Eliade* found in Culianu's Nachlass, a Romanian translation of which ("Cuvînt înainte") was published in Culianu, *Mircea Eliade*, 3rd ed., pp. 169–71.
73. Ioan Culianu, "The Fall: 1933–43," Chapter 7 to *The Unknown Mircea Eliade*, published in ibid., pp. 243–61.
74. Culianu, "Mircea Eliade und die Blinde Schildkröte," p. 239 (emphasis added).
75. Culianu, from Chapter 10 of *The Unknown Mircea Eliade*, in Culianu, *Mircea Eliade*, 3rd ed., p. 283.
76. Mihai Miroiu, *Romanian Practical Dictionary: Romanian-English/English-Romanian* (New York: Hippocrene Books, 2010), p. 170.
77. Culianu, Chapter 7 of *The Unknown Eliade*: "The Fall: 1933–43." in Culianu, *Mircea Eliade*, 3rd ed., p. 155.
78. On the relation of Ionesco's play to his experience of watching Eliade and others embrace the Legion, see Dorothy Knowles, "Eugene Ionesco's Rhinoceroses: Their Romanian Origin and Their Western Fortunes," *French Studies 28* (1974): 294–307, and Matei Călinescu, "Ionesco and *Rhinoceros*: Personal and Political Backgrounds," *East European Politics and Societies 9* (1995): 393–432. On the shifting relations between the two men over the course of their lives, see Sergiu Miculescu, "Deux ennemis rapprochés: Eugène Ionesco et Mircea Eliade," *Recherches ACLIF: Actes du Séminaire de Didactique Universitaire 7* (2010): 133–43, and Laignel-Lavastine, *Cioran, Eliade, Ionesco*.
79. Eugène Ionesco, letter to Tudor Vianu, September 19, 1945, in *Scrisori către Tudor Vianu*, vol. 2 *(1936–1949)*, ed. Maria Alexandrescu Vianu and Vlad Alexandrescu (Bucharest: Minerva, 1994), p. 274.
80. Andrei Oişteanu, *Religie, politică şi mit*, p. 75. The questions are presented in similarly adulatory and uncritical fashion by Moretti, *Il sacro, la conoscenza, e la morte*, p. 30.
81. Ioan Culianu, "Convorbiri Întrerupte," a set of twenty-one questions submitted to Mircea Eliade as part of *The Unknown Mircea Eliade,* in Culianu, *Mircea Eliade*, 3rd ed., pp. 291–98 (ellipsis in the original).
82. Ibid.
83. Mircea Eliade, *Journal*, vol. 4: *1979–1985*, trans. Mac Linscott Ricketts (Chicago: University of Chicago Press, 1990), p. 22.
84. Culianu, Chapter 7 of *The Unknown Eliade*. in Culianu, *Mircea Eliade*, 3rd ed., p. 255.
85. Eliade, *Forbidden Forest*, p. 171. Cf. pp. 117–18, 148–49, and 161–62.
86. Culianu, "Convorbiri Întrerupte."
87. Ibid.

88. Culianu to Gianpaolo Romanato, letter of November 9, 1978, in Romanato, "Ricordo di un amico," p. 119.

89. Eliade to Culianu, letter of February 14, 1985, responding to Culianu's letter of February 3 in Culianu, *Dialoguri întrerupte*, pp. 275 and 279–80, respectively.

90. In his last years, Eliade suffered from severe arthritis that made it difficult for him to write, also from bouts of depression, as he confided to Culianu in several of his letters.

Chapter 5

1. A bibliography of Culianu's published work (up to 2001) is included in Antohi, *Religion, Fiction, and History*, vol. 2, pp. 542–56. His relations with Eliade have been discussed, inter alia, in Anton, *Eros, Magic*; Culianu-Petrescu, "Ioan Petru Culianu"; Idel, *Mircea Eliade*; De Martino, *Mircea Eliade Esoterico*, esp. pp. 443–66; Dan Petrescu, "Ioan Petru Culianu şi Mircea Eliade," in Antohi, *Ioan Petru Culianu*, pp. 410–58; Sorin Antohi, "Postface" to Ioan Petru Culianu, *Mircea Eliade*, 3rd ed., pp. 351–69; Oişteanu, *Religie, politică şi mit*, pp. 75–82; Liviu Bordaş, "Ioan Petru Culianu, Mircea Eliade şi felix culpa," *Studii de istorie a filosofiei româneşti 9* (2013): 319–78; Liviu Bordaş, "'Întotdeauna far într-o lume nihilistă,'" and Liviu Bordaş, "Il cuore del saggio e la sua statua: Quando Culianu omaggiava Eliade," *Antarès: Prospettive antimoderne 18* (2021): 56–59.

2. Culianu, "Foreword" to *The Unknown Mircea Eliade* in Culianu, *Mircea Eliade*, 3rd. ed., p. 170. Eliade's *Journal*, vol. 3, records meetings with Culianu in September 1974 (Paris), February–May 1975 (Chicago), September 1976 (Paris), June 1979 (Paris), July 1984 (Paris), and August 1984 (Groningen).

3. Eliade to Culianu, letter of May 3, 1977, in Culianu, *Mircea Eliade*, 3rd ed., pp. 5–7; *Journal*, vol. 3, p. 305 (April 4, 1978); and letter of December 31, 1981, to Constantin Noica in *Europa, Asia, America,* vol. 2, p. 415.

4. Eliade, *Journal*, vol. 4, p. 97 (entry of August 1, 1984).

5. Wendy Doniger, personal communications, February 20 and March 15, 2019. The University of Chicago's files on Culianu remain closed until fifty years after his death, but Associate Provost Jason Merchant inspected them in response to my inquiry and told me they include no indication of a full search, but a dozen letters unanimously supporting the appointment (personal communication, May 14, 2019).

6. Lanternari, "Ripensando a Mircea Eliade."

7. Vittorio Lanternari to Ioan Culianu, letter of April 5, 1987, in Bordaş, "Culianu-Ricketts Correspondence," pp. 172–74.

8. Ibid. The manuscript to which Lanternari referred was Radu Ioanid's then-forthcoming article "Mircea Eliade e il fascismo," *La critica sociologica 84* (January–March 1988): 16–29, which discussed six of Eliade's legionary articles.

9. Lanternari, "Ripensando a Mircea Eliade," p. 79, with reference to *Storia sacra e storia profana*, p. 22.

10. Ioan Culianu to Vittorio Lanternari, letter of April 28, 1987, in Bordaş, "Culianu-Ricketts Correspondence," pp. 175–77.

11. Culianu, "Mircea Eliade und die Blinde Schildkröte," p. 234. For Culianu's subsequent statements on this point, see Table A.3 in the appendix.

12. Ioan Culianu, letter of April 28, 1987, to Lanternari and of April 29, 1987, to Arnaldo Momigliano in Bordaş, "Culianu-Ricketts Correspondence," pp. 175–77 and 178, respectively.

13. Ioan Culianu to Mac Linscott Ricketts, April 29, 1987, in Bordaş, "Culianu-Ricketts Correspondence," p. 125.

14. For Ricketts' reflection on the history of his relation to Eliade, see his "Mircea Eliade, My Professor: A Memoir," in Mihaela Gligor and Mac Linscott Ricketts, eds., *Întâlniri cu Mircea Eliade / Encounters with Mircea Eliade* (Cluj-Napoca: Casa Cârţi de Ştiinţă, 2005), pp. 133–40.

15. Ricketts described his archival research in the Introduction to *Mircea Eliade: The Romanian Roots*, p. 3.

16. The articles Ricketts sent to Culianu were the same ones he listed in his letter of August 23, 1981, to Theodor Lavi, in Mihaela Gligor and Miriam Caloianu, eds., *Theodor Lavi în corespondenţă*, pp. 326–28. Missing from this set are three of the most troubling pieces: ""Meditaţie asupra arderii catedralelor" ("Meditation on the Burning of Cathedrals"), *Vremea 10*, no. 474 (February 7, 1937): 3; "De unde începe misiunea României?"; and "Piloţii orbii."

17. Mac Linscott Ricketts to Ioan Culianu, letter of May 5, 1987, in Bordaş, "Culianu-Ricketts Correspondence," pp. 126–28.

18. Ioan Culianu to Arnaldo Momigliano, letter of April 29, 1987, in ibid., p. 178.

19. Ioan Culianu to Mac Linscott Ricketts, letter of May 13, 1987, in ibid., pp. 129–30.

20. Ricketts, *Mircea Eliade*.

21. Adriana Berger to Ivan Strenski, letter of December 14, 1987, archived in the Special Collections of the University of Chicago's Regenstein Library.

22. Ricketts, *Mircea Eliade*, pp. 881–930. See also Ricketts's letter to Theodor Lavi of April 17, 1982, in Gligor and Caloianu, eds., *Theodor Lavi în corespondenţă*, pp. 348–49, where he stated: "I now believe that Eliade was extremely naive in connection with the Iron Guard—which does not excuse his association with it. However, I do not believe he was an anti-Semite." Lavi's response of May 19, 1982, in ibid., pp. 350–51 is also worth citing: "In contrast to you, I do not believe that Eliade was naive regarding the Iron Guard, since it was, I would say, the bloody, murderous personification and materialization of anti-Semitism. It is not possible that he did not take account of the fact that through adherence to the Iron Guard one also accepted its judeophobic credo."

23. The panel included presentations by Ricketts, "The Spiritual Revolution That Failed: Eliade's Involvement in the Romanian Nationalist Movement of the 1930s," and Berger, "Mysticism and Politics in Eliade's Writings," with Strenski

as respondent. Ricketts paper, which closely follows Chapter 22 of his book, is included in Box 139, Folder 3 of the Eliade archive of the Regenstein Library's Special Collections. A copy of Berger's paper is included in Box 3, file 3 of Regenstein's Culianu archive.

24. Ioan Culianu to Mac Linscott Ricketts, letter of May 20, 1987, in Bordaş, "Culianu-Ricketts Correspondence," p. 133.

25. Mac Linscott Ricketts to Ioan Culianu, letters of June 4, 1987, in ibid., p. 134.

26. Ivan Strenski, "Love and Anarchy in Romania: A Critical Review of Mircea Eliade's Autobiography," *Religion 12* (1982): 391–403, esp. pp. 396–402.

27. Adriana Berger, letter of April 27, 1987, to Ivan Strenski, archived in the Special Collections of the University of Chicago's Regenstein Library.

28. Ivan Strenski, *Four Theories of Myth*, esp. Chapter 4: "Eliade and Myth in Twentieth-Century Romania," pp. 70–103. Professor Strenski detailed to me the difficulties he encountered in getting the book published (personal communication, April 29, 2019).

29. Adriana Berger, "Le temps et l'espace dans l'oeuvre de fiction de Mircea Eliade" (PhD dissertation in comparative literature at the Sorbonne, Université de Paris IV, 1982), pp. 255–58 (emphasis in the original). A copy is preserved in Box 112, Folder 2, of the Eliade Archive in the Special Collections of the University of Chicago's Regenstein Library.

30. Berger's letters to the Eliades from March 1980 until March 1986 have been published in Mihaela Gligor and Liviu Bordaş, *Postlegomena la Felix Culpa: Mircea Eliade, Evreii şi Antisemismul* (Cluj-Napoca: Presa Universitară Clujeana, 2012), vol. *1*, pp. 299–408.

31. Berger's admiring articles were "Eliade's Double Approach: A Desire for Unity," *Religious Studies Review 11* (1985): 9–12, and "Cultural Hermeneutics: The Concept of Imagination in the Phenomenological Approaches of Henry Corbin and Mircea Eliade," *Journal of Religion 66* (1986): 141–56. Her curriculum vitae gives the book's title as *Mircea Eliade: The Inner Quest of a Radical Traditionalist* and describes it as "accepted for publication by Harper and Row, scheduled to appear in June 1988."

32. It is not entirely clear what she found and there were other strains in the relationship. Both Ivan Strenski and Kenneth Zysk, who was Berger's husband during those years, suggested that frustration at Eliade's failure to help her find an academic position contributed to her turning against him (personal communications, April 29, 2019 [Strenski], May 1 and 2, 2019 [Zysk]).

33. According to Wendy Doniger (personal communication, March 3, 2018): "When Christinel found out how much money Eliade had been giving Adriana—thousands and thousands of dollars—she made him stop giving her any money." Adriana's last letters to the Eliades, dated December 27, 1985, and March 1, 1986, in Gligor and Bordaş, *Postlegomena la Felix Culpa*, pp. 401–4 and 404–8, indicate financial hardship, continued dependency, and serious strains in the relationship, without making clear their cause. According to Doniger once more, Mrs. Eliade refused Berger admission to the hospital

room where Professor Eliade passed his last week of life, provoking bitter resentment.

34. Adriana Berger to Ivan Strenski, letter of April 17, 1987, archived in Special Collections of Regenstein Library.

35. Cf. Berger's letters to Ivan Strenski, of April 27, May 7, May 13, May 23, and November 8, 1987, archived in Special Collections of Regenstein Library.

36. As she saw it, "the Chicago mafia" included Christinel, Culianu, Wendy Doniger, Saul Bellow, David Tracy, Frank Reynolds, Charles Long, Jerome Long, Kees Bolle, and Mary Gerhart. Cf. Berger's letters to Strenski of April 27, 1987, November 5, 1987, and May 6, 1988. A letter she received from Harper & Row after the AAR panel, archived in Special Collections of Regenstein Library (as are all the others), suggests that her suspicions were probably justified. It is surely the case that Harper & Row, having published many of Eliade's books, would have wanted to protect his reputation and would have been sensitive to pressure from these people.

37. Cf. Berger's letters to Strenski of April 17, 1987, September 21, 1987, and December 14, 1987, archived in Special Collections of Regenstein Library.

38. Alexander Ronnett, "Mircea Eliade," in Gabriel Stănescu, ed., *Mircea Eliade în conştiinţa contemporanilor săi din exil* (Norcross, GA: Criterion Publishing, n.d.), pp. 288–94. Eliade confirmed the fact that he kept a "secret journal" in a May 1983 discussion with Mac Linscott Ricketts, for which see Bordaş, "On the *Hadīth* corpus of Mircea Eliade," pp. 85–86. To date, that document has not come to light.

39. Adriana Berger to Ivan Strenski, letter of April 17, 1987, archived in Special Collections of Regenstein Library.

40. Ioan Culianu to Mac Linscott Ricketts, letter of January 19, 1988, in Bordaş, "Culianu-Ricketts Correspondence," pp. 147–48.

41. Mac Linscott Ricketts to Ioan Culianu, letter of February 1, 1988, in ibid., p. 150.

42. Adriana Berger, "Fascism and Religion in Romania," *Annals of Scholarship 6* (1989): 455–65, and Adriana Berger, "Mircea Eliade: Romanian Fascism and the History of Religions in the United States," in Nancy A. Harrowitz, ed., *Tainted Greatness: Antisemitism and Cultural Heroes* (Philadelphia: Temple University Press, 1994), pp. 51–74.

43. Ioan Culianu to Mac Linscott Ricketts, letters of December 4, 1990, and March 4, 1991, in Bordaş, "Ioan Petru Culianu, Mircea Eliade şi felix culpa," both on p. 367. The information regarding Berger's dealings with potential publishers comes from Kenneth Zysk, who observed, "This seems to point to a conspiracy to prevent publication, especially as a direct threat was issued against us back in January 1990" (personal communication, May 9, 2019).

44. Stelian Pleşoiu, interviewed by Catalina Iancu, "În căutarea omului total," *Jurnalul National* (April 6, 2009), and by Cristina Scarlat, "În America, pe urmele lui Mircea Eliade—convorbire cu Stelian Pleşoiu," *Hyperion 10* (2011): 25, both of which were republished and are available at https://www.academia.edu/8179557/%C3%8En_America_pe_urmele_lui_Mircea_Eli

ade-_convorbire_cu_Stelian_Ple%C5%9Foiu_%C3%AEn_Hyperion_nr._10-
11-12_2011_pp._23-28. In the interview with Scarlati and one with Gabriel
Stanescu in *Centrul Cultural Pitești*, republished on the same website, Pleşoiu
described how the Eliades asked him to destroy his photograph of Mircea and
Adriana Berger (Figure 5.3) after she became persona non grata.

45. Kenneth Zysk, personal communication, May 2, 2019.

46. Adriana Berger to Ivan Strenski, letter of April 27, 1987, archived in Special
Collections of Regenstein Library.

47. Mac Linscott Ricketts to Christinel Eliade, letter of December 11, 1986,
in the Eliade Archive, Special Collections of Regenstein Library, Box 87,
Folder 29.

48. Adriana Berger to Ivan Strenski, letter of December 14, 1987, archived in
Special Collections of Regenstein Library. David Tracy, professor of theology
at the University of Chicago, was a friend of the Eliades and particularly close
to Christinel.

49. The episode is described in Adriana Berger to Ivan Strenski, letter of May
13, 1987, archived in Special Collections of Regenstein Library. Ricketts's
acknowledgment appears at p. xxi of the "Translator's Preface" to Eliade,
Autobiography, vol. 2.

50. Pierre-Emmanuel Lacocque, "Mircea Eliade Remembered," *McGill Journal of
Education 22* (1987): 124, quoting Christinel Eliade.

51. Ibid. Mrs. Eliade had this to say on the first point: "He had a good friend, Nae
Ionescu, who had, for reasons I do not recall, taken objections to Judaism. But
these were not anti-Semitic slurs, they reflected only philosophical-theological
differences." And on the second: "You know he was even imprisoned for this
accusation. He refused to sign confession papers in exchange for freedom
because he was outraged at the charges against him."

52. Cf. Monica Lovinescu, *Jurnal 1985–1988* (Bucharest: Humanitas, 2002),
p. *162* (September 26, 1986) and p. 312 (August 8, 1988); Monica Lovinescu,
Jurnal 1990–1993 (Bucharest: Humanitas, 2003), p. 351 (June 1, 1993); Monica
Lovinescu, *Jurnal 1994–1995* (Bucharest: Humanitas, 2004), pp. 226–27 (June
6, 1995), and p. 302 (October 16, 1995).

53. Lovinescu, *Jurnal 1985–1988,* pp. 217–18 and 312 (June 3, 1987, and August 8,
1988, respectively), Lovinescu, *Jurnal 1990–1993*, p. 351 (June 1, 1993).

54. Lovinescu, *Jurnal 1994–1995*, pp. 18 and 226–27 (March 6, 1994, and June 6,
1995, respectively).

55. Norman Manea, "Happy Guilt: Mircea Eliade, Fascism, and the Unhappy
Fate of Romania," *New Republic* (August 5, 1991), pp. 27–36. Manea described
the controversy that the Romanian translation of this article provoked in
"Blasphemy and Carnival," *World Policy Journal* (Spring 1996), pp. 71–82.
See also Michael Shafir, "The Man They Love to Hate: Norman Manea's
Snail House between Holocaust and Gulag," *East European Jewish Affairs 30*
(2000): 60–81, and Irina Livezeanu, *Romania's Cultural Wars: Intellectual
Debates about the Recent Past* (Washington, DC: National Council for
Eurasian and East European Research, 2003), pp. 17–23.

56. Manea, "Happy Guilt," p. 33, quoting from Eliade, "De ce cred în bîruinţa mişcării legionare," and "Strigoi" ("Vampires"), *Cuvântul 15*, no. 3120 (January 21, 1938): 2.

57. Lovinescu, *Jurnal 1990–1993*, p. 89 (April 2, 1990).

58. Monica Lovinescu, "Cîteva confuzii," *223*, no. 10/III (March 19, 1992): 13. In her journal, Lovinescu went further, describing the legionary articles as "incriminating," rather than "regrettable." Cf. *Jurnal 1990–1993*, pp. 89, 219, 296 (February 14, February 16, and December 1, 1992, respectively), and *Jurnal 1998–2000* (Bucharest: Humanitas, 2006), pp. 432–33 (October 30, 2000). On her role in the debates about Eliade, see Livezeanu, *Romania's Cultural Wars*, pp. 19–21.

59. Lovinescu, *Jurnal 1990–1993*, p. 296 (December 1, 1992).

60. Lovinescu, *Jurnal 1994–1995*, pp. 226–27 (June 6, 1995). Cf. related discussions in *Jurnal 1990–1993*, pp. 89, 219, and 296 (April 2, 1990, February 16, 1992, and December 1, 1992, respectively), and *Jurnal 1994–1995*, pp. 226–27 (June 6, 1995).

61. Lovinescu, *Jurnal 1990–1993*, pp. 250–51 (June 13, 1992) and *Jurnal 1994–1995*, p. 226 (December 1, 1992).

62. Lovinescu, *Jurnal 1994–1995*, p. 302 (October 16, 1995).

63. Ioan Culianu to Mac Linscott Ricketts, letter of May 13, 1987, in Bordaş, "Culianu-Ricketts Correspondence," pp. 129–30.

64. Ioan Culianu to Mac Linscott Ricketts, letter of October 22, 1987, in ibid., pp. 138–39. According to Prof. Scagno, Culianu did not seek to involve him in such a project and Italian translations of Eliade's legionary articles were not circulating in 1987, when the originals were still tightly controlled. He thus found the content of Culianu's letter of October 22 to Ricketts "incomprehensible" (personal communication, July 12, 2023).

65. Ioan Culianu to Adrian Marino, letter of October 11, 1987, in Călinescu, *Despre Ioan P. Culianu şi Mircea Eliade*, pp. 27–28.

66. Mac Linscott Ricketts to Ioan Culianu, letter of November 3, 1987, in Bordaş, "Culianu-Ricketts Correspondence," p. 141.

67. Mac Linscott Ricketts, memo of November 6, 1988, in ibid., p. 151 (emphasis in the original).

68. Mac Linscott Ricketts to Ioan Culianu, letters of November 29, 1988, and January 19, 1989, in ibid, pp. 152–53 and 154, respectively. In a letter of February 26, 1988, published in Bordaş, "Ioan Petru Culianu, Mircea Eliade şi *felix culpa*. Supplementa," p. 17, Culianu acknowledged receipt of the articles, indicating that Wendy Doniger had also received copies.

69. "Iudaism şi Anti-Semitism—preliminarii la o discuţie," "Doctorul Gaster," and "Moartea Doctorului Gaster," were all included in the packet I received from Mark Krupnick, although one of Eliade's most disturbing articles—"Meditaţie asupra arderii catedralelor"—was not. I believe (but am not 100% certain) this was also true of "Piloţii orbii," but most of the other legionary articles were included.

70. One sees the same struggle to reconcile admiration and loyalty with the hard evidence of troubling documents in Călinescu's account of his reaction to the legionary articles: "The fact is that in 1988 I read them and I was initially shocked by some passages—just a few, it's true, and not lacking, in context, certain ambiguities." Călinescu, "Culianu: Eliade: Culianu," p. 236.

71. Wendy Doniger, personal communications, October 13, 2017.

72. Călinescu, *Despre Ioan P. Culianu și Mircea Eliade*, pp. 25–26.

73. Wendy Doniger, personal communication, November 1, 2017.

74. In Article II of his will, Eliade left all his property to Christinel, and in Article V he appointed her executor of his estate. Culianu was aware of the will's provisions, since a copy of it is included in Box 2, Folder 6 of the Culianu archive in Regenstein Library's Special Collections.

75. Mircea Eliade, letter of February 3, 1983, to Jean-Luc Pidoux-Payot, his Parisian publisher. He informed Culianu of this decision in a letter of March 28, 1983, which included a photocopy of his letter to M. Pidoux-Payot. Both documents are reproduced in Culianu, *Dialoguri întrerupte*, pp. 243–45.

76. Ioan Culianu to Henry Pernet, letter of May 21, 1986, in Bordaș, "Culianu-Ricketts Correspondence," p. 370.

77. Agreement signed by Mrs. Georgette [Christinel] Eliade and Mr. I. P. Culianu, June 9, 1986, a copy of which is in Box 2, Folder 6 of the Culianu Archive in the Special Collections of the University of Chicago's Regenstein Library.

78. Calvin Sawyier, Esq., Affidavit on behalf of Georgette (Christinel) Eliade, February 28, 1989, a copy of which was transmitted to Culianu, as evidenced by its presence in Box 2, Folder 6 of his archived papers in Chicago's Regenstein Library.

79. Culianu, "L'Albero della conoscenza." For the extent to which these concessions departed from positions Culianu took earlier, see the appendix.

80. For the extent to which these assertions were consistent with the positions he maintained in previous publications, see Tables A.1, A.4, and A.5 in the appendix.

81. Ioan Culianu to Mac Linscott Ricketts, letter of June 7, 1989, in Bordaș, "Culianu-Ricketts Correspondence," p. 157 (emphasis in the original).

82. T. David Brent, personal communication, October 16, 2017. In the years after Mrs. Eliade's death (1998), the legionary articles have been republished multiple times in the original Romanian, most accessibly in Eliade, *Textele 'legionare'*, but also in Mircea Handoca, ed., "Să lăsăm textele să vorbească," *Revista Vatra* 6–7 (2000): 28–37, and Mircea Handoca, "Anchetele Bunei Vestiri," *Revista Vatra* 6–7 (2000): 37–58, and Mircea Handoca, *"Dosarul" Eliade, vol. 5: (1936–1944): Jos Farsa! Partea Doua* (Bucharest: Curtea Veche, 2001), pp. 228–64. German translations of four of the articles appeared in Müller, *Der frühe Mircea Eliade*, pp. 75–107, English translations of two others in Bryan Rennie, ed., *Mircea Eliade: A Critical Reader* (London: Equinox, 2006), pp. 412–22.

83. Gregory Spinner, "The Use and Abuse of Morphology," in Antohi, *Religion, Fiction, and History*, vol. 2, pp. 172–73.

84. Culianu-Petrescu, "Ioan Petru Culianu," p. 46, gives a brief account of this episode. Humanitas had acquired exclusive rights to Eliade's work in Romania, consistent with its promotion of the "great interwar authors." See further Livezeanu, *Romania's Cultural Wars*, pp. 25–26.

85. Culianu-Petrescu, "Ioan Petru Culianu," p. 46, slightly modified to include information present in the original Romanian text that was omitted from the English translation. Cf. Anton, *Eros, Magic*, pp. 174–75, and Călinescu, *Despre Ioan P. Culianu și Mircea Eliade*, pp. 25–28.

Chapter 6

1. The phone call, which lasted one minute, has occasioned much discussion since it was placed to a number in Medellin, Colombia. Some take this as evidence the murder was drug-related, while others believe Culianu was instructed to make the call by those threatening him, thus creating a false track for police to follow. For the latter view, see Anton, *Magic, Eros*, pp. 24, 238, 240–41, and 249.
2. Chicago Police report dated May 22, 1991, and FBI report dated June 18, 1991. These and other files on the case were released on March 29, 2018, and remain available at https://archive.org/stream/IoanCulianu/IoanCulianu Part 01 of 01_djvu.txt, https://archive.org/stream/IOANCULIANU/Ioan%20Culi anu%20Part%2001%20of%2001_djvu.txt, and https://vault.fbi.gov/ioan-culi anu. Many pages have been deleted, along with the names of most individuals who were interviewed and much other information.
3. The threats were mentioned by many of the people interviewed by the FBI. See further Anton, *Eros, Magic*, pp. 23, 194, 205–6, 208, and 238.
4. FBI report of information received at the Baton Rouge office, June 18, 1991, available online at https://archive.org/stream/IoanCulianu/Ioan Culianu Part 01 of 01_djvu.txt.
5. Thus Anton, *Eros, Magic*. Cf. Umberto Eco, "Murder in Chicago," *New York Review of Books* (April 10, 1997), Matei Călinescu, "O crimă perfectă?," in *Despre Ioan P. Culianu și Mircea Eliade*, pp. 7–9, and others. In proper dialectic fashion, this theory spawned an inversionary antithesis, whereby Culianu was taken to be a covert agent who infiltrated right-wing groups in the West on behalf of Securitate and was killed by the CIA. Cf. Ezio Albrile, "Diafane Sovversioni: Ioan Petru Culianu e la disintegrazione del sistema," *Rivista di Studi Indo-Mediterranei 1* (2011), available online at http://archivindomed.altervista.org/alterpages/Albr ile-Diafane.pdf, and Ezio Albrile, "Smeraldi sognanti: Un altra ipotesi sul professor Culianu," available at http://www.asfer.it/upload/dl/ASFeR/ Culianu_Smeraldi.pdf.
6. Lovinescu, *Jurnal 1990–1993*, pp. 141–43 (May 26, 1991).
7. Petrescu-Culianu, Tudoran, and Călinescu were regularly quoted in news articles treating the murder, as were Andrei Codrescu, Vladimir Tismăneanu, and a few others from the same circle. See, inter alia, Teresa Wiltz, "Romanians Link Politics, Prof's Death," *Chicago Tribune* (June 2, 1991); Andrew Borowiec, "Ceaușescu Terrorists Unchecked," *Washington Times*, June 3, 1991; Sharon Cohen, "Political Intrigue Is One Theory in Killing of

Romanian-Born Professor," *Los Angeles Times* (June 30, 1991); and Ted Anton, "The Killing of Professor Culianu," *Lingua Franca 2*, no. 6 (September–October 1992): 28–34.

8. Culianu's columns for *Lumea Liberă* and his other political writings have been republished in Ioan Culianu, *Păcatul împotriva spiritului: Scrieri politice* (Iași: Polirom, 2013).

9. Cea mai proastă inteligență" ("The Stupidest Intelligence Service"). Both these articles were published in two parts: "Dialogul morților in *Lumea liberă* nos. 91 and 94 (June 30, 1990 and July 21, 1990), "Cea mai proastă inteligență" in Lumea liberă nos. 94 and 96 (July 21 and 28, 1990). The two are reprinted in Culianu, *Păcatul împotriva spiritului*, pp. 119-25 and 152-55, respectively.

10. Ioan Culianu, "Fantapolitica," *Lumea liberă*, no. 100 (September 1, 1990): 9, reprinted in Culianu, *Păcatul împotriva spiritului*, pp. 135–41. Cf. Culianu, "Cea mai proastă inteligență" and "Cel mai mare român în viață," and ("The Greatest Living Romanian"), *Lumea liberă*, no. 104 (September 29, 1990): 9, reprinted in Culianu, *Păcatul împotriva spiritului*, pp. 119–25 and 152–55, respectively.

11. FBI interview with Dan Costescu and Cornel Dumitrescu, June 19, 1991, available online at https://archive.org/stream/IoanCulianu/Ioan Culianu Part 01 of 01_djvu.txt.

12. FBI reports dated May 31 and June 7, 1991, available online at https://archive.org/stream/IoanCulianu/Ioan Culianu Part 01 of 01_djvu.txt.

13. Ioan Culianu, "Eliade *koan*," *Lumea liberă* (September 8, 1990); "Elie Wiesel," *Lumea liberă* (September 15, 1990); "Iadul și civilizația" ("Hell and Civilization," on Moshe Idel, Kabbalah, and exile), *Lumea liberă* (October 13, 1990); "Umberto Eco și biblioteca din Alexandria" ("Umberto Eco and the Library of Alexandria"), *Lumea liberă* (October 20 and 27, 1990); "François Furet și revoluția franceză" ("François Furet and the French Revolution"), *Lumea liberă* (November 10, 1990); "Grazia Marchianò," *Lumea liberă* (November 24), 1990, all reprinted in Culianu, *Păcatul împotriva spiritului*.

14. Ioan Culianu, "Somnul cel de moarte" ("The Sleep of the Dead"), *Lumea liberă* (September 22, 1990); "Grandoarea și mizeriile structuralismului" ("Greatness and Sufferings of Structuralism"), *Lumea liberă* (November 17, 1990); "Patruzeci de secole" ("Forty Centuries"), *Lumea liberă* (August 25, 1990); and "Arcadia," *Lumea liberă* (December 1, 1990), all reprinted in Culianu, *Păcatul împotriva spiritului*.

15. Ioan Culianu, "Inchiziția? Cel mai bun tribunal din lume" ("Inquisition? The Best Court in the World"), *Lumea liberă* (November 3, 1990), reprinted in Culianu, *Păcatul împotriva spiritului*, pp. 174–76.

16. Ioan Culianu, "Adio," *Lumea liberă*, no. 116 (December 22, 1990): 9, reprinted in Culianu, *Păcatul împotriva spiritului*, pp. 196–97.

17. Ibid.

18. Chicago Police report, May 22, 1991, available online at https://archive.org/str eam/IoanCulianu/Ioan Culianu Part 01 of 01_djvu.txt.

19. Gabriela Adameşteanu, interview with Ioan Petru Culianu. The interview is most readily available in Gabriela Adameşteanu, *Obsesia politicii* (Bucharest: Editura Clavis, 1995), pp. 192–202, and Culianu, *Pacatul împotriva spiritului*, pp. 39–74, but the text of these two versions differs at numerous points. Adamesteanu discussed the circumstances under which the interview was conducted in "Istorie unui interviu după zece ani," in Antohi, *Religion, Fiction, and History*, vol. 1, pp. 258–84.

20. Liviu Turcu, quoted by Cornel Nistorescu, "O crimă în dispută politică," *Expres 2*, no. 27 (July 9–15, 1991): 8–9.

21. Lovinescu *Jurnal 1990–1993*, pp. 141–43 (May 26, 1991).

22. Lovinescu made disparaging remarks about Culianu in her journal entries of April 25, 1983 (*Jurnal 1981–1984*, pp. 196–97), June 17, 1987 (*Jurnal 1985–1988*, pp. 220–21), June 11, 1991 (*Jurnal 1990–1993*, pp. 145–46), May 2, 2001 (*Jurnal 2001–2002*, p. 91), and June 15, 2001 (*Jurnal 2001–2002*, p. 117).

23. Note also Lovinescu's journal entry of June 11, 1991 (*Jurnal 1990–1993*, pp. 145–46), where she entertains the idea that Ms. Wiesner had her fiancé killed in order to collect on his life insurance and gain control of their joint accounts, suspicions that reflect tropes of unscrupulous Jewish greed.

24. On Lovinescu's position in the Parisian community of Romanian exiles and the attack on her, see Camelia Crăciun, "Monica Lovinescu at Radio Free Europe," in John Neubauer and Borbála Zsuzsanna Török, eds., *The Exile and Return of Writers from East-Central Europe* (Berlin: de Gruyter, 2009), pp. 276–306.

25. Antohi was a core member of the dissident group centered in Iaşi and was subject to harassment as such. In 2006, he resigned from the Presidential Committee for the Analysis of the Communist Dictatorship in Romania and acknowledged that between 1976 and 1982 he intermittently cooperated with Securitate under pressure, while struggling to give them only worthless information. His admiration for Culianu led him to organize and edit two *Gedenkschriften* in his honor: *Religion, Fiction, and History: Essays in Memory of Ioan Petru Culianu* (Bucharest: Nemira, 2001) and *Ioan Petru Culianu: Omul şi opera* (Iaşi: Polirom, 2003).

26. Sorin Antohi, personal communication, March 18, 2019.

27. Idel, *Mircea Eliade*, pp. 213–19.

28. Nistorescu, "O crimă în dispută politică."

29. Ronnett, "Mircea Eliade," and Alexander Ronnett, "Mircea Eliade şi Mişcarea Legionară," in Stănescu, *Mircea Eliade în conştiinţa contemporanilor săi din exil*, pp. 295–96. See also Mac Linscott Ricketts, "An Afternoon with Mircea Eliade's Doctor, Dentist, and Confidant," in Ricketts, *Former Friends and Forgotten Facts* (Norcross, GA: Criterion Publishing, 2003), pp. 93–107.

30. Ronnett, "Mircea Eliade," p. 291. When Mrs. Eliade—who wished to defend her husband against all hints of legionary involvement—took offense at placement of St. Michael's Cross, the legionary equivalent of the Roman fasces and Nazi swastika, on the medal, Ronnett says he responded brusquely: "Ma'am, this medal is for Mircea and if you don't like it, don't look at it."

31. Marta Petreu, "Cioran şi Eliade în vizorul Legionarilor din exil," in *De la Junimea la Noica*, pp. 468–70.

32. Sorin Antohi, personal communication, March 18, 2019. Cf. Călinescu, "Culianu: Eliade: Culianu," pp. 235–36.

33. Codreanu, *Pentru legionari*, p. 112.

34. Ibid., p. 311.

35. Idel, *Mircea Eliade*, p. 215. Legionaries never forgot it was King Carol II, Michael's father, who suppressed the Legion and ordered Codreanu's murder. Michael inherited their antipathy, although he himself had taken no major actions against the movement.

36. Ioan Culianu, "Jormania liberă," *Agora* (Philadelphia) 3, no. 2 (July 1990), reprinted in Culianu, *Păcatul împotriva spiritului*, pp. 34–38.

37. Ioan Culianu, "O şansă unică" ("A Unique Opportunity"), *Lumea liberă*, no. 105 (October 6, 1990): 9, reprinted in Culianu *Păcatul împotriva spiritului*, pp. 156–61. The controversy described here arose from Culianu's article "Some Considerations on the Works of Horia Stamatu," *International Journal of Roumanian Studies* 2 (1980): 123–34, which Stamatu found deeply offensive. More fully on the controversy, see Bordaş, " 'Întotdeauna far într-o lume nihilistă,' " pp. 314–15.

38. Ioan Culianu, "Ku Klux Klan Ortodox," *Meridian 1*, no. 1 (May–June 1991): 64, reprinted in Culianu, *Pacatul împotriva spiritului*, pp. 261–64. Culianu adapted ideas from Martin Riesebrodt, *Pious Passion: The Emergence of Modern Fundamentalism in the United States and Iran* (Berkeley: University of California Press, 1993) to better fit the case of Romania. Thus, Riesebrodt's most important argument—that "fundamentalism" constitutes a panicked religious defense of patriarchal values and power—disappeared from Culianu's discussion, while xenophobia—a relatively minor theme for Riesebrodt—became central.

39. Eliade, "Meditaţie asupra arderii catedralelor."

40. See Mac Linscott Ricketts, memo of November 6, 1988, Mac Linscott Ricketts to Ioan Culianu, letters of November 29, 1989, and January 19, 1989, Ioan Culianu to Mac Ricketts, letter of June 7, 1989, all in Bordaş, "Culianu-Ricketts Correspondence," pp. 151–57; Petrescu-Culianu "Ioan Petru Culianu," pp. 45–46; Călinescu, *Despre Ioan P. Culianu şi Mircea Eliade*, pp. 25–28.

41. Ioan Culianu to Vittorio Lanternari, letter of April 28, 1987, in Bordaş, "Culianu-Ricketts Correspondence," pp. 175–77.

42. Ioan Culianu, letter of May 13, 1987, to Mac Linscott Ricketts in Bordaş, "Culianu-Ricketts Correspondence," pp. 129–30.

43. See herein, Chapter Five, Section V.

44. See herein, Chapter Five, Section VI.

45. Dorin Tudoran, "Într-adevăr . . . ," in Antohi, *Religion, Fiction, and History*, vol. 1, p. 308.

46. Culianu-Petrescu, "Ioan Petru Culianu," p. 46.

47. Călinescu, "Culianu: Eliade: Culianu," p. 244.

48. Stelian Pleşoiu, interviewed by Silvia Vrinceanu, originally published in *Ziarul de Iaşi* (August 22, 2005), republished in *Ziaristi online* and available at https://www.ziaristionline.ro/2012/03/09/cum-au-trait-si-murit-sotii-eli

ade-o-colectie-de-marturii-ale-omului-de-casa-al-lui-mircea-eliade-adunate-de-ziaristi-online/. Ellipsis in the original.

49. Cf. Adriana Berger to Ivan Strenski, letters of April 17, April 27, May 13, November 5, 1987, and May 6, 1988, archived in Special Collections of Chicago's Regenstein Library.

50. Lovinescu, journal entry of May 28, 1986 (*Jurnal 1985–1988*, p. 141).

51. Lovinescu, journal entry of June 3, 1987 (*Jurnal 1985–1988*, pp. 217–18).

52. Lovinescu, journal entry of September 26, 1986 (*Jurnal 1985–1988*, p. 162).

53. Lovinescu, journal entry of August 8, 1988 (ibid., p. 312).

54. Lovinescu, journal entries of June 1, 1993 (*Jurnal 1990–1993*, p. 351), June 6, 1995 (*Jurnal 1994–1995*, pp. 226), October 16, 1995 (ibid., p. 302).

55. Lovinescu, journal entries of October 18, 1988 (*Jurnal 1985–1988*, pp. 325–26), June 13, 1992 (*Jurnal 1990–1993*, pp. 250–51), December 1, 1992 (ibid., p. 296), and June 6, 1995 (*Jurnal 1994–1995*, pp. 224–27).

56. Lovinescu, journal entry of June 3, 1987 (*Jurnal 1985–1988*, pp. 217–18).

57. Lovinescu, journal entry of June 1, 1993 (*Jurnal 1990–1993*, pp. 351).

58. Wendy Doniger, personal communication, January 31, 2023.

59. These groups included the World Anti-Communist League and the Anti-Bolshevik Bloc of Nations, on which see Ross Bellant, *Old Nazis, the New Right, and the Republican Party* (Boston: South End Press, 1991); Scott Anderson and Jon Lee Anderson, *Inside the League: The Shocking Exposé of How Terrorists, Nazis, and Latin American Death Squads Have Infiltrated the World Anti-Communist League* (New York: Dodd, Mead, 1986); and Kyle Burke, *Revolutionaries for the Right: Anticommunist Internationalism and Paramilitary Warfare in the Cold War* (Chapel Hill: University of North Carolina Press, 2018). Dr. Ronnett bragged of his involvement with these groups, as well as the international legionary movement and his connections at high levels of the US government, military, and intelligence services. Cf. Ronnett, "Mircea Eliade," pp. 289, 290, and 292; Ricketts, "An Afternoon with Mircea Eliade's Doctor, Dentist, and Confidant," p. 97; and Bellant, *Old Nazis*, pp. 42–43, 75, and 115–19.

60. T. David Brent, personal communication, September 26, 2022.

61. Regarding Culianu and Wiesner's collaboration on this novel, see Anton, *Eros, Magic*, pp. 149–51 and 157–59.

62. I. P. Couliano and H. S. Wiesner, *The Emerald Game*, p. 170, unpublished manuscript now in the Culianu Archive of the University of Chicago's Regenstein Library. A Romanian translation of the novel was ultimately published: *Jocul de Smarald* (Iași: Polirom, 2005).

INDEX

———◆◆◆———

For the benefit of digital users, indexed terms that span two pages (e.g., 52–53) may, on occasion, appear on only one of those pages.

Tables and figures are indicated by *t* and *f* following the page number